2005

BECOMING

ADULT LEARNERS

BECOMING
ADULT LEARNERS

Principles and Practices
for
Effective Development

Eleanor Drago-Severson

Teachers College
Columbia University
New York and London

Published by Teachers College Press, 1234 Amsterdam Avenue, New York, NY 10027

Library of Congress Cataloging-in-Publication Data

Drago-Severson, Eleanor.
    Becoming adult learners : principles and practices for effective development /
Eleanor Drago-Severson.
       p. cm.
    Includes bibliographical references (p.) and index.
    ISBN 0-8077-4485-9 (cloth : alk. paper) — ISBN 0-8077-4484-0 (pbk. : alk. paper)
       1. Adult education—United States.   2. Functional literacy—United States.
    3. Continuing education—United States   I. Title.

    LC5251.D72 2004
    374'.012'0973—dc22   2004046096

ISBN 0-8077-4484-0 (paper)
ISBN 0-8077-4485-9 (cloth)

Printed on acid-free paper

Manufactured in the United States of America

11   10   09   08   07   06   05   04   8   7   6   5   4   3   2   1

For all who immigrate to America,
And especially for my ancestors,
Who led our family to learning.

For David,
My loving husband,
And touchstone.

For Robert Graham Kegan,
Exemplary mentor and inspiring teacher.

Contents

Foreword by *Laurent A. Parks Daloz*   ix
Acknowledgments   xiii

1. Introduction:
Aims, Purposes, and Intentions of This Book   1
   The Field of Adult Basic Skills Development   3
   The Adult Development Team Study   8
   The Content of this Book   10
   Contributions of this Research to the ABE/ESOL Field   14

2. Understanding Constructive-Developmental Theory   17
   The Nature of Transformational Learning: Development of Self   18
   Kegan's Constructive-Developmental Perspective on Adulthood   20
   Kegan's "Ways of Knowing"   23
   Why Ways of Knowing Matter in the Classroom   33
   The Holding Environment: A Dynamic Context for Growth   35
   Summary   36

3. Research Method   37
   Site and Participant Selection   37
   Research Questions: What Did We Want to Learn?   40
   Data Collection   40
   Data Analysis   48
   Summary   51

4. The Polaroid Learning Site   55
   About Polaroid   55
   About CEI's Adult Diploma Program   58
   The 1998–1999 CEI Program at Polaroid   64
   Cohorts and Collaborative Learning Defined   67
   Summary   70

5. "Not I Alone": The Power of the Cohort
and Collaborative Learning   72
   "Everybody Thinks Differently": The Cohort as a Holding Environment
      for Learning and Teaching   73

"Like a Family": The Cohort as a Holding Environment
    for Emotional Support   90
"I Have a Better Appreciation for People": The Cohort as a Holding
    Environment for Perspective Broadening   94
Conclusion   99

6. **"Good Teachers Understand Their Students":
A Developmental View of Learners' Expectations
of Their Teachers**   **103**
How Learners Conceptualized Teacher-Learner Relationships   105
Summary and Conclusions   124

7. **"We're Trying to Get Ahead": Changes in Learners'
Conceptions of Themselves, Their Skills, and Their
Relationship to Work**   **129**
How Program Learning Influenced Learners' Work Lives   131
Conclusion   150

8. **Implications of a New Pluralism for Program Design,
Curriculum Development, Practice, Policy, and Research**   **154**
Designing Programs that Center on the Cohort and Collaborative
    Learning   155
Creating a Developmental Curriculum   160
Contextualizing the Curriculum: Goal Setting   164
Conceptualizing Competency as a Developmental Continuum   167
Creating Opportunities for Development in the Classroom:
    Teaching Practice   168
Policymaking in Support of Developmental Learning   171
Promising Avenues for Developmental Research   175
An Appetite for Learning   177

Epilogue.   Graduation: A Red-Letter Day   **181**
Notes   **187**
References   **191**
Index   **205**
About the Author   **223**

A New Kind of Pluralism

IT IS A MATTER of quiet pride to me that my daughter, Kate, teaches
Adult Basic Education students under the shadow of New York's Citibank building. "In my classes," she loves to remind her father who raised
her in snow-white Vermont, "there are more languages than students."
And I must say that when I sat in her classroom not long ago, the cultural
diversity was in your face and stunning: a tall, dignified Senegalese civil
servant sat beside a reserved middle-aged Polish secretary; a young Bengali
woman watched cautiously as a 20-something street kid in $200 Nikes
slouched in his seat in the back; a smartly dressed Latino man thumbed
through a worn textbook, while beside him a short, balding man with a
thick accent of uncertain origins stared blankly into the middle distance.
As she prepared to begin the class, the students teased Kate about the Red
Sox's latest loss to the Yankees. She took it with threadbare humor, then
turned and said, "OK, remember that it's a dollar fine for anyone whose
cell phone goes off in class." And they were off.

Some of the best teaching I know goes on in scruffy classrooms in the
shadows of our society as underpaid instructors struggle to help their students heal from the wounds of toxic schooling, stark poverty, and oppressive regimes at home and abroad. More than even their instructors, many
of these students hold a poignant Jeffersonian dream as old as our nation
that education will lift them out of their condition. And the best of their
teachers share and feed that hope as they remind their students over and
over that they are not dumb, that they often already know the answers or
can figure them out, and that they can reach their dream of passing the
GED, and perhaps achieve much more.

Powerful as the cultural diversity is in these classrooms, however, what
Ellie Drago-Severson brings us in this work is recognition of another kind
of diversity: What she calls "a new kind of pluralism." More than yet
another form of difference threading an already complex classroom, this is
the difference between who our students are and who they can become. To
help our students close this gap is what our work is about.

When he was a young teacher at Harvard, William Perry—whose
work undergirds much of the thinking here—made what he wryly referred
to as the shocking discovery that *every student in his class had a different
teacher*. Some saw him as an all-knowing authority; some as a dithering,

feathery academic; and still others as a guide to their ongoing learning. Likewise, some of the students whom we are about to meet view their education as simply a ladder to success; others see it as a way to become more accepted and to help others; still others believe it will help them to think for themselves and to become more independent. Importantly, these differences may show up across people who share the same culture, age, or gender. More importantly still, we will watch some of those people change as the ways in which they view their teachers, their education, and their world are transformed over time.

Constructive-developmental theory, as this body of work is known, has been applied with growing influence and effectiveness in higher education over the past two decades, particularly among adult educators. It offers a rich, new interpretation of what it means for adult learners to change in significant ways, and it illustrates how educators can go beyond simply teaching facts or skills to cultivate human growth itself. To my knowledge, this is the first time it has been applied in a systematic way to adults with less formal schooling. What is telling is that the very same broad patterns appear among Adult Basic Education and pre-GED students as appear in Harvard students. It is abundantly clear that although formal education may strongly affect development, it is by no means a sine qua non. The wag's comment that there may be more wisdom in a window washer than the White House reminds us to ask whether our teaching is transforming or simply informing our students.

The research on which this book is based had its genesis in a federally funded study conducted by the Adult Development Research Group headed up by Robert Kegan at Harvard University. The group was made up of three teams, each studying a different site. Ellie Drago-Severson, who headed the Polaroid team, took on the task of writing this book, but the research is representative of the collective wisdom of many of her colleagues. The research was, she emphasizes, "a huge team effort."

One of the great gifts of this book is that the language is clear and its ideas are accessible. Although the intellectual underpinnings of the developmental shifts described here are elaborate, subtle, and complex, the terms *instrumental, socializing,* and *self-authoring* used to describe the levels of development are straightforward and direct. And while Drago-Severson makes it abundantly clear that these categories can be fluid and overlapping, we finish the book informed and empowered as teachers, ready to move back into our classrooms or student conversations with new eyes and ears. Moreover, she includes grounded descriptions of the characteristics of each of these "cultures of mind" that are intuitively apparent to anyone who has spent time working with adult learners. The book is marbled with poignant and often moving stories of struggle, loss, and triumph—the true grit of this world of adult learning. The material is compelling as well as readable, and the stories are told with deep sensitivity and always with respect.

Another gift is the sheer practicality of the theory presented here, for a good developmental map enables us not only to make valuable inferences about how our students are making meaning, but also how they are moving—about what constitutes progress and what may be a backwater. It helps us to recognize that a hand up for one student might be dead weight for another and that any given lesson will be read differently by different students. It makes visible differences that are deeper than clothing, accent, gender, or skin color, so that the enterprising teacher can orchestrate discussions more richly, tailor responses more artfully, and ask questions more powerfully. Teaching becomes not only more practical and effective, but more satisfying as well.

A third gift is what we learn here about the power of learning communities. Heretofore, much of the research on student development has focused on the isolated individual rather than on the context of that development, particularly the power of diverse communities to promote transformative learning. By emphasizing the power of the cohort as a "holding environment" within which learners may or may not undergo developmental change, Drago-Severson sheds fresh light on the profound influence that elemental aspects of life such as friendships, marriage, and parenting have on the quality of learning. What and how well we learn in formal settings invariably affects and is affected by the larger and more intimate worlds in which our lives are steeped.

Why does all this matter? Public discourse about adult education rings with assertions about the need for workers to "learn new skills" in order to cope effectively with today's rapid social and technological change. And although there is no question about the importance of such skills, any thoughtful critic of our times knows that simply to train more workers to slip silently into the dark waters of the current cultural and corporate-driven economy is to fail not only the learners themselves but our shared future as well. To address the multiple demands of the 21st century with courage, imagination, and hope will require far more than new skills. What is asked of us demands fundamental transformation in the very ways we understand the world. This book not only expands our understanding of human development and contributes significantly to our field, but it provides a lush map for the territory that lies ahead as well as practical guidelines for how adult educators can work together to make a real and positive difference in the world.

LAURENT A. PARKS DALOZ

Acknowledgments

A COMMUNITY OF PEOPLE and organizations came together self-lessly in generous contribution over many years leading to this book. I am honored to acknowledge their insights and inspirations, and I ask forgiveness for failing to mention others who also made a difference to the success of this project.

I thank the former Office of Educational Research and Improvement (OERI), the National Center for the Study of Adult Learning and Literacy (NCSALL), World Education, and Harvard Graduate School of Education (HGSE). (Research cited in this book was drawn from a larger study that was funded by the U.S. Department of Education, Prime Cooperative Agreement No. R309860002.) I especially thank John Comings of NCSALL for his leadership and thoughtful counsel.

The spirit of this project lives in the 19 courageous adults who allowed our team to learn from them over countless hours. They patiently helped us understand what their learning meant to them. Confidentiality agreements, though, prevent me from acknowledging each by name. My gratitude goes to all of you.

It was the welcoming stance offered by the Polaroid Corporation that provided our opportunity to learn. I thank William Munzert, Brenda Mc-Gill, and Elizabeth Foote at Polaroid. At the Continuing Education Institute (CEI), I thank its director, Lloyd David, and also Kathy Hassey Bell, Matthew Puma, and Jean Bancroft, Mark Donnelly, and Mary Ann Sliwa.

Throughout this research, Robert Kegan of HGSE brought and held our adult development team together. As principal investigator, he modeled for us his transformational leadership. Our leadership team consisted of Bob Kegan, Maria Broderick, Nancy Popp, Kathryn Portnow, Deborah Helsing and me. I thank these distinguished scholars, and in particular Maria, for the individual and collective contributions that strengthened our research. Maricel Guiao Santos, Jennifer Garvey Berger, and Elana Peled were also members of our adult development team who served on the Polaroid team. This work could not be as strong without these exemplary thinkers. Thanks in particular to Maricel, who generously gave her thinking to developing some of the ideas presented in the final chapter.

Ann Diamond, James Hammerman, and Katie Pakos Rimer contributed greatly to data collection and analysis. Our extended research team included those who helped with data collection: Laura Carmen Arena, Marlene Major Ahmed, Stephanie Beukema, Lisa Boes, Carla Brown, Chris Soto, Robert Goodman, Anne Harbison, Lisa Lahey, Alan Medville, Svetlana Nikitina, David Severson, Mary Jane Schmitt, Faina Smith, David Eddy Spicer, Linda Booth Sweeney, and Julie Veins. Transcription was provided by Arlington Transcription Service (ATM, Inc.), Lisa Boes, Deborah Helsing, Annie Howell, Ann Amatangelo Korte, Elana Peled, Joanne Pearlman, Katie Pakos Rimer, Maricel Guiao Santos, Erin Seaton, Chris Soto, and Ellen Theriault. Marcia Brownlee, Faith Harvey, Karen Manning, Joelle Pelletier, Karen Rowe, and Chris Soto provided administrative support. India Koopman and her thoughtful suggestions accompanied my writing and my spirit.

I thank those who provided valuable consultation: Beth Bingham, Laurent Daloz, Wendy Luttrell, and Sondra Stein.

Carol Kolenik, the dynamic leader of HGSE's Bridge to Learning and Literacy Program, offered a contagious energy and love for her work in addition to information about it. Thanks to Sondra Cuban of NCSALL for helpful listening and good company through the journey. Enduring appreciation and gratitude go to Howard Gardner of HGSE for his inspiration and encouragement. I also thank Eleanor Duckworth for generously sharing her knowledge as part of our friendship.

I am grateful to my students for all that they teach me. Among the excellent students who supported me in this work, Sue Stuebner Gaylor and Kristina Pinto stand out like yellow tulips blossoming in sunshine. Thank you Kristina and Sue for your clarifying suggestions, help with manuscript details, and your colleagueship. I have benefited enormously from your teachings.

It was Brian Ellerbeck of Teachers College Press who saw the promise of this work and offered wisdom that helped make this research accessible to all educators. My appreciation also goes to Wendy Schwartz and also to Aureliano Vázquez, Jr. of TCP for their editorial expertise.

My acknowledgments conclude with deepest gratitude for the love and support of those who have most shaped my life—family. Rosario and Betty Drago are my parents and greatest teachers. With wisdom, they taught me to learn as models of lifelong learners. Holding me each step of the way, they helped me stand for something. Just as they taught me about ancestors and family values, they also encouraged me to shape and pursue my own dreams. It is on their shoulders that I now stand in order to see farther. I thank them for showing me the value of both roots and wings.

My five brothers and only sister walked some of my paths before I did. I thank my six siblings for teaching me about family, and for being loves.

I now express deepest gratitude to my cherished husband, David Severson, who lovingly accompanies me through this project and life. Thanks to him for being here, being there, for being wherever he is next needed, and for sacrifices he makes with good cheer. David's way of attending to our lives of learning and growth together carries us.

The dedication of this book only scratches the surface of my deep gratitude to David, to Bob Kegan, and to my parents and ancestors. Thanks to all of them for the different ways they help me learn and grow.

CHAPTER 1

Introduction: Aims, Purposes, and Intentions of This Book

> Who comes into a person's life may be the single greatest factor of influence to what that life becomes. Who comes into a person's life is in part a matter of luck, in part a matter of one's power to recruit others, but in large part a matter of other people's ability to be recruited.
>
> —Kegan, 1982, p. 19

MY FATHER, Rosario P. Drago, was a doctor, a pediatrician who selflessly gave himself to the children and families of our Bronx, New York, community for more than 50 years of practice so that life, learning, and living might be a little better for these families and those who came after. My mother, Betty L. Brisgal Drago, is a nurse who, in addition to joining my father in the raising and nurturing of seven children, also joined him in serving the medical needs of our community over those same years, spanning the last half of the 20th century.

My father's parents came to the United States from Italy. They gave themselves to the futures of their children by working hard with a value for education and sacrificing much over many years. Their dream was that life, learning, and living be a little better for their children and for their children's children. Beyond an enormous hope and a courage that humbles, my grandparents' story—and the stories of countless others like them who left their homelands and transformed themselves in the process—was and continues to be primarily a story of dreams, dreams of bright futures for posterity.

The boldest dreams of my grandparents and immigrants to new lands everywhere could be realized only by means of investing lifetimes into the special kind of hard work, sacrifice, and relentless perseverance that must begin with learning a new language. The same kinds of hopeful journeys that my grandparents traveled continue today. Countless numbers of equally courageous and relentlessly persistent people continue to invest their time and energies and selves in the first steps of realizing dreams for their children and families. The first steps begin with literacy, learning, and development.

My most vivid memory of my paternal grandmother, Eleanora Locasia Drago, rings with song as well as with sympathy. Grandma would sing songs to me and my siblings—always in her beautiful Italian—as we all curled up together with her on a sofa much too small to hold us. "What does it mean?" we would ask her, as the music of a place we did not know called Italy came to a stop. "Who taught that song to you?" one of us would ask. "Did your Mom sing it to you?" We wanted to know. I remember how my Grandma's eyes seemed to change instantly from happiness of joyful song to frustration of silence in response to our questions. This woman of dreams and courage searched her mind in vain for words she did not know. She so much wanted to tell us her story of people and times and memories she treasured, but she could not do it in our language, English.

In this book I present the voices of people not unlike my grandparents in their courageous pursuit of their dreams. Many are immigrants trying to become fluent enough to sing their songs in English; all are learners wanting to improve their literacy so as to expand their lives. Literacy today, though, means something quite different from what it did in my grandparents' time. In the early 1900s individuals were considered literate if they could write their names (Comings et al., 2000). What it means to be considered literate in the 21st century, particularly in the workplace, includes familiarity with technology and critical thinking skills. As Comings and colleagues (2000) write,

> The main literacy problem of U. S. workers is not that of illiteracy in the traditional sense. Instead, it is a problem of limited skills that restrict workers' ability to perform higher skilled jobs and take on more complicated duties that are required of workers in the New Economy. (p. 18)

In the United States, 64 million working adults between the ages of 18 and 64 (in excess of 90% of our nation's workforce) are in need of improved language skills (the language challenge group), a high school diploma (the educational challenge group), or enhanced basic skills that will allow them to meet the demands of the modern workplace (the new literacy challenge group) (Comings, Reder, and Sum, 2001). While these skills and competencies are needed to be an effective and competent worker in today's world, they are equally important to the roles of family member and community member. Comings, Reder, and Sum (2001) describe our national human resource in this way: "The 64 million working-age adults who fall into the estimate of the three challenge populations are not a problem; they are a national resource" (p. 8).

As we move more fully into this 21st century, we need to support and strengthen one another's capacities to meet the demands of work, family, and community life. The federally funded adult basic education (ABE) program is the principal support for helping 40 to 44 million adults (Kirsch et al., 1993) in need of basic literacy education (Comings, Reder, & Sum, 2001). Beder, Medina, and Eberly (2000) emphasize that while the National Adult Literacy Survey (NALS) and the National Evaluation of the Adult Education Program (NEAEP) have provided information about adult literacy education programs and their adult learners, little is known about what actually occurs in adult literacy education classrooms. Recent research efforts are beginning to address this gap in our knowledge, and this book is a contribution to those efforts.

This study is the first in-depth study of adult learning in ABE/ESOL settings that applies Robert Kegan's (1982, 1994) constructive-developmental theory to understand how adults make sense of their learning experiences and their lives. While our larger study examined the learning experiences of adults in three ABE/ESOL programs (a community college, a family literacy site, and a workplace site), the research reported here focuses on a group of adult learners at the workplace site. These adults were employed as shop-floor workers and enrolled in a high school diploma program sponsored by their employer, the Polaroid Corporation. Importantly, learnings from this research have broader implications for adult learners in other educational settings.

In this introduction I will situate the study illustrated in this book in relationship to research on adult literacy and learning needs, specifically prior work on adult basic skills development and the expanding ABE/ESOL field. I will also introduce the nature and findings of the study and how it contributed to a larger study conducted by the Adult Development Team of the National Center for the Study of Adult Learning and Literacy (NCSALL), which is housed at the Harvard Graduate School of Education and of which I was a leader. I conclude by presenting a description of each chapter in this book.

THE FIELD OF ADULT BASIC SKILLS DEVELOPMENT

At least 40% of American working-age adults lack the necessary skills and education for success in their jobs and community (NCSALL website). Comings and colleagues (2000) assert that without multiple skill sets or the training sufficient to develop them, workers in today's information age will lose their places as new technological positions replace manual jobs.

The new economy of the 21st century requires that, in order to thrive in their roles as workers, learners, parents, and citizens, adults must have both educational credentials and enhanced basic skills (Comings, Reder, & Sum, 2001). To build a "level playing field" for all adults, we must give adults the chance to develop the basic skills and competencies needed to benefit from the opportunities offered in the new century. Comings, Reder, and Sum (2001) assert that the basic skills needed to work effectively in today's complex world include math, English literacy, an aptitude for thinking critically, collaborative problem-solving, and the use of computers and other technology.

Researchers (Ciulla, 2000; Evers, Rush, & Berdrow, 1998; Gowen, 1992) commonly cite three major changes that have led to current workplace conditions: "the shift to . . . technology requir[ing] highly skilled workers"; "significant shifts in the ethnic and gender distribution as well as the size of the future workforce"; and "the familiar contention that the nation is in the throes of a major decline in basic skills" (Ciulla, 2000, p. 8). Comings, Reder, and Sum (2001) refer to "basic skills" as cognitive skills (e.g., reading) and the knowledge (e.g., vocabulary) needed to use the skill. In this book, I adhere to their definition.

Work on today's shop floors has changed dramatically since Frederick Winslow Taylor published his treatise on efficiency in the workplace, *The Principles of Scientific Management*, in 1911. While Taylor admired the skills of the workers and craftsmen of his day, his goal was to design work so that "almost any person could do any job with maximum efficiency" (Ciulla, 2000, p. 93). Today, work requires more.

Recent national attention has been devoted to the complex nature of the 21st-century workplace and the need to better support workers as they grow, enhancing their skills and competencies to meet the demands of the changing nature of work. The authors of a study sponsored by the nonpartisan research group Massachusetts Institute for a New Commonwealth (Comings, Sum, & Uvin, 2000) report that Vaishnav and Greenberger's (2001) research indicates that one third of Massachusetts's 3.2 million workers age 25 to 64 lack the "basic technical skills" (p. 1) required to meet the demands of the modern workplace. Of these, 58% have a high school diploma and 17% have limited English skills. Comings and colleagues (2000) also report that 1.1 million workers will be at risk of losing their jobs as companies across the country come to demand skills that they do not have. Managers across the nation are seeking employees who can "adapt to the rapid pace of modernization" (Vaishnav & Greenberger, 2001, p. 22).

Murnane and Levy (1996) conducted research to examine the minimum skills workers need to attain a middle-class job and found that the "new basic skills" include the ability to:

- Read at the ninth-grade level or higher.
- Use math at the ninth-grade level or higher.
- Solve semistructured problems where hypotheses must be formed and tested.
- Work in groups with coworkers from different backgrounds.
- Communicate effectively, both orally and in writing.
- Use personal computers to carry out simple tasks such as word-processing.

(cited in Comings et al., 2000, p. 2)

To improve the economic health of our nation and to support those who are striving to meet the complex demands and conditions of the modern workplace, we must attend to workers' learning needs. Research suggests "substantial productivity payoff to workplace literacy programs. They also help workers by teaching them the basic skills that often translate into opportunities to advance in their jobs" (Comings et al., 2000, p. 49).

The results of the research I report in this book point to a new and promising way to help prepare learners in adult basic education (ABE) and English for speakers of other languages (ESOL) programs—and all adults, for that matter—for the demands of the modern workplace. This research emphasizes the need for attending to a more subtle form of diversity in the classroom: the learner's "way of knowing"—an internally consistent meaning-making system that we all use to make sense of, or interpret, our experience (Kegan, 1982, p. 5). In this writing, I use the terms "way of knowing," "meaning-making system," and "developmental level" inter-changeably. Kegan (1982, 1994) and other constructive-developmental theorists regularly employ these terms to describe an internally consistent meaning-making system from which we, as human beings, interpret our experience.

The Expanding Field of ABE/ESOL

This research, conducted by the Adult Development Team (hereafter referred to as "the research team") and sponsored by NCSALL, empirically explores how a person's way of knowing constitutes a lens through which ABE/ESOL learning and teaching experiences are filtered and how that way of knowing can change and become more complex over time given developmentally appropriate supports and challenges (see, e.g., Kegan, Broderick, Drago-Severson, Helsing, Popp, & Portnow, 2001a, 2001b).

As a research team, we situate our study in the growing field of ABE/ESOL research, in which there is a call for in-depth qualitative studies that explore the internal experiences of adult learners, the idea being to round out the equally important though perhaps overrepresented large-sample, quantitative, demographic, and summary approaches to research (Horsman, 1991; Hunter & Harman, 1979; Rockhill, 1982; Skilton-Sylvester & Carlo, 1998; Valentine, 1990; Wikelund, Reder, & Hart-Landsberg, 1992).[1] It is important to note that both qualitative and quantitative studies are needed to explore different sorts of research questions.

Several of the researchers and practitioners noted above highlight the need for in-depth qualitative studies because

> the learner's perspective tends to be considered in light of a program's expectations or the U. S. host society's definitions of the learner's needs, rather than considering the perspectives of learners as *they* would define their own experiences, their own hopes, their own needs. (Kegan et al., 2001a, p. 3)

Similarly, Malicky and Norman (1997) urge researchers to ask questions that will help us understand adult literacy learners' lives and the ways in which they perceive changes in their lives as they learn. Lytle and her colleagues (Lytle, 1991; Lytle & Cochran-Smith, 1990; Lytle, Marmor & Penner, 1986; Lytle & Schultz, 1990) encourage researchers to join them in building a literature that will help us to better understand "adults' own evolving conceptual frameworks or theories about language, literacy, teaching, and learning" (Lytle, 1991, p. 120). The research team focused on just such an exploration (Kegan et al., 2001a, 2001b).

This longitudinal research, in which we tracked learners' experiences in their programs and the meaning they made of program learning, represents an effort to address this important call. Put simply, the adult learner and the meaning he or she makes of a learning experience are the starting point and orienting compass of this research. While the team recognized that other theories can and do shed light on the many features of adults' lives,[2] *this* work focuses on a constructive-developmental approach in the hope of better understanding the adult learner's experience in ABE/ESOL settings.

In the ABE/ESOL field, researchers and practitioners engage in lively discussion about key questions, pleas, and debates regarding instruction, best practices, assessment, and competency and skill development. While the main focus of our research team was to develop a better understanding of how adult learners make sense of their ABE/ESOL learning experiences, and how such learning may transfer to the other social roles they assume as citizens, parents, family members, and workers, we also came to believe that our research might shed light on some of these much-debated areas of investigation and discussion (Kegan et al., 2001b). For example:

- *Motivation to learn.* We detect in the literature a growing restlessness with the way ABE/ESOL participants' *motivations to learn* are conceptualized. Peirce (1995), e.g., regards the widespread distinction between "instrumental" and "integrative" motivation (Gardner and Lambert, 1972) as too static and unidimensional (Ullman, 1997). How can our "cultures of mind" [or constructive-development] approach help us to see a wide variety of qualitatively different ways of knowing which may lie behind a learner's motivation to, e.g., secure a new job (an example of the "instrumental" stance) or, e.g., become more a part of the PTA at one's children's school (an example of the "integrative" stance)? The literature suggests that despite the conceptually neat distinction between these kinds of motivations, real learners trouble this neatness by demonstrating both kinds of motives. How can a "cultures of mind" approach help us to see the consistency in a given person's "motive mix"? (Kegan et al., 2001a, p. 8)

- *Classroom community.* There is a growing recognition in the literature that, even for adults, positive relationships between the student and teacher and among fellow students, are important to learning (Chevalier, 1994; Atwell, 1987; Brookfield, 1995; Calkins, 1986; Graves, 1991; Heard, 1989; Meyers and Erdmann, 1985; Wrigley and Guth, 1992; Kegan, 2000). But what constitutes "positiveness" is different for different learners. It can be puzzling for well-intentioned teachers to find that the same behaviors which leave one student feeling well-attended-to leave another feeling abandoned. A student who wants to be helpful to her fellow learners can find that some people feel supported and others condescended to by the identical behaviors on her part. How can a "cultures of mind" approach help us better understand the differing criteria students will bring to their constructions of supportiveness or trustworthiness in a teacher? Within one's cohort of fellow learners? (Kegan et al., 2001a, p. 8–9)

- *Classroom pedagogy.* Do all adult learners prefer and benefit from student-centered, teacher-as-coach, "democratic" classroom designs? Sometimes the literature seems to suggest that a capacity and appetite for these kinds of pedagogical designs comes along automatically with the "condition" of adulthood (Knowles, 1970, 1980, 1984; Grow, 1991; Mezirow, 1991). The implication is that if you are going to be an effective teacher of grown-ups you must eschew the teacher-centered, teacher-as-expert, "authoritarian" designs, which, if ever appropriate, are only so for children and youth. Similarly, discussions about "cooperative" vs. "collaborative" vs. "traditional teacher transmission" models (Hamilton, 1994; Flannery, 1994; Eble and Noonan, 1983) tend to frame the possibilities in terms of philosophical differences and ideological preferences among educators, on the one hand, and on unresearched assumptions about "how the adult mind works," on the other. But is it possible the question of optimal classroom teaching designs should not be one of "either-or," but optimal matches to the learner's current way of knowing? Can a "cultures of mind" approach help us create a more "plural" set of teaching designs in any one classroom? (Kegan et al., 2001a, p. 9)

- *The purpose and outcome of ABE/ESOL learning.* Goals for ABE/ESOL programs range from helping adults to become better prepared to join and/

or participate in the work force or civic life, to increasing skill development, to developing personal empowerment, to engaging in social and political change (Evers, Rush, & Berdrow, 1998). While increasing "competence" is the hoped-for outcome of any adult learning program, with so varied an assortment of favored goals, "competence" comes to mean a host of different things (Green, 1995; Chappell, 1996; Ecclestone, 1997; Hyland, 1994; Kerka, 1998). And yet, whether one's favored goals orient to the acquisition of basic skills or to the personal growth of the learner, whether goals are first derived from a consideration of academic disciplines that need to be mastered or from consideration of the adult's real-life demands, the fact remains that whatever learning one seeks to promote must go on in the mental home of the learner. How can a "cultures of mind" approach help us better to engage the learner's "mental home," whether our goal is, e.g., to increase the accessible skill base within that home, or e.g., to facilitate the learner's move to a qualitatively more expansive and complex mental home? (Kegan et al., 2001b, p. 11)

THE ADULT DEVELOPMENT TEAM STUDY

We have learned much over the last four decades about how individual human beings grow and develop cognitively over time. For a number of years this knowledge, often drawn from narrow or intuitive samples, remained in graduate seminars, scholarly journals or the occasional academic text. During the 1970's, however, and into the 1980's, it began to make its way into . . . applied realms and many of us in the field found our teaching transformed. But there remained a number of questions limiting the further extension of the work: *How adequate is it for students with less formal education? What is the interaction of cultural differences with this understanding of development? What role does the larger social context play in development? How do communities of learners affect development? And why can't they put it all in simple English?* (L. Daloz, personal communication, June 2, 2001 [emphasis in original].)

After reading the team's research monograph (Kegan et al., 2001b), Dr. Laurent Daloz shared his view, as the above passage illuminates, that the work of the Adult Development Team of NCSALL addresses these questions in a promising manner. The research I present here is rooted in and benefits from the collective wisdom, expertise, and shared investigation of a larger research team. This Adult Development Team, of which I was honored to be a lead researcher and collaborator under the aegis of principal investigator Robert Kegan, was part of NCSALL. Housed at Harvard Graduate School of Education (HGSE) since 1996, NCSALL assists adults in achieving their potential through improved practice and policy. Linking research with practice through university affiliations, NCSALL strives to strengthen programs and level the playing field, giving all adults in the United States the opportunity to move toward reaching their potential as learners, workers, parents, partners, and citizens.

By conducting systematic, high-quality research directed toward strengthening practice, NCSALL aims to increase the knowledge base in the field of adult literacy education and provide teachers, program directors, program designers, and policymakers with a research-informed basis for decision making, so that we can all better support and serve adult learners. This research is part of that effort.

As with NCSALL, our research benefited from partnering with Equipped for the Future (EFF), a standards-based ABE reform initiative the goal of which is to enhance the ABE literacy system so that all adults can better assume their roles as parents, workers, and citizens (see, e.g., Bingman & Stein, 2001; Nash & Gillespie, 2002; Stein, 2000, 2002). The Adult Development Team shares EFF's conception of adult literacy as something more sophisticated than acquiring basic skills (Kegan et al., 2001a, 2001b; Portnow, Popp, Broderick, Drago-Severson, & Kegan, 1998). In our collaboration with EFF, we have aligned with the reconceptualization of adult literacy and support for lifelong learning by employing a constructive-developmental framework (Kegan 1982, 1994) to inform how we think about the ways in which adults, with different meaning-making systems, will demonstrate skills and competencies differently (see, e.g., Popp & Boes, 2001). We assert that various forms of support and challenge may facilitate adult learners' development as they grow and become able to demonstrate skills and competencies in more complex ways (see, e.g., Drago-Severson, 2001; Drago-Severson & Berger, 2001; Helsing, Broderick, & Hammerman, 2001; Portnow, Diamond, & Rimer, 2001).

As adult developmental psychologists and educators engaged in adult education, our research team carefully followed for a year or longer 41 ABE/ESOL learners from many different parts of the world to understand their processes of learning and the ways in which those processes changed as they participated in three distinctly different ABE/ESOL programs: one at a community college, Bunker Hill Community College in Boston, Massachusetts; one at a family literacy site, an Even Start program in Massachusetts, that prefers to remain anonymous; and another at a workplace site, the Polaroid Corporation in Waltham, Massachusetts. Each of the three programs was intended to help learners improve their English-language proficiency and competencies, increase their content knowledge, and enhance their effectiveness as students, parents, or workers. In this book, I report longitudinal findings from the workplace site (the Polaroid Corporation), where I was research captain with support from distinguished doctoral students.

As a team, we were especially interested in how these participants made sense of their learning processes; their motives, aspirations, and goals for learning; their expectations of teachers and of themselves as learners; and their definitions of and understanding of themselves in their social roles as students, parents, and/or workers. Of great importance was the goal of understanding how these adults perceived what we call "program learning." In other words, the team examined how adults learners from all three study sites experienced learning in their programs; how this learning transferred to the ways in which they enacted their social roles as students, parents, or workers; how they experienced the supports and challenges to their learning, which were embedded in their programs; and how, if at all, this learning helped them to change and grow (Drago-Severson et al., 2001a; Kegan et al., 2001a). By attending to participants' experiences for a year or longer, the team was able to track the processes of their learning and, in some cases, of their transformation—that is, their evolution to a way of knowing that allowed them to comprehend the world with greater complexity.

Drawing on constructive-developmental theories (Daloz, 1983, 1986, 1999; Kegan, 1982, 1994; Kegan & Lahey, 1984, 2001), the research team looked at the interplay between a learner's developmental capacity and his or her experience in a program. The results of our study show that adults with different preferences, needs, and developmental orientations do indeed need different forms of support and challenge in order to learn and grow. This book focuses on our team's involvement with the group at the workplace site and thus also focuses on the relevance of the program at that site to the learners' growth as workers, although their growth as learners, parents, and even as human beings is also touched on.

In employing Kegan's (1982, 1994) constructive-developmental theory, our team sought to better understand how adult learners make sense of their learning experiences. How do learners with different developmental capacities experience programs aimed at supporting their learning? How do these adults make sense of the various supports and challenges these programs provide? How can such programs be organized and develop structures to better support adult learners with different developmental capacities?

THE CONTENT OF THIS BOOK

In the chapters that follow I explore these and other questions and invite the reader to consider the ways in which a developmental approach might shed light on a number of especially prominent areas of exploration and debate. While the research team examined similar questions at all three of the study's sites, I focus on how adult learners at the Polaroid site made sense of these issues.

A constructive-developmental approach can help practitioners and policymakers to better understand and support adult learning, given the complex demands upon us in the 21st century. These demands require not simply skill, knowledge, and competency acquisition (content knowledge)—though these are important as well—but also more complex ways of knowing (structure of knowledge).

Our team's research is based on the assumption that in every ABE/ESOL classroom of adult learners, there will be developmental diversity, that an adult's developmental level (or meaning-making system) will shape the ways in which he or she experiences the learning and teaching enterprise, and that effective classrooms are not only environments where adults gain skills; they are also dynamic "holding environments" (Kegan, 1982, p. 115) where adult learners can grow to better manage the complexities of their lives and roles as students, parents, and workers (Kegan et al., 2001a, 2001b). This research suggests that programs designed to recognize adult learners' developmental diversity—and support adults' growth accordingly—will be especially effective.

The three core research findings explored in this book address

1. the variety of importantly different ways of knowing that adults bring to the ABE/ESOL classroom
2. the importance of the cohort, what I call a community of connection, for adult learning
3. the possibility and variety of significant change for adults in ABE/ESOL settings, even during as short a period of about 1 year.

In addition to the many forms of diversity that are present in an ABE/ESOL classroom—and that good teachers strive to recognize and include (e.g., gender, age, race, religion, and cultural origin), the team's research suggests the importance of another form of diversity. This form of diversity is a new kind of pluralism, namely the differing ways of knowing, or meaning making, that adults bring to both their learning experiences and their lives as a whole. All three of the study's major findings revolve around the importance of this new variable for thinking about and improving teaching and learning in the ABE/ESOL classroom—and in other adult learning contexts as well. These three core findings are explored in the chapters that follow. They are: (1) the variety of ways of knowing that adults bring to the ABE/ESOL classroom; (2) the importance of the cohort, or community of connection, for adult learning; and (3) the possibility and variety of significant change for adults in ABE/ESOL settings, even during as short a period as 1 year.

Here, in Chapter 1, I have situated the study illustrated in this book in relation to the field of adult literacy, specifically, prior research on adult basic skills development and the expanding ABE/ESOL field. I have also discussed the nature and general findings of the study and how it contributed to a larger study conducted by the Adult Development Team of the National Center for the Study of Adult Learning and Literacy, of which I was a lead researcher and captain of the Polaroid site. This chapter also presents an overview of the chapters in this book and introduces three distinct ways in which this research makes important contributions to the ABE/ESOL field.

Chapter 2 discusses the key principles of Kegan's (1982, 1994) constructive-developmental theory. I describe the various ways in which adults make sense of their experiences and Kegan's (1982) concept of the "holding environment."

Chapter 3 describes the three research settings in which the team was welcomed. In addition to stating our criteria for selecting each of the programs as research sites, the chapter offers an overview of our methodology.

Chapter 4 introduces the reader to the workplace site and the educational program on which the book is focused; namely, the Continuing Education Institute's Adult Diploma Program at the Polaroid Corporation in Waltham, Massachusetts. Chapters 5, 6, and 7 highlight common patterns in the Polaroid learners' descriptions of aspects of their learning experiences.

Chapter 5 explores how learners at the Polaroid site experienced the cohort and collaborative learning differently depending on their "way of knowing." Illustrated by case examples, we found that peer support seemed importantly defined by their way of knowing, while the learner cohort supported the learners' academic development and emotional well-being regardless of their way of knowing. This chapter illustrates one of this study's core findings: *the importance of creating a learner cohort—what I call a community of connection*—for adult learners in ABE/ESOL classrooms.

Chapter 6 explores how learners at the Polaroid site perceive their goals for learning and the teacher-learner relationship—and how, in many cases, these perceptions changed during the course of the program. In presenting the culturally diverse and rich cases of the learners at the Polaroid site, I will illustrate that while their descriptions of effective teaching vary, the learners maintained perspectives that transcend their cultural and personal differences. The chapter shows how learners' ways of knowing profoundly shape their conceptions of their motives for learning, what they want to learn, how they want to learn, how they learn best, and what they expect from their teachers and themselves as students.

This chapter illustrates a core finding of this study—namely, the variety of different ways of knowing that adults bring to the ABE/ESOL classroom. This new pluralism calls for *a diversity of pedagogical approaches* that attend to diverse ways of knowing.

Chapter 7 discusses the study's third finding: the varieties and types of significant changes these learners exhibited during the 14-month program. Learners changed in at least three important ways: informative (i.e., increases in knowledge and skills), transformative (i.e., increases in mental capacities that enable adults to better manage the complexities of life and work), and with regard to acculturation.

All learners were seeking new kinds of information, skills, and ideas, which they hoped would contribute to improvements in their lives, including their identity, careers, social and economic status, home life, and self-confidence.

In experiencing transformational change, some of the learners not only made gains in *what* they knew but modified the shape of *how* they knew— that is, they grew to demonstrate new and more complex ways of knowing. Remarkably, while prior research (see, e.g., Kegan, 1994) would not indicate that such qualitative development in the complexity of ways of knowing would occur over the course of only 1 year, several of the learners at each site did undergo such development. While many of the 41 learners in the team's study underwent acculurational changes, these were most apparent at the community college site (see, e.g., Helsing, Broderick, & Hammerman, 2001) and the family literacy site (see, e.g., Portnow, Diamond & Rimer, 2001), where learners were recent immigrants to the United States. Most of the learners at the Polaroid site had been in the United States for a number of years, though their English fluency did improve over the course of the program.

This chapter deals with the fact that the participants' experience of these changes was related to their ways of knowing. The case examples provide a contextualized view of how learners experienced different types of change. These examples also illustrate the developmentally driven similarities and differences in the learners' experiences.

Chapter 8 summarizes lessons from previous chapters and their practical implications for ABE/ESOL—and adult education, in general—teaching, program design, and policymaking. This chapter explores the promise of building cohorts within ABE/ESOL settings and suggests the implication of doing so for both teacher practice and program design. In this chapter, I suggest that this kind of developmental attentiveness may allow us to better serve adults with a diversity of learning needs and ways of knowing.

Attending to the diversity of ways in which adults interpret their experience—in addition to other, more visible and important types of diversity—has the potential to offer new and meaningful insights into learners' experiences. This chapter discusses how this type of understanding can help teachers, program designers, and policymakers to better respond to adult learners' strengths and learning needs.

It is with deep respect and admiration and an awareness of the space between us (Josselson, 1992) and the connections we share that I describe these learners' stories of hope, struggle, learning, literacy, emerging new competency, and development.

CONTRIBUTIONS OF THIS RESEARCH TO THE ABE/ESOL FIELD

This research contributes to the field in three distinct ways.[3] This, to our team's knowledge, is the first comprehensive study that explores adults' perspectives on their own learning experiences in three different ABE/ESOL programs by employing a constructive-developmental approach to understanding adult's meaning making. Prior studies of adults that have employed Kegan's theory of adult development (1982, 1994) and research methods (Lahey et al., 1988) have been composed largely of white, college-educated, middle-class, native-English-speaking adults, the majority of whom are American. Our team's research (Kegan et al., 2001b) extends the use of this framework to ABE/ESOL settings and applies a constructive-developmental perspective of adult growth and learning to a diverse sample of adults who are not economically privileged, mostly not American, and mostly nonnative English speakers. In other words, this study was, among other things, an effort to understand whether and how this particular theory, which was developed by studying samples with strikingly different characteristics, would apply to economically disadvantaged immigrants and less well educated Americans and help us to understand their learning experiences.

The team found that despite the fact that learners in any single setting were primarily of similar age and oriented to a common and particular social role (at the family literacy site, all participants were parents, and at the Polaroid workplace site, all participants were workers), they were diverse in their ways of knowing—an intriguing and less visible new form of pluralism (Kegan et al., 2001a, 2001b). At the same time, these learners demonstrated a range of ways of knowing that was similar to the range found in previous studies with samples of native-English-speaking adults with similarly widespread socioeconomic status (see, e.g., Kegan, 1994). In other words, ABE/ESOL learners were *not* found to have developmental

CHAPTER 2

Understanding
Constructive-Developmental Theory

THE STUDY FOCUSED on in this book investigated the learning experiences of a group of shop-floor workers enrolled in an adult diploma program at the Polaroid Corporation. The theoretical framework used by our research team to guide the project at Polaroid and the other two research sites was built on the principles of psychologist Robert Kegan's constructive-developmental theory of adult growth and learning (1982, 1994). This framework illuminates an ongoing process of meaning-making that Kegan argues may be an essential, universal account of personality growth. It helped the team understand how the adult learners in the study made sense of their learning; their motives and goals for learning; their expectations of themselves and their teachers; their understanding of themselves in their social roles as students, workers, and parents; and their development as learners over time.

In introducing this framework here I hope to familiarize readers with its theoretical principles and the three essential adult "ways of knowing" that it identifies. As noted in Kegan and colleagues (2001a, 2001b), the important work of Belenky and colleagues, especially *Women's Ways of Knowing* (1986), has achieved such prominence in the field of adult education that it is useful to point out that in this book I use the term *ways of knowing* in its customary sense. The foundation of a way of knowing (as distinguished from something that is known), or an epistemology, is the subject-object relationship: What can a person with this way of knowing reflect on, look at, have perspective on (Kegan's "object" [1982])? What is a person with this way of knowing embedded in, identified with and not able to reflect on (Kegan's "subject")? The qualitatively different ways of knowing described in this book are distinctly different ways of organizing the subject-object balance (Kegan, 1982; Kegan et al., 2001a, 2001b). I will discuss three of Kegan's five epistemologies: instrumental, socializing, and self-authoring ways of knowing. I will also explicate the central features of a "holding environment" (Kegan, 1982, 1994), which, according to Kegan, is the surrounding context that can be shaped to offer both developmentally appropriate supports and challenges that can help learners, who make sense of their experiences in qualitatively different ways, grow.

Research[1] suggests that adult learners enter ABE/ESOL classrooms—or any learning environment, for that matter—with a number of already established, qualitatively different "philosophies," or ways of knowing (Kegan et al., 2001a). My goal in this chapter is to describe the look and feel of these different ways in which adult learners make sense of their experiences. First, though, I want to introduce the concept of transformational learning, which is crucial to any discussion of constructive-developmental theory as applied to adults in a learning situation.

THE NATURE OF TRANSFORMATIONAL LEARNING: DEVELOPMENT OF SELF

In order to understand transformational learning, one must conceive learning as development, even among adults, who are often conventionally thought to have fully developed by their 20s. Granott (1998) emphasizes our need, as adults, to continue learning, both in and outside of school and in and outside of the workplace. Granott further challenges the conventional distinction between learning and development and highlights the need to examine and recast the relationship between learning and development "into a differentiation between developing processes (which can occur through learning as well) and nondeveloping processes" (p. 16). Granott (1998) also points to research on microdevelopment—development that takes place during short time periods, whether minutes, hours, or days (Fischer, 1980; Fischer & Granott, 1995; Granott, 1994), and argues that *"developing learning*—learning that has clearly identifiable developmental characteristics—does occur in adult learning" (p. 16, emphasis in original). Granott (1998) identifies three attributes of "developing learning":

> *Growth trajectory*: Developing learning clearly shows a progress to more advanced knowledge levels.
>
> *Fundamental restructuring*: Developing learning undergoes restructuring that results in qualitative shifts in knowledge reorganization.
>
> *Self-scaffolding*: Developing learning generates knowledge that supports unguided construction of more advanced knowledge.
>
> (p. 18)

In elaborating on these attributes, Granott suggests that while learning can take place through "interaction with a more knowledgeable partner, the learner has an active role in the process" (1998, p. 18). Granott urges educators, researchers, program designers, and leaders of workplace training programs to consider "the developmental nature of adult learning in order to design better learning experiences for the adult population" (p. 16).

Learning as development is an essential feature of transformational learning, because such learning can contribute to the development of the self through reconfiguring the individual's way of knowing. Crucial to an understanding of transformational learning is an understanding of a corollary theory, informational learning, which are increases in knowledge and skills that are thought to bring about changes in adults' attitudes and even their competencies. Kegan (2000) writes that learning which develops skills or knowledge introduces new cognitive resources, or deepens the resources available within an existing way of knowing. This type of learning brings new contents into a preexisting way of knowing the world.

While the research team was interested in and did examine informational learning, our primary purpose was to see how adult learners might undergo transformational learning, adhering to Kegan's (1994) definition of the concept:

> An informational stance leaves the form [of a person's way of knowing] as it is and focuses on changing what people know; it is essentially a training model for personal change. I would contrast this with a transformational stance, which places the form itself at risk for change and focuses on changes in how people know; it is essentially an educational model for personal change. . . . While *training* increases the fund of knowledge, *education* leads us out of or liberates us from one construction or organization of mind in favor of a larger one. (pp. 163–164)

In short, informational learning—new skills and information—adds to *what* a person knows, whereas transformational learning changes *how* a person knows. When a person's way of knowing changes, the person comprehends information in a different way and has enhanced his or her capacities (cognitive, interpersonal, and intrapersonal) to manage the complexities of work and life. Increases in developmental capacity widen the learner's perspective on both himself and others (Kegan, 1982, 1994). For such changes to occur, the educator needs to pay attention to the ways in which a learner is interpreting, or making meaning of, his or her experience, and then provide both supports and challenges that are developmentally appropriate to that way of making meaning.

Many scholars point to the intimate connection between transformational learning and self-examination (Brookfield, 1987, 1995; Cranton, 1994, 1996; Mezirow, 1991, 1994, 1996, 2000). As Cranton (1996) writes about her own and Jack Mezirow's (1991) work, transformational learning occurs after an individual realizes, upon reflection, that previously held assumptions are flawed and require revision. According to Kegan (1982, 1994), transformational learning involves a shift in how a person constructs reality—a change in the very way a person knows and understands and makes sense of her experience. To the learner, this kind of profound change may feel less like the self that he or she knows has simply become more capable and more like that self has changed in some essential way. The learner has undergone a development in the very way he or she constructs and makes sense of experience; this type of change is at the heart of constructive-developmental theory, as Kegan describes it (1982, 1994).

KEGAN'S CONSTRUCTIVE-DEVELOPMENTAL PERSPECTIVE ON ADULTHOOD

The constructive-developmental view of adult growth and development derives from a 30 year theoretical and methodological tradition that closely tracks the ways in which individuals make sense of their internal and external experiences (Basseches, 1984; Baxter-Magolda, 1992; Belenky et al., 1986; Gilligan, 1982; Kegan, 1982, 2000; Kitchener & King, 1994; Kohlberg, 1969, 1984; Perry, 1970; Piaget, 1952; Weathersby, 1976).[2] Constructive-developmental theory builds on the work of Swiss psychologist Jean Piaget (1952, 1963, 1965), who throughout his career examined the cognitive development of children's knowledge (the nature and origins of knowledge) and later in life focused on their social and moral reasoning. Many of the ideas that form the foundation of Piagetian theory also form the foundation for constructive-developmental theory.[3]

Constructive-developmental theory attends to the ways in which people make sense of their experiences with respect to cognitive, intrapersonal (the self's relationship to itself), and interpersonal lines of development. It attends to both the structure and the process of a person's meaning-making system and is based on two fundamental ideas: *constructivism*, which takes the view that people actively construct, or make sense of, their experiences (that is, reality), and *developmentalism*, which proposes that the ways in which people make meaning (that is, their constructions of reality) can develop over time according to regular principles of stability and change (Kegan, 1982). From a constructive-developmental perspective, a person's "way of knowing," or meaning-making system, is the lens through which he or she actively interprets life (Daloz, 1983, 1986, 1999; Kegan 1982, 1994; Kegan & Lahey, 2001; Mezirow, 2000). In Kegan's (1982) words, "There is no feeling, no experience, no thought, no perception independent of a meaning-making context" (p. 11).

Constructive-developmental theory relies on several premises, which I outline here. (For additional discussions of the premises and constructive-developmental theory in general, see Drago-Severson, 2004; Drago-Severson et al., 2001a; Kegan, 1982, 1994, 2000; Popp & Portnow, 2001.)

Premises about the Nature of Growth and Development

The first premise is that growth and development are lifelong processes; they do not end in late adolescence, but continue throughout our lives. Kegan (1982) defines growth in terms of the process of increasing differentiation and internalization—that is, the process through which there is a constant renegotiation between what is "self" and what is "other."

Development, from a constructive-developmental perspective, involves more than acquiring new knowledge or learning new skills (informational learning). Kegan and Lahey (1984) describe it as follows: "Development is always a process of outgrowing one system of meaning by integrating it (as a subsystem) into a new system of meaning" (p. 203). According to this theory, the self "is" what it is subject to, and the self "has" what it can take as object. In other words, we are unable to take a perspective on what we are subject to; we are embedded in it and identified with it. It is not separated from ourselves.

What we can take as "object," on the other hand, are components of our knowledge that are discrete from our selves, such that they can be examined, controlled, manipulated, or in some way acted upon (Kegan, 1994). What we are subject to, we do not question and cannot *see*; it is a part of the self, and though we may be able to name something that we are subject to, we cannot reflect on it. Thus, meaning making, Kegan (1982) explains, is a "simultaneously epistemological and ontological activity" concerned with both ways of knowing and being (p. 45).

Another premise of constructive-developmental theory is that these kinds of growth processes are gradual and progressive (they occur step-by-step). Moreover, they occur in the direction of greater complexity—that is, adults evolve gradually from a simpler way of knowing to another, more complex way of knowing, and they do so at their own pace, depending on the supports and challenges provided by the environment. Importantly, adults with different ways of knowing experience the same events and situations in qualitatively different ways. While these developmental processes are sequential, people of similar ages and life phases can be at different developmental places (Broderick, 1996; Drago-Severson, 1996, 2004; Kegan, 1982, 1994; Popp, 1993; Portnow, 1996; Portnow et al., 1998; Stein, 2000).

Regardless of the way that a person is making sense of experience, the self strives to make itself cohere; it organizes experiences in ways that are reflective of its meaning-making system. This coherence is preserved until the self is no longer able to incorporate new experiences into the existing meaning-making system. This is the point at which the subject-object balance is gradually renegotiated and a new, more complex subject-object balance evolves. Transition from one developmental stage or level to another is an incremental progression of increasing complexity in an individual's cognitive, emotional, interpersonal, and intrapersonal capacities. During transitions from one stage to the next, the self gradually incorporates the former way of knowing into a newer, larger and more complex way of organization. For example, in the transition from an instrumental to a socializing way of knowing, an individual will begin to empathize with the perspectives of others, which are typically not considered in this way when making meaning with an instrumental worldview.

A frequent debate concerns whether a higher, more complex stage is also considered to be a better stage. Perhaps the best way to look at this issue is in terms of the natural learning challenges that people encounter in life. If the complexity of a person's meaning system is sufficient to meet the challenges that he or she encounters, then it would not necessarily be better for that person to construct experiences through a more complex way of knowing. If that meaning system is not sufficient to meet those challenges, then a change in the person's way of knowing in the direction of greater complexity would indeed be better, in the pragmatic sense. This is not to say that a person is a better person for having a more complex way of knowing (Drago-Severson et al., 2001a).

From the research team's perspective, this sort of development involves transformational learning, a qualitative shift in one's understanding of oneself, the world, and the relationship between the two. Transformational learning makes it possible for a person to take broader perspectives on different aspects of the self and others (Cranton, 1994; Kegan, 1982, 1994; Kegan & Lahey, 2001; Mezirow, 1991). In the view of the research team, transformational learning is intimately linked to the way in which people conceive of and enact their adult responsibilities. It enhances their capacities to manage the complexities of their lives as learners, parents, and workers. In the team's view, transformational development occurs across domains. Thus, in general people tend to, but may not always (in exceptional circumstances), exercise the same meaning systems across all domains of life. (For a more detailed discussion of this, see Kegan, 1994.) Because our research focused on understanding how adults made sense of and interpreted their learning experiences, we employed Kegan's framework—a theory that considers the way people construct or made sense of the reality in which they live and the way that these constructions can potentially change or develop over time.

Our ways of knowing organize how we understand our experiences of ourselves, others, and life situations. Like Kegan's (1982, 1994) prior work, our team's research suggests that a person's relationship to his or her ways of knowing is not accidental or random. In other words, we do not tend to take our way of knowing on and off from one day to the next, like putting on and removing a coat (Kegan et al., 2001a). Rather, meaning systems are stable and consistent for a period of time, reflect an identifiable inner logic and a coherent system, and may feel more to us like the way we *are* rather than something we *have* (Kegan et al., 2001a). Each way of knowing is qualitatively different from and builds upon the previous way of knowing by incorporating the former into its new, more complex meaning system. As human beings we are actively building our own meaning through our way of knowing (including our experiences of learning in the classroom; and our relationships with loved ones, supervisors, and colleagues). Understanding how a person is making meaning creates an opportunity to support that person's growth in a way that will be experienced as supportive.

KEGAN'S "WAYS OF KNOWING"

Kegan's constructive-developmental theory is composed of six qualitatively different systems of thought, or ways of constructing reality.[4] The first, "Stage 0," termed *incorporative*, occurs in the first years of life when infants are identified with their reflexes (i.e., sensing, moving). The second of these six ways of knowing, termed *impulsive*, describes the meaning making of young children. The last, mostly theoretical stage is known as *interindividual*, and is not ordinarily found in any population (Kegan, 1994) and, if it is, has not been detected before midlife. Therefore, I will focus on describing the three broadly and qualitatively different ways of knowing that are most prevalent in adulthood: the *instrumental*, the *socializing*, and the *self-authoring* ways of knowing. There are also four distinct and identifiable transition points between each of these main ways of knowing, which I discuss below.

The Instrumental Way of Knowing

A person who relies largely on an instrumental way of knowing tends to maintain a what-do-you-have-that-can-help-me/what-do-I-have-that-can-help-you perspective of life. A strength of this meaning system is that the person understands that observable events, processes, and situations have a reality independent of his or her own perspective or vantage point (e.g., when a person is in an airplane moving away from Earth, objects look smaller, but the person knows that the buildings and trees are not *actually* becoming different or shrinking).

People with this way of knowing are able to have a perspective on and to control their impulses. They do not, however, have this same sense of perspective on their own or others' needs, wishes, and interests. In general, another person's needs and interests are important only if they interfere with the interests of the instrumental knower. Instrumental knowers are aware that they have preferences and feelings that remain consistent over time (I love car racing but I hate riding in buses). They also recognize and understand that other people have their own preferences and beliefs. Experiences of self, others, and the world are understood and organized by concrete attributes, events, and sequences (I am good at my job, I like basketball); by noticeable actions and behaviors (good students follow rules, study hard, and get the right answers); and by one's own point of view, needs, interests, and preferences (if I do this at work, I will have a better chance of getting a raise).

While people with this way of knowing recognize that other people have feelings, beliefs, and desires, they do not yet have the developmental capacity to hold—or accommodate—both their perspective and the perspective of another person simultaneously (what you have can help me, and what I have can help you in completing this assignment and then I may get a high score or better grade, or promotion), nor do they have the capacity for abstract thinking or for making generalizations. Instrumental knowers derive meaning and structure in their lives from concrete rules. They generally want to learn "the rules" so that they will be able to do things in "the right way," whether it is performing a task on the job, solving a math problem, or helping their children with homework.

Features of the Instrumental Meaning-Making System. Popp and Portnow (2001) describe key features of the instrumental way of knowing as follows:

- Characterized by a very concrete orientation to the world. The self is identified with and defined through one's self-interests; by concrete needs, purposes, plans, wants. One tends to describe herself in concrete, external, or behavioral terms such as one's physical characteristics, one's concrete likes and dislikes, the kind of job one has, the kind of car one drives.
- Characterized by dualistic thinking such as right versus wrong, and arbitrary either/or distinctions.
- Concerned with concrete consequences, such as: "I want to get my GED so I can get a better job/make more money." "If I do/don't do this, will I get fired?" "Will I get caught or punished?"
- Others are seen as either pathways or obstacles to getting one's concrete needs met. For example, "if you like me, there's a better chance that you'll help me get/do what I want. If you don't like me, you won't help me get what I want." Interactions with others are understood in terms of their concrete elements (the facts of what transpired), the concrete give-and-take (what I help you with, what you help me with), and concrete outcomes (I get a better grade).

- Strong reliance on rules to know how to accomplish something and to do it the right way.
- Thinks through categories. Not capable of abstract thinking or making generalizations.
- Understanding of the Golden Rule[5] has a tit-for-tat mentality: "I'll do to you what you do to me." (p. 58)

While instrumental knowers orient toward their own concrete goals, interests, and needs, they should not be pejoratively construed as solipsistic; they are also often very kind and giving, even if in a concrete manner.

The Socializing Way of Knowing

A person who makes meaning predominantly with a socializing way of knowing has developed a greater capacity for reflection than a person with an instrumental way of knowing. Socializing knowers are able to think abstractly, to make generalizations, and to reflect on their actions and the actions of others.

Socializing knowers have developed the capacity to be conversational and to participate in a shared reality. They have the capacity to subordinate their needs and desires to the needs and desires of other people—an advance from the instrumental way of knowing. When people have grown into a socializing way of knowing, they can identify with and internalize other people's feelings (What does my boss want me to do? Will my spouse still love me if I disagree with her?). Kegan (1994) asserts that for people making sense of their experiences with this way of knowing, "winning the approval and acceptance of others" is of ultimate importance (p. 171).

In other words, other people are experienced not merely as resources to be used by the self but as sources of internal validation, orientation, or authority. The self is identified with, or made up by, its relationship to other people (family, important friends, supervisors, or colleagues) or ideas (religious, political, or philosophical ideologies) (Drago-Severson, 2004; Drago-Severson et al., 2001a; Kegan et al., 2001a).

With this way of knowing, the self, others, and the world participate in a swirl of values, loyalties, and longer-term purposes that are seen to underlie events, attributes, and immediate preferences. Socializing knowers are not, however, able to externalize another person's point of view; that is, they do not have the capacity to consider that point of view from a distance and evaluate it or have perspective on it. In other words, the major limitation to this way of knowing is that a person does not yet have the capacity to consult herself about the shared reality. "One's self-definitions, purposes, and preoccupying concerns are essentially co-defined, co-determined, and co-experienced" (Kegan & Lahey, 1984, p. 203). A socializing knower cannot evaluate other people's points of view without risk to his or her own self; the self does not know itself as separate from the interpersonal context in which it is embedded.

A person making meaning with this way of knowing represses anger rather than expressing it, and avoids conflict because it is a risk to the interpersonal relationship—and a threat to the person's very self. Put simply, when a socializing knower experiences a conflict between herself and one other person or between herself and several other important and valued people (e.g., a loved one, a supervisor, a colleague), she will feel torn—and as she tries to figure out what to do. People with this way of knowing identify with other people's expectations of themselves and do not yet have the capacity to look inside themselves and consider their own expectations for themselves. Kegan (1982) summarizes the socializing knower's embeddedness in interpersonal relationships in this way: "You are the other by whom I complete myself, the other whom I need to create the context out of which I define and know myself and the world" (p. 100).

Features of the Socializing Meaning-Making System. Popp and Portnow (2001) describe the socializing way of knowing in the following way:

- Self is defined by an abstract sense of identity: "I am a sensitive person." "I am shy." "I feel confused a lot." Sense of self is defined by opinions and expectations of others: "If she gets mad at me I feel like I am a really bad person and that she doesn't like me anymore."
- Feels empathy; feels responsible for other's feelings; experiences others as responsible for own feelings. "I made him feel terrible; it's my fault he feels bad." "She made me feel good about myself."
- Concerned with abstract psychological consequences: "Am I still a good person?" "Am I meeting your expectations of me?" "Do you still like/love/value me?" "Do I still belong?"
- Intolerant of ambiguity. Needs a clear sense of what others expect and want from him- or herself and feels a strong obligation and duty to meet those expectations.
- Others are experienced as co-constructors of the self: "What you think about me tells me who I am and what kind of person I am."
- Reliance on external authority and important others for standards, values, acceptance, belonging, and sense of identity.
- Capable of abstract thinking, thinking about thinking.
- Criticism is experienced as destructive to the self: "If you don't like what I did/said/am, I am not a good person."
- Understanding of the Golden Rule deals with issues of mutuality and loyalty

and obligation: "I should do for you what I hope and need and expect you should do for me." (p. 60)

A socializing knower has the capacity to think about the self abstractly and defines his or her own identity in terms of others' expectation and perceptions. Unlike instrumental knowers, a person with a socializing way of knowing orients to abstract and psychological consequences, with concern for one's sense of belonging.

The Self-Authoring Way of Knowing

People with predominantly self-authoring ways of knowing have the capacity to take responsibility for and ownership of their own internal authority and to make up their own system of beliefs rather than being "made up by" someone or something outside themselves. They have the capacity not only to identify (and identify with) abstract values, ideals, and longer-term purposes, but also to prioritize and integrate competing values; to apply the expectations and demands of others to their own internal bench of judgment; and to author—and internally generate—an overall system of belief or personal ideology.

A person with a self-authoring way of knowing is able to take the interpersonal context as object—to hold it out and look at it, to reflect on it. Thus, a self-authoring knower "authors a self which maintains a coherence across a shared psychological space and so achieves an identity" (Kegan, 1982, p. 100). Self-authoring knowers are able to take responsibility for and regulate their own feelings rather than seeing others as the generators of their feelings. Simply put, they have made the evolutionary (or constructive-developmental) move from " 'I am my relationships' to 'I have relationships' " (Kegan, 1982, p. 100).

Self-authoring knowers can control their feelings and emotions and can discuss their internal states. They can reflect on and regulate their relationships. While a preoccupying concern for socializing knowers is how well they are liked, self-authoring knowers concern themselves with the stability of their internal structure of beliefs and values. They have self-regulating capacities, including the capacity to reflect on their roles, representing a developmental advance from the socializing way of knowing, in which a person identifies with others' expectations. Self-authoring knowers are able to construct a theory about their relationships and have a way of understanding how the past, present, and future relate.

A limitation to this way of knowing is that the self identifies with its ideology; it is embedded in its own assertions, theories, ideals, and principles. Self-authoring knowers are not able to reflect on the purposes of the organization they are running. Self-authoring knowers can generate their own values and personal standards (internally). Competence, achievement, and responsibility are the most important concerns of people who make meaning in this way.

Features of a Self-authoring Meaning-Making System. Popp and Portnow (2001) summarize the strengths and limitations of the self-authoring way of knowing as follows:

- Self is defined by its own internal authority, and by the capacity to differentiate between parts of itself and parts of others.
- Can hold contradictory feelings simultaneously. Self can disagree with itself, feel two or more contradictory or conflicting things at the same time.
- Concerned with consequences for personal integrity and meeting one's own standards: "Am I competent?" "Am I living/working/loving up to my full potential?" "Am I upholding my own values and standards?" The self is the evaluator of its own performance and the holder of its own standards and values. "I evaluate myself according to what I have decided is important."
- Integrates others' perspectives, including criticism, as one perspective among many. Evaluates and uses criticism and other perspectives according to own internally generated standards and values.
- Others are experienced as autonomous entities with their own psychological agendas and standards. Differences with others are experienced as a given, are appreciated as such and are taken as opportunities for growth and creativity.
- Reliance on own authority. "I am my own authority on my values and standards and goals, and especially on what I know, what I need to know, and what I don't know, and can choose to consult with others to enhance my own authority."
- Understanding of the Golden Rule deals with the recognition, acknowledgment, and respect of different values and standards: "Doing for each other supports each of us in meeting our own self-defined values, ideals, and goals, and helps preserve the social order." (pp. 61–62)

Unlike socializing knowers, self-authoring knowers strive to meet their own self-determined expectations and standards and internally evaluate attainment of these, with concerns for competency.

Table 2.1 summarizes the essential qualities that make for an instrumental, a socializing, or a self-authoring way of knowing.

Transitions: Subphases in Constructive-Developmental Theory

Although development is a gradual process and the complete evolution from one comprehensive way of knowing to another may take years

Table 2.1. How Adults with Different Ways of Knowing Construct Knowledge and the Meaning of Education

Way of Knowing/ Underlying Structure of Thinking [1]	Guiding Orientation: Considerations and Concerns	Orientation to and Construction of Knowledge	Meaning of Education
Instrumental Knowers (S = Needs, interests, wishes; O = Impulses, perceptions)	• Orient to self-interests, purposes, wants, & concrete needs. • Dependence on rules, decisions are based on what the self will acquire. • *"Will I get punished?"*	• *"What's in it for me?"* • Knowledge is a kind of possession, an accumulation of skills, facts, and actions that can yield solutions—a means to an end. Once I get it, then I have it. • Knowledge is right or wrong. • Knowledge comes from external authority that tells me the right skills, facts, and rules I need to produce the results to get what I need/want. • Knowledge helps me meet my own concrete needs and goals and obtain instrumental outcomes.	Education is pursued to acquire something.
Socializing Knowers (S = Needs, interests, wishes; O = Impulses, perceptions)	• Orient to valued others' (external authority) expectations and opinions. • Dependence on external authority. • Acceptance and affiliation are crucial. • Self feels responsible for others' feelings and holds others responsible for own feelings. • Criticism & conflict are threats to the self. • *"Will you (a valued other/ authority) still like/value me?"* • *"Will you still think I am a good person?"*	• *"What do you think I should know?"* • Knowledge is general information one should know for the required social roles and to meet expectations of teachers and authorities. • Knowledge is equated with objective truth. • Knowledge comes from high authorities and experts who hand down truth and understanding. Authorities and experts are the source of the legitimate knowledge and informed opinions. • Knowledge helps one to meet cultural and social expectations, gain acceptance and entry into social roles, and feel a sense of belonging.	Education is pursued to be someone.

(continued)

Table 2.1. (continued)

Way of Knowing/ Underlying Structure of Thinking [1]	Guiding Orientation: Considerations and Concerns	Orientation to and Construction of Knowledge	Meaning of Education
Self-Authoring Knowers (S = Authorship, identity, psychic administration, ideology; O = The interpersonal, mutuality)	• Orient to self's values, internal authority. • Reliance on own internal values. • Criticism is evaluated according to personal standards. • Concern with one's own competence and performance. • Can hold contradictory feelings simultaneously. • *"Am I maintaining my own standards and values?"* • *"Am I competent?"* • *"Am I living, working, loving to the best of my ability?"* • *"Am I achieving my goals and reaching for my ideals?"*	• *"What do I want and need to know and learn; what is important for me to know to keep learning and growing?"* • Knowledge is understood as construction, truth, and a matter of context. Bodies of knowledge and theories are seen as models for interpreting and analyzing experience. • Knowledge comes from one's interpretation and evaluation of standards, values, perceptions, deductions, and predictions. • Knowledge comes from a self-generated curiosity and sense of responsibility for one's own learning. • Knowledge helps to enrich one's life, to achieve a greater competence according to one's own standards, to deepen one's understanding of self and world to participate in the improvement of society.	Education is pursued to become someone.

[1] "S" refers to Subject, or that which a person is identified and "O" refers to Object, or that which a person can hold, examine, and perceive.

Adapted from Drago-Severson (2002b); Kegan (1982); and Portnow, Popp, Broderick, Drago-Severson, & Kegan, (1998).

(Kegan, 1994), there are identifiable and significantly different steps along the way, each creating a new frame of reference for how adults think about themselves in their various roles as parents, learners, workers, and so forth. While the pace of this development varies from one person to another, its course is predictable (Kegan, 1982, 1994, 2000). Included in this course are four steps referred to by Lahey and colleagues (1988) as transitional phases. In fact, for most of our lives, as we grow and develop from one way of understanding to the next, we make meaning in these transitional phases, the spaces between each of the three well-defined ways of knowing described above.

In *A Guide to the Subject-Object Interview: Its Administration and Interpretation*, Lahey and her colleagues (1988) propose a system for understanding these transitional phases. In this system, X is a person's current way of knowing, and Y the evolving way of knowing. The notations $X(Y)$, X/Y, Y/X, and $Y(X)$ are used to indicate what Lahey and colleagues refer to as "transitional ways of knowing" and the evolution from one meaning system to the next. Movement through the transitional space from X (e.g., a socializing way of knowing) to Y (a self-authoring way of knowing) is typically represented in the following manner: $X \rightarrow X(Y) \rightarrow X/Y \rightarrow Y/X \rightarrow Y(X) \rightarrow Y$.

The transition from X to Y begins with a dominant X, with a sense that Y may contribute a better way of knowing, though lacking an ability to articulate Y fully (Popp & Portnow, 2001). Y acts as a hunch or feeling in this $X(Y)$ state. Once operating as X/Y, each way of knowing works to promote the other; X fosters the developing Y, and Y works to transform X. In the shift from socializing to self-authoring, this might manifest as the strength of considering others' perspectives balancing with the commitment to one's own point of view. In a Y/X stance, for instance, Y is dominant and other perspectives are important but not crucial in the emergent self-authoring identity. Before fully attaining Y status, the individual acts from a $Y(X)$ position, in which the X is merely a trace of a previous mindset, just as Y was a hunch in the $X(Y)$ perspective.

As mentioned earlier, moving from one phase to the next is a gradual, sequential, and incremental process. In fact, in all of the longitudinal data our research team and Kegan have reviewed, movement from one transitional phase to the next has not occurred in a timeframe of less than one year[6]; there is, however, no maximum amount of time in which an evolution may occur. The descriptions that follow are brief; for a complete description of this process, see Lahey et al., 1988.

Transitioning from an Instrumental to a Socializing Way of Knowing

Recall that instrumental knowers are unable to coordinate more than one perspective at a time; thus, people with this way of knowing consider another person's perspective mainly in terms of how it affects their ability to meet their own needs. Lahey and colleagues (1988) argue that evolution from a wholly operating instrumental way of knowing entails introducing another's perspective to the self, which requires a capacity to hold two points of view simultaneously, amidst ambiguity. As Popp and Portnow (2001) explain, thinking shifts from concrete to abstract, from relationships as means to ends in themselves, and from self-reference to empathy. The individual can reflect on his or her own thinking and understand that more than one feeling can exist at one time.

Transitioning from a Socializing to a Self-Authoring Way of Knowing

The evolution from a socializing way of knowing to a self-authoring way of knowing is characterized by a developmental move from *being* identified with one's relationships to *having* the capacity to reflect on and hold a perspective on relationships. Kegan (1982) writes that the individual can discern more of a self than was previously possible in a context of "interpersonalism" (p. 100). An authority over one's own identity marks the attainment of a self-authored way of knowing, which can retain its integrity in the company of others.

In the transition from these two whole meaning structures, the self gradually renegotiates the subject-object balance in that the self is now able to have a perspective on the interpersonal relationships with which it had been closely identified. During this transition, the self develops the capacity to look to its own internal value "generator" as the source of feelings and principles.

When people first begin to grow toward making sense of their experiences with a self-authoring way of knowing, they may feel the limitations of their present way of knowing. As Popp and Portnow (2001) note, however, such people are in a state of "not being able to construct anything beyond it yet—just knowing that there must be a different way to think and feel about things, and not wanting to be so caught by the concerns and issues that feel so ultimate and fundamental to who one is" (p. 67).

In other words, during the transition from the socializing way of knowing to the self-authoring way of knowing, the socializing way gradually diminishes and the self-authoring becomes more dominant. Popp and Portnow (2001) explain that while individuals feel more confident in engaging with others and integrating or opposing their values without a loss of self, development does not indicate the disposal of psychological conflicts or difficulty. Other people's opinions and expectations are still important; however, they no longer define a person's self. Instead, a person grows to have the capacity to reflect on and consider the expectations of others as separate from his or her own.

WHY WAYS OF KNOWING MATTER IN THE CLASSROOM

Learners construct knowledge in qualitatively different ways, depending on their way of knowing. For example, as Table 2.1 indicates, adults who are instrumental knowers construct knowledge as something that is right or wrong, and something that is obtained from an external authority. Knowledge is seen as a possession that a person can accumulate (the more knowledge, facts, and skills, the better) rather than something that is internally generated. Like instrumental knowers, socializing knowers consider knowledge to be the property of authorities. Unlike instrumental knowers, socializing knowers conceive of knowledge as something a person should have in order to meet the goals and expectations of external authorities (such as a teacher or a supervisor) and/or valued others (a friend or family member). Adults with a self-authoring way of knowing see knowledge as context dependent. They see others as sources of knowledge, but they also see themselves as sources of knowledge.

People's ways of knowing influence the way they see themselves and the expectations they have for themselves. What constitutes the expectations a learner with a particular way of knowing holds for herself differs for a learner with a different way of knowing. Each learner needs developmentally appropriate supports and challenges in order to grow and learn. For example, instrumental knowers may view teacher comments and questions as evidence that they were either "right" or "wrong," whereas self-authoring knowers may review, and even seek out, teachers' comments to enhance their own learning. As such, it is vital for teachers to consider students' individual expectations of themselves as learners to provide them with the most effective support. Teachers need to attend to this developmental diversity (in addition to other, more visible forms of diversity, such as race and ethnicity) (Drago-Severson et al., 2001c; Kegan et al., 2001a, 2001b).

Table 2.2 shows how adults with different ways of knowing make decisions and experience the decision-making process. Adults with different ways of knowing have qualitatively different capacities for self-reflection and perspective taking. For example, instrumental knowers will focus on following the correct steps and rules in order to make the "right" decisions so that they can achieve concrete goals that are based upon their concrete desires. Socializing knowers will look to valued others or authorities for direction, guidance, and confirmation of progress when faced with decisions. For socializing knowers, decisions are based on a sense of loyalty or allegiance to valued others. In contrast, self-authoring knowers have the capacity to look internally to their self-generated values when making decisions. With this way of knowing, a person is able to hold and coordinate multiple perspectives and to balance them with her own when making decisions. Self-authoring knowers think about conflict as a natural part of dialogue, whereas socializing knowers perceive conflicting views of valued others as a threat—both to themselves and to their relationships with oth-

Table 2.2. Decision-Making Skills: How Learners with Different Ways of Knowing Make Decisions and Solve Problems (e.g., When Using Technology, Understanding Mathematical Techniques, Conducting Research, and Planning)

INSTRUMENTAL KNOWER	SOCIALIZING KNOWER	SELF-AUTHORING KNOWER
Focus is on naming concrete goals and setting the right concrete steps to get there. Goals are based on concrete needs and desires.	*Focus* is on realizing an abstract goal and figuring out best ways to achieve it. Goals are based on a sense of loyalty or obligation to another person or group or cause.	*Focus* is on identifying one's own independently conceived and desired goal(s) and considering all of the possible ways to accomplish it/them.
Works to follow correct steps and rules and make sure to do each one in the right way (there being only one right way).	*Works* to follow guidance from experts or other authority regarding best way to plan for and reach goal. Looks externally for support, encouragement and validation of progress.	*Works* toward considering the multiple ways of achieving one's goal and deciding on which makes most sense to do given all of the complexities of the goal and of one's own talents and resources.
Emphasizes following through on those concrete procedures and doing so in the proscribed manner. Deviation is experienced as doing it wrong.	*Emphasizes* setting up a plan and steps to get there based on what the experts or authorities recommend. Successful achievement of goal is based on positive evaluation from others or other external measure.	*Emphasizes* following one's own standards and values for reaching the goal, recognizing when and where one needs others' expertise and seeking that out.
Challenge is to recognize, accept, and be flexible enough to follow very different paths to reach a goal; to see the goal and the steps toward it in abstract terms with a variety of meanings and ways to get there.	*Challenge* is to independently create and use one's own goal, procedures, and standards for evaluation separate from and possibly in contradiction to external experts/authorities.	*Challenge* is to recognize the relative and constructive nature of one's goals and plans, and to be able to pursue, with equal investment, goals that once felt antithetical to who one is.

Adapted from Popp (2001).

ers. When faced with conflict, instrumental knowers will focus on concrete identification on the conflict (Who is right? Who is wrong?), and orient toward a "tit for tat" construction of fairness.

Simply put, adults with different developmental orientations need different forms of support and challenges. Taking into account the way a person makes sense of the world creates an opportunity to offer support and challenge in a way that is developmentally appropriate (see, e.g., Drago-Severson, 2004). By focusing on the supports and challenges to a person's current way of knowing, learning can be greatly enhanced and transformational learning made possible.

THE HOLDING ENVIRONMENT: A DYNAMIC CONTEXT FOR GROWTH

D. W. Winnicott (1965) originally used the term *holding environment* to refer to the kinds of special relationships in the psychosocial environment that are needed to support the robust development of infants. Such environments, according to Winnicott, needed to be responsive to an infant's processes of growth and development, so that he could thrive. Kegan (1982) extended its application to a human being's entire lifespan.

A good holding environment serves three functions, according to Kegan (1982, 1994). First, it must "hold well"—meaning that it recognizes and confirms who the person is and how the person is currently making meaning, without frustration or urgent anticipation of change. As Kegan explains, holding does not refer to circumscribing or confining, but rather to buttressing or supporting who a person is and how a person is making meaning. Holding without confining may be challenging, but it may also be a necessary ingredient of what it means to care, he notes.

Second, when a person is ready a good holding environment needs to "let go," permitting and stimulating a person to move beyond his or her existing understandings to more complex ways of knowing, so that growth is promoted. Third, a good holding environment "sticks around," providing continuity, stability, and availability to the person who is in the process of growth. This means that whenever possible, the holding environment remains in place so that relationships can be reknown and reconstructed in a new way—a way that supports who the person has grown to become. While this third feature of a good holding environment may be challenging to provide in shorter-term programs, any classroom or program can include the other two features—namely, high support and challenge (Drago-Severson & Berger, 2001; Drago-Severson et al., 2001a; Kegan et al., 2001a). Both are essential for good holding.

SUMMARY

In introducing constructive-developmental theory here I hope that I have helped to familiarize readers with its theoretical principles, the three essential adult "ways of knowing" that it identifies, the process of transformational learning, and the central features of a "holding environment" (Kegan, 1982, 1994). I have tried to acquaint readers with the look and feel of a number of qualitatively different "philosophies" or ways of knowing through which adult learners make sense of their experiences.

Our relationship to our ways of knowing is not at all casual. In other words, we do not tend to take them on and off from one day to the next like sweaters from a drawer. The world we construct through our way of knowing (including the learning and teaching world of the classroom) may seem to us less the way things *look to us*, and more like the way things *are*. Learning new information or skills can be difficult, and when it is accomplished we may feel like the person we know ourselves to be knows more and has more capabilities. But changing our fundamental way of knowing—in essence, developing a whole new way of knowing—can be qualitatively even more difficult; it can feel less like the self we know has taken on greater capabilities and more like the self we knew has changed in some fundamental way. This is "constructive-development." We have undergone a development in the fundamental way we construct experience.

This chapter implies the kinds of benefits to practitioners and policymakers that may result from better understanding how adults make sense of their learning experiences. I discuss this more fully in the chapters that follow.

CHAPTER 3

Research Method

Understanding the narrative and contextual dimensions of human actors can lead to new insights, compassionate judgment, and a creation of shared knowledge and meaning that can inform professional practice.
—H. McEwan and K. Egan, *Narrative in Teaching, Learning, and Research,* 1995

A S DEVELOPMENTAL PSYCHOLOGISTS AND EDUCATORS, the research team embarked on a process-based research study. Our aim was to carefully track the way learners made sense of their program learning experiences over time. Our team had the privilege of developing a contextualized understanding of learners' experiences—as described in the above quotation—that we hope will inform teaching and learning practices, program designs, and policy.

Like other researchers who have examined adult development and transformational learning, we employed a variety of research methods and tools that enabled us to deeply examine participants' internal, or psychological, processes of change. Our methods built on and extended techniques for conducting developmental case analyses of transformational learning developed and validated by Selman and Schultz (1990).[1]

SITE AND PARTICIPANT SELECTION

In 1997, our research team identified three settings in which to study implementing adult basic education (ABE) and English for Speakers of Other Languages (ESOL) programs that were widely considered to employ best practices (see, e.g., Harbison with Kegan, 1999). Each program had an established history of practices focusing on learner-centered curricula and pedagogical approaches that appeared to be developmental in nature. Moreover, the program designs in part allowed for long-term growth in students' understanding, thereby allowing us to examine the developmental dimensions of transformational learning over time.

In addition to having learner-centered curricula, each of these programs intentionally incorporated a diversity of supports and challenges to facilitate adult learning. Our team carefully considered the ways in which program design, teacher practice, learner expectations, and curricula might support and challenge learners with different ways of knowing and possibly lead to transformation. The programs we selected also incorporated curricula and pedagogical practices that were directed toward supporting the enhancement of adults' competency in one of three social roles: student, parent, and worker. Through our methodology, we were able to trace changes in the ways that participants understood and fulfilled these roles.

Participation in each of the programs was voluntary. We began this study with 58 adult learners—17 at the community college site, 22 at the family literacy site, and 19 at the workplace site. During the research, 17 participants (across sites) either withdrew or temporarily stepped out. Our team was able to conduct what we refer to as "non-completer" interviews with several of these participants after the programs ended for that year.

Each program had specific goals: (1) to prepare learners for enrollment in a GED (general education development) program or to help students learn ESOL (the family literacy site); (2) to prepare learners for entry into academic coursework at the college level (the community college site); or (3) to earn a high school diploma (the workplace site). Thirty-eight of these participants were non–native English speakers, and most were from a lower socioeconomic background. This sample was diverse with respect to race, ethnicity, age, past educational experience, and social role.

The Bunker Hill Community College Site

The research team negotiated a relationship with Bunker Hill Community College (BHCC) in Chelsea, Massachusetts, during the summer of 1998. Throughout the 1998–1999 academic year, we looked at the experience of a group of recently immigrated young adults, most in their late teens or mid-20s, in a pilot program at BHCC intended to prepare them for traditional academic coursework in college. These 17 adults, 11 women and 6 men, were originally from world regions that included Africa, Asia, the Caribbean, Central America, and Europe.

These learners were enrolled as a *cohort*—a tight knit group—in the same two classes at BHCC during their first semester, an ESOL class, and an introductory psychology class designed for ESOL learners. During the second semester the group disbanded and each learner independently selected courses from the full range of offerings at BHCC. As part of this pilot program, all learners also engaged in coursework at BHCC's Self-Directed Learning Center. This center is open all year and is staffed with tutors and computers to assist students with their coursework.

Much like the learners at the other two sites that the team researched, all of the adults enrolled in this program were primarily from lower socioeconomic backgrounds, and all of them spoke English as a second language. Unlike the learners at the other two sites, these had already earned a high school diploma and were matriculating for an associates degree or a certificate of study. Our interest was in learning how participation in the program influenced their conception of the role of student. (For a discussion of learnings from this site, see Helsing, Broderick, & Hammerman, 2001.)

The Even Start Family Literacy Site

During the summer and early fall of 1998 we negotiated a research relationship with an Even Start Family Literacy Program in Massachusetts (administrators did not want to reveal the name or exact location of the site). To enroll in this program, participants had to come from a lower socioeconomic background and have at least one child who attended the facility.

Thirteen of the parents who participated in the research from start to finish were women and two were men. They were mostly in their 30s and had emigrated from various regions of the world (Asia, Africa, the Caribbean, and Central and South America). All of them, except for one woman who was born in the United States, spoke English as a second language and had been living in the United States for an average of 9 years.

At this site, we carefully followed two cohorts of parents. Those in one cohort attended a preparatory GED class, and those in the other were enrolled in an ESOL class, which ran from the fall of 1998 through July 1999. The literacy program the parents attended had five components: a pre-GED or ESOL class; a class for their child or children; home visits from site administrators; parent and child meetings; and a parent discussion group, in which the two cohorts of adults met each week. Although we conducted our research with these parents over the course of a year, several learners had been participating in this family literacy program for several years. Our interest was in learning how participation in the program affected the ways in which these adults conceived of and enacted their roles as parents. (For a discussion of learnings from this site, see Portnow, Diamond, & Rimer, 2001.)

The Polaroid Workplace Site

We selected the Polaroid Corporation of Waltham, Massachusetts, as our workplace site in the fall of 1997. At this site we studied a group of shop-floor workers who participated in a 14-month diploma program designed and delivered by the Continuing Education Institute (CEI) of Watertown, Massachusetts.

Eight men and eight women completed the program. Most of them were in their 30s and 40s, had lived in the United States for more than 20 years, were married, and had children. Two men were born in the United States and spoke English as their first language. The remainder of the learners in this cohort spoke English as a second language and had emigrated from different regions of the world, including Asia, the Caribbean, and West Africa. More details on the context of Polaroid as a workplace and on the CEI Adult Diploma Program are provided in Chapter 4. The learners who completed the program at Polaroid are introduced in Table 4.2.

RESEARCH QUESTIONS: WHAT DID WE WANT TO LEARN?

By carefully examining the developmental dimensions of transformational learning, the team sought to understand, from the learners' perspective and from our developmental perspective, how the mixture of supports and challenges provided by the three programs helped these adults in their learning (Kegan et al., 2001b). The following research questions guided our exploration:

1. How does the developmental level, or way of knowing, shape adults' experiences and definitions of the core roles they assume as learners, parents, and/or workers? What are the regularities in the ways in which adults at similar levels of development construct the role demands and role supports in each of these domains?
2. How do adult learners' ways of knowing shape their experience and definition of programs dedicated to increasing their role competence? What are adult learners' motives for learning, definitions of success, conceptions of the learner's role, and understandings of their teachers' relationship to their learning?
3. What educational practices and processes contribute to changes in the learner's relationship to learning (vis-à-vis motive, efficacy, and meaning system) and, specifically, to any reconceptualization of core roles?
4. To what extent does the level of a person's development and/or transformation predict success and competence? Are the similarities in experiences across roles related to developmental levels (ways of knowing)?

DATA COLLECTION

To each adult learner at each site on at least three different occasions during the program, we administered a variety of data collection methods and tools. Our methods included various types of in-depth qualitative interviews, structured exercises, classroom observations, focus groups, and quantitative survey measures.

The first round of intensive data collection at the community college site occurred in early October 1998, the second in December 1998, and the last in May 1999. In addition, at this site we conducted observations of classes during the academic year and teacher interviews at the start and toward the end of the academic year. At the family literacy site, the first wave of data collection took place in November 1998, and the second and third occurred in March and July 1999, respectively. We also conducted periodic classroom observations. In addition, teacher and program director interviews took place at the beginning and end of this program. At the workplace site, we had four rounds of data collection (March-April 1998, September 1998, March 1999, and June 1999). Just as we did at the other two sites, we conducted periodic classroom observations for the duration of the CEI program. In addition, we conducted interviews with program teachers at the start and end of the program. In total, we conducted and analyzed approximately 670 hours of semistructured qualitative interviews and developmental assessments (tape-recorded and transcribed), 160 hours of quantitative survey type measures, 25 hours of observations, and analysis of various site documents.

While our team considered interviewing each learner in his or her first language, because of the diversity of the sample across the three sites and the expense associated with hiring interviewers who spoke each of the represented languages, this was not feasible. We administered all interviews individually and conducted all of them in English. Talking with adults at different points during their programs helped us to learn about their program learning experiences (i.e., how they experienced learning in their programs; how learning transferred to their social roles as parents, workers, or learners; how they made sense of program supports and challenges); and their internal experiences of change.

For example, questions included: What are your purposes in pursuing this learning? What supports in the program are helping you to learn? What, in your view, makes a person a good teacher? What do you think makes a good student? How do you know when you have learned something? What effect is your learning having on your work, in your relationship with your child, or in your thoughts about what it means to be a lifelong learner? These and other questions helped our team examine what their processes of learning looked like, how learners with different developmental levels experienced such processes, and what practices learners found to be supportive of these changes. Revisiting the same participant over time enabled us to ask about any changes and to trace these changes by examining previously collected data and using it to inform future questions.

Following are short descriptions of the measures we administered before the start of each program and what we hoped to learn from each. (For a discussion of what we learned from employing various measures with this sample of learners, see Drago-Severson, 2002a.)

1. *Pre-Program Learner Focus Groups.* In the focus groups, which we designed and facilitated, smaller groups (n = 8) of participants were asked questions about their hopes and expectations for learning in their programs.

2. *Experiences of Learning Interview.* We designed this qualitative interview to help us understand a learner's previous learning experiences and theories of teaching and learning processes. This interview was tailor-designed for each site, and it helped us to gather information on learners' motives for program participation, their learning goals, and their current understanding of a targeted role (that of student, parent, or worker). Additional topics woven through this interview included educational history, conceptions of support for learning, and demographics.

3. *Subject-Object Interview* (See Lahey et al., 1988, for a complete description of administration of this protocol.) We administered the subject-object interview (SOI) to participants at all three sites during our first and final rounds of data collection to help us assess whether or not a learner's way of knowing changed during the program. The SOI is a semistructured, developmental interview created to explore the ways in which an adult makes sense of his or her experience. Administration of this interview takes about one hour, and it is conversational in nature. Dr. Robert Kegan and his associates at the Harvard Graduate School of Education developed the original SOI. The interview is structured around a uniform set of probes that encourage the interviewee to talk about the ways in which he or she makes sense of real-life situations and issues. In the team's research the participant was invited to jot down his or her thinking on five different probes (e.g., important to me, success, and worried/anxious) on five different index cards. The interviewer then explored the meaning that each of the experiences (written about on the cards by the participant) had for the participant and how meaning is organized. Through the SOI assessment procedure, the team was able to distinguish five gradations between each way of knowing.[2] Our analysis of this measure included a developmental comparison of each participant's meaning making during our initial and final data collection, as we were especially interested in assessing changes in the ways in which participants made sense of their experiences.

4. *Loevinger's Ego Development Sentence Completion Test.* Loevinger and Wessler (1970) developed this measure to explore how people make sense of themselves and the world. Usually, participants write down their first response, which allows administration of the measure to larger groups of people. Occasionally, the researcher writes down participants' verbal answers. Loevinger and Wessler identify six stages of ego development, or complex thinking, and their measure is scored in accordance with these stages. We administered the short form of this measure, which is composed of 18 sentence stems. Participants are asked to complete a sentence stem in any way they wish by responding spontaneously to the stem. Each individual sentence stem is scored to assess the participant's ego development level. For example, the female version of the Loevinger asks a participant to respond to the following questions:

A wife should _____

A man feels good when _____

A person's response to these sentence stems is thought to reveal his or her way of interpreting events. Our team administered this developmental measure as an additional assessment of a participant's developmental level.[3]

5. *Vignettes.* We created three different role-specific vignettes, one for each of the three sites, as developmental measures. Each was a hypothetical problem-solving measure that we used to assess an individual's way of knowing and role competence in specific domains. The *learner vignette,* which we administered at the community college site, is a developmental student-situated dilemma we created to understand a student's decision-making ability, problem-solving skills, and sense of competency as related to their construction of authority. It presented a student/classroom dilemma and invited each participant to respond to a set of questions designed to help our team understand the reasoning underlying the decisions a person would make. The *parent vignette,* which we administered to parents at the family literacy site, is a developmental role-situated dilemma created to explore a parent's decision-making ability, problem-solving skills, and sense of competency as related to a person's construction of authority. It presented a parental dilemma and invited participants to respond to a set of questions designed to help us understand the reasoning underlying the decisions a parent would make. The *worker vignette,* which we administered to adults at the Polaroid site, is a developmental work-situated dilemma

created to explore a worker's decision-making ability, problem-solving skills, and sense of competency as related to his or her construction of authority. It presented a workplace dilemma and invited participants to respond to a set of questions designed to help the team understand the reasoning underlying the decisions a person would make. We analyzed these vignettes qualitatively for role competency themes and also scored participants' responses in accordance with Kegan's constructive-developmental theory (see Popp & Boes, 2001).

6. *Quantitative Survey Measures.* We administered several well-established and highly regarded quantitative measures to help us assess participants' levels of satisfaction, feelings of self-efficacy and success, and locus of control.

   - *Satisfaction with Life Scale (SWLS)*: Diener, Emmons, Larsen, and Griffin (1985) created the SWLS, which is a five-statement questionnaire (that is, a Likert scale) administered to ascertain a person's subjective judgment of his or her global life satisfaction. The scale for this measure is 1–5, ranging from "Strongly Disagree" to "Strongly Agree." A person is asked to select the number that best describes his or her degree of agreement with each statement. This global evaluation is directed toward assessing individuals' satisfaction and dissatisfaction with life.
   - *Perceived Self-Efficacy Scale (PEBS)*: The PEBS, created by Riggs, Warka, Babasa, Betancourt, and Hooker (1994), assesses individuals' thinking about their capacity to successfully perform the role-related tasks within a particular sphere (for instance, as a worker, as a parent, as a learner). The PEBS is a ten-statement questionnaire that helped the team to better understand and assess possible changes in individuals' belief in their ability to do the tasks and skills necessary to perform successfully in their primary social role.
   - *Locus of Control Scale (LOC)*: The LOC is a seven-statement questionnaire administered to assess people's beliefs in their ability to control life circumstances, events, and problems. The LOC, created by Pearlin and Schooler (1978), assesses the extent to which people believe their life experiences are under their own control (internally determined) as opposed to the result of things outside themselves (externally determined or controlled by fate).

7. *Self as Learner, Parent, or Worker Map.* We created and administered three mapping interviews to explore participants' perceptions of their roles as learners, parents, or workers. In this mapping exercise we asked participants to place descriptor labels (some prepared and some created

by the participant) on a piece of paper with two concentric circles (the inner circle was labeled "me" and the outer circle was for labels that the participant did not associate as closely with his or her self). These maps helped the team to explore the participant's current conception of the core elements of a particular role (learner, parent, or worker), his or her perception of the relationships between these core elements, and his or her way of making sense of the role. We employed this tool to establish and then track participants' perceptions of themselves in their roles and changes in their perceptions of how they were enacting their roles, their view of role relationships, their central emotions and beliefs associated with a particular role, and the activities of their role.

Near the start of the program, we also administered to program teachers a qualitative interview, the Teacher Experience Interview, which focused on their goals for their students and their classes, their philosophy of teaching, and their methods for assessing learners' progress.

During each of the programs, we administered the following measures to participants at each of the three sites (as noted, at the Polaroid site we conducted two rounds of data collection during the middle months of the program):

1. *Focus Groups.* Our team administered two types of focus groups to participants in each program. One type invited participants to reflect on and discuss their learning experiences in their program classes, and the other type invited them to describe any changes they noticed in themselves, as learners and as they enacted a particular social role. Regarding the second kind of focus group, one of our hopes was to understand how adults at each site believed their participation in a particular program was or was not influencing their perceived performance in a particular role (as worker, parent, or learner). We designed this protocol to explore individuals' perceptions of their roles and role-related responsibilities.

2. *During the Program—Experiences of Learning Interview.* The team designed this semistructured, qualitative interview to understand each participant's learning experiences in the program and to see how, if at all, the individual thought the learning experience was making a difference in his or her thinking about and enactment of his or her role as worker, parent, or learner.

3. *Reflecting on Changes in Self as Learner, Parent, or Worker Map.* We designed this protocol to help us continue exploring participants' perceptions of their roles as workers, parents, or learners, in their own

words and also through the lens of developmental theory (Kegan, 1982, 1994). Moreover, this protocol created an opportunity for individuals to reflect on and add to the picture/map/diagram created during the first round of data collection, which showed learners' initial conceptions of the core elements of a particular role, his or her perception of the relationships between these core elements, and his or her way of making sense of the role. When administering this protocol, we asked learners to add to or modify their prior map in any way that seemed appropriate, based on changes they noticed in themselves and in the ways in which their learning in the program was affecting their sense of themselves in a particular role. This protocol helped us to track learners' changing perceptions of themselves in that particular role, changes in the ways in which they valued or devalued their work, changes in their views of role relationships (e.g., with peers and supervisors), and changes in the central emotions and beliefs they associated with work.

4. *Classroom observations.* We conducted observations of learners in each of their program classes on one occasion or more during each semester.

Near the end of or shortly after each program's end, we administered the following protocols:

1. *Subject-Object Interview.* We administered a final SOI to each participant in order to assess his or her developmental level (way of knowing) at program completion and to compare it with our initial assessment of each individual's developmental level. We compared scores and emergent themes from these final interviews with initial SOI scores and themes.

2. *Final Learning Experience Participant Interview.* We designed and administered this open-ended, semistructured interview to better understand how participants at each site were thinking about their program experiences, how they believed they had changed since beginning their program, and how they felt about themselves as learners and in their social role at program completion. This enabled our team to gain a deeper understanding of how participants made sense of changes they noticed in themselves and what they experienced as sources of challenge and support in their student and social (parent, worker, or learner) roles. In addition, we asked learners to reflect on their overall program experience—that is, how their learning influenced their perceived role competencies, their learning goals, and their overall satisfaction with the program.

3. *Teacher Interview on Changes Noticed in Students.* We administered this qualitative, semistructured interview to program teachers at or near the end of each program. We designed this protocol to help us understand any changes program teachers noticed in each of their students during the program. When administering this protocol to program teachers at each site, we asked them to describe the changes they noticed in each of the learners, and to what or whom the teachers attributed the changes.

4. *Quantitative Survey Measures.* At program completion, we administered the same quantitative measures that were administered at the start of the research. Our goal was to assess each participant's levels of satisfaction, feelings of self-efficacy, and locus of control. We noted changes in these measures from the initial assessment.

5. *Vignettes.* At program completion, the same vignette from our initial round of data collection was administered to each learner individually at each site. Learner responses were examined for role competency themes and also scored in accordance with Kegan's constructive-developmental theory.

6. *Reflecting on Changes Map.* A final mapping interview (entitled, "Reflecting on Self as Student, Parent, or Worker Map") was administered to each participant at each site. We designed three distinct mapping exercises (one for participants at each of the three sites). These enabled our research team to talk with participants about the changes they noticed in their perceptions about themselves in a particular social role. We probed participants' end-of-program thinking about their perceptions of role competence. We also asked them about any changes relating to their self-regard. This measure helped the team to continue exploring participants' perceptions of their role as workers, parents, or learners, in their own words and through the lens of our theory. As we had administered at least two prior mapping protocols to participants at each site during prior data collection, this final mapping gave participants a chance to discuss their current perceptions about their social roles.

At each site, learners were asked to review two past diagrams (maps) that they created and to add to or modify the map in any way that seemed appropriate, based on changes they noticed in themselves and in the ways in which they saw their program learning influencing their sense of themselves in a particular role. We carefully examined the evolution of learners' perceptions of themselves in a particular role, changes in the ways in which they valued or devalued their role, changes in the ways in which they viewed their role relationships, changes in the central emotions and beliefs they associated with a particular role, and changes in how they understood their role activities and responsibilities.

We also created a qualitative interview that we administered after program completion to several participants who did not complete their program (called a "non-completer interview"). Our goal was to understand how these participants thought about their experiences during the year, how and why they had decided to leave the program, and what were their current conceptions about learning. We wanted to learn more about what was different or had changed for them since the beginning of the program year and after leaving the program. This interview was designed to help us learn more about the heart of participants' experience—and the differences in how learners thought or felt about themselves at the end of the official program year versus the beginning of the program. We probed participants' responses to understand how they made sense of any changes they noticed in themselves, and to learn how they were making sense of the supports and challenges in their lives.

DATA ANALYSIS

Our team engaged an early and a substantive phase. Research gains depth and focus when data collection and analyses are continuously integrated (Coffey & Atkinson, 1996; Strauss & Corbin, 1998). Our study benefited from this kind of purposeful integration and triangulation of data.

The Early Phase of Data Analysis

Data analysis began by coding participant interviews and learner-generated role maps from the Polaroid site's first round of data collection, since it was the site from which the team had collected the first full set of data. We generated theoretical codes (etic codes) and examined codes that emerged from the participants (emic codes) (Geertz, 1974; Miles & Huberman, 1994). We did this because we wanted to develop a coding schema and to refine our analytic framework in such a way that we could later employ it to analyze data from all three sites. We then compiled a list of emerging themes derived from both types of codes and applied them to data from all three sites.

In this early phase we focused on identifying consistencies and discrepancies within and across participants' data (Maxwell, 1996). Next, we reduced our code list to 12 central categories and their subconcepts while drawing out distinctions between participants (e.g., participants' thinking about their motives for learning and the ways it may have changed over time). We then built matrices to illustrate participants' responses to key interview questions across the sample site data and created narrative summaries (Coffey & Atkinson, 1996; Maxwell & Miller, 1991) that illuminated the critical themes and main points from interviews. After each data collection round at each site, the research team wrote analytic memos (Strauss & Corbin, 1998; Maxwell, 1996). Shortly after each round of data collection for each site, the full team met to discuss learning, assess protocols, and develop preliminary strategies for the next round of data collection. The analytic memos and tape-recorded team discussions were vital to both the early and substantive phases of analysis. The collective wisdom and diversity of the research team served as an invaluable resource, strengthening both study design and data analyses (see, e.g., Drago-Severson, 2002a).

To explore the possible relationship between learners' developmental levels and their experiences of change in the program, we examined the subject–object interviews and vignettes and related these to learnings from analysis of the quantitative measures that were administered. The subject–object interviews and vignettes were scored using methods described by Lahey and colleagues (1988) in *A Guide to the Subject-Object Interview.* Initially, we scored one full set of SOIs and vignettes using multiple scorers to establish inter-rater reliability. (Similar methods were used during the substantive analytic phase.) The preliminary quantitative and qualitative analyses, analytic memos, and full-team analytic discussions enabled us to identify patterns of transformation and develop an analytic framework for the intensive analytic phase.

The Substantive Phase of Data Analysis

The substantive phase of data analysis was guided by the refinement of an analytic framework that we developed in light of learning from the early phase. During this phase, research team members divided into analytic subteams (one subteam analyzed data from each of the three research sites). We focused on one participant per site per week and created thick narrative summaries in response to our research questions. Because this analysis pivoted around our developmental perspective, we sequenced the exploration of the participants (in each subteam) purposively. In other words, all individual analytic subteams first considered those participants with common initial SOI scores (i.e., all subteams started by examining data from participants who demonstrated an instrumental way of knowing). Our analysis helped us to gradually build a picture of the commonalities and differences across that meaning-making world. After completing these analyses, sub-teams moved on to another common subject-object world to examine contrasts and commonalities across ways of knowing. In this exploration, team members closely examined both social role-related analytic questions and learning- and teaching-related analytic questions. In addition, we carefully explored how participants' conceptions of their roles changed over time.

Creating analytic memos for each of the two role-related sets of questions and discussing these memos in site subteam weekly meetings enabled us to share interpretations, entertain alternative interpretations, and incorporate additional discoveries and ideas noticed by the subteam. These analytic role memos (which included data and interpretations) were then enhanced and elaborated on by integrating subteam discussions. During this intensive individual week-by-week participant analysis, analytic subteams also met periodically as a full research team to discuss what we were learning from participants at each site and to identify key findings within and across sites. (These discussions were tape-recorded.)

To explore the influence of learners' ways of knowing on how they made sense of their program experiences, and in some cases their experiences of change during the program, our team examined the subject-object interviews and vignettes. Also, scores from the formal measures of stress, life satisfaction, and ego development (collected as pre and post assessments before and at the end of each program) were used to establish baselines as well as changes in these core constructs over time (see, e.g., Kegan et al., 2001a, 2001b). These assessments of variability were also correlated with changes in SOI scores. The degree of change and the direction of change were captured in our quantitative analysis through descriptive statistics (see Kegan et al., 2001b, for a full description of the statistical analyses and their results).

Our team used the developmental and qualitative data to expand our definition of transformation and the holding environment, so that they were informed by data from the study itself (Strauss & Corbin, 1998). We looked for relationships between participants' experiences of changes as they related both to developmental level and to the timing of their occurrence in the trajectory of development from one way of making meaning to the next. We built matrices that linked patterns in ways of knowing across the groups to other aspects of participants' experience (e.g., other ongoing supportive contexts and their conceptions of the teacher-learner relationship). We examined patterns that emerged across the maps to track frequent and compelling descriptions of self and role in each context.

Having identified the learners whose experiences appeared to be transformational and those whose experiences had changed in other ways (e.g., skill acquisition), our research team examined how learners described the supports and challenges that coincided with both kinds of changes. Sub-teams then selected a set of participants whose stories served as examples. These case examples extended earlier narrative summaries of participants' experience, concentrating on key information that participants gave about changes they experienced during the program. We integrated data from various sources and crafted a storyline for each case, summarizing a person's experience in the program; descriptions of his or her skills; how, if at all, he or she generalized to the concept of role competence; his or her reported changes during the program; and his or her recent experiences of real success.

Throughout our analysis, we also looked for and examined discrepant data to test both the power and scope of our developing grounded theory (Maxwell, 1996; Merriam, 1998). By attending to the data at the level of the individual narrative, group patterns, and case write-ups, our research team built a theory that accounts for the many levels of data and role-specific perspectives on its interpretation (Glaser & Strauss, 1967).

SUMMARY

In this chapter I have described the three research settings to which we were welcomed. In addition to stating the team's criteria for selecting each of the programs as research sites, I have discussed demographic characteristics of the participants at each the site. The chapter also offers a brief overview of the team's research questions, tools for data collection, and how we made sense of the participants' experiences.

Employing a variety of data collection methods and analytic tools enabled our research team to deeply examine participants' internal, or psychological, processes of change, as well as the profound ways in which program learning influenced their lives. Carefully attending to *both* the learners' perspectives and our constructive-developmental perspective while assessing the multiple qualitative and quantitative measures enabled us to understand the ways in which participants made sense of their experiences from program start to program completion. Engaging in several rounds of data collection over an extended period of time at each site allowed us to talk with participants about their ongoing learning experiences and to trace the changes they noticed in their perceptions about themselves as learners and in a particular social role. By attending to the evolution of participants' conceptions of themselves as students in these programs and in a particular social role over time we were able to examine the developmental dimensions of transformational learning. In addition, we learned how the mixture of supports and challenges provided by the three different programs helped these adults in their learning and development. Our research team's purposeful integration of using learnings from each round of data collection to inform both the next round of data collection and analyses as well as our attention to alternative interpretations of data helped us to expand our definition of transformation and the holding environment, so that they were informed by data from the study itself.

Since this was the first time constructive-developmental theory was employed as a lens to understand ABE/ESOL learners' experiences and also the first time that we administered many of the measures that we designed for this study, we experienced some challenges in administrating measures and learned many lessons about how to adapt both standardized and our own measures in an effort to improve their administration. Using multiple measures helped us triangulate data and assess validity.

Administration of the various protocols gave rise to four key issues: logistical issues, language issues, cultural issues, and contextual issues (see Drago-Severson, 2002a, for a full discussion of how we adapted protocols to better match the needs of ABE/ESOL learners, how using a range of measures helped in assessing development, and what we learned from employing each measure over time). Below I provide an overview of these issues:

1. *Logistical Issues*. Time constraints for collecting data made it necessary to alter certain protocols so that they could be administered to learners within the time we had for administration at each site. Pairing the same interviewer and interviewee, whenever possible, helped build relationships. Gaining access to participants who did not complete a program was sometimes difficult.

2. *Language Issues*. Especially at the programs' start, we learned that participants' levels of expressive English (e.g., vocabulary, grammar, difficulty and/or ability to fully express ideas) varied. This influenced both our choice of measure and the ways in which we modified them—especially developmental measures—to better suit participants.

3. *Cultural Issues*. When we administered some of the paper and pencil measures, including the Loevinger sentence completion test, cultural issues emerged. Subject-object interviews (Lahey et al., 1988), in which participants select the content issues to be discussed, encouraged participants to discuss cultural issues.

4. *Contextual Issues*. Focus groups provided a rich context in which participants could express feelings and concerns that would not necessarily

emerge in individual interviews. For example, at the Polaroid site, recent downsizing and layoffs were discussed in-depth during focus groups; several workers voiced concerns about being "let go." At the community college site, the focus groups provided a context in which individuals and groups of students expressed their thoughts about the importance of community.

In this summary, I highlight a few of the key theoretical and methodological lessons learned from this work.

Our team developed strategies to deal with challenges associated with language issues. We learned that some of the paper-and-pencil measures contained vocabulary words unfamiliar to participants. For instance, one of the questions in the PEBS asked learners to state their degree of agreement or disagreement with the following sentence: "I feel threatened when I have to present my work in class." Several learners did not understand the meaning of the word "threatened." We altered administration of these measures from large- to small-group administration so that we could attend to these types of language issues (Drago-Severson, 2002a).

We also learned about cultural issues after administering several paper-and-pencil measures during the first round of data collection, which caused us to think carefully about how to administer the measures in the final round (Drago-Severson, 2002a). For instance, a few participants told us that the statement "I am an excellent student" was hard for them to agree or disagree with because of their home country's cultural norms that a person should "not speak in this way about himself."

Another very important lesson concerns the value of using an array of measures (e.g., in-depth qualitative interviews, subject-object interviews, role maps, focus groups, quantitative measures, vignettes, observations, and learner-centered interviews) to help triangulate data from multiple sources, track both content-related and developmental changes over time, and assess validity (Drago-Severson, 2002a). For example, our "Experiences of Learning" interview administered to participants during each round of data collection was not initially intended as a developmental assessment tool (although we included several developmental questions within the protocol). And the subject-object interview was not originally designed to examine participants' experiences in the program. However, as we analyzed data from these interviews, we learned that taken together they gave us a fuller picture of participants' learning experiences and in some cases a broader and richer picture of their lives, helping us to understand how they saw themselves in various social roles. Using multiple developmental assessment measures (e.g., role-based vignettes administered before program entry and also at program completion) helped us to assess developmental change over time (Drago-Severson, 2002a). The longitudinal nature of our study and the design of our protocols enabled us to revisit the same participants at different points, allowing us to carefully trace changes in their thinking and to ask of data and participant, Are there changes in learner views?

In summary, our methods and findings have important implications for future research. For example, our research demonstrates that language-based research measures can be administered if the effectiveness of the measures is carefully monitored and assessed, if they are properly adapted, if the students' expressive English skills are adequate, and if multiple measures are used to triangulate findings and assess validity (Drago-Severson, 2002a). Also, validity can be strengthened if participants are frequently asked during interviews how well they feel they are expressing the full complexity of their ideas in English. This creates an additional check on the data quality.

I hope that our research methods and findings illuminate how a constructive-developmental perspective can be used as an analytic lens for better understanding how adults experience ABE/ESOL program learning and how this learning helps them grow better able to enact their roles as learners, parents, and workers. By better understanding adults' learning experiences, we can better support and guide them. By using a constructive-developmental framework to inform research in the ABE/ESOL and the adult education field, in general, I hope that our methods serve as a helpful map so that we can enhance educational practices to more closely match and attend to the developing capacities and experience of adult learners.

CHAPTER 4

The Polaroid Learning Site

TO BEST UNDERSTAND the learners at this site and their experiences in this program, it will be helpful to understand the dynamic of Polaroid as a workplace and the nature of the CEI program. This chapter provides a brief history and explanation of both, discusses the concepts of the cohort and collaborative learning and introduces the Polaroid cohort. Learners' experiences of the cohort as a support to their academic learning, emotional well-being, and cognitive development will be discussed in the next chapter.

ABOUT POLAROID

In November 1997 our research team met with the Polaroid Corporation's workplace education manager, Steve Williams,[1] to take care of the final details of our research partnership. At that time, Mr. Williams was part of the workplace education team, which was responsible for all programs offered to nonexempt (nonsalaried, hourly) employees. The learners participating in this research would come from this group.

Mr. Williams's team developed a "Star Model" for skill competency development for Polaroid's nonexempt employees. The five components of this model are: team participation; task management; functional; high-performance workstyle; and information. Each component hinges on a set of core skills. Polaroid also had an "Applied Knowledge Program" (AKP), in which employees were rewarded with "credit" (in the form of points) from their supervisors for developing the skills listed in the Star Model, which would help them to do their jobs more effectively. Table 4.1 lists these core skills associated with each component of Polaroid's Star Model for success.

In 1997, when we met with Mr. Williams, approximately 5 to 10% of Polaroid's employees lacked these core skills. In other words, Polaroid hired them with the understanding that they had limited literacy skills or were lacking in the "core skills" outlined in the Star Model. These employees were invited to apply for the Continuing Education Institute (CEI) Adult Diploma Program; however, program attendance was not part of

Table 4.1. Polaroid's Competency Development Star Model

COMPONENT	SKILLS SET
Team participation	• Works well with diverse team • Active listening, feedback skills • Negotiation • Basic conflict management techniques • Teaches others, gives presentations • Problem-solving skills • Responds to customer needs
Task management	• Organizes work, ranks priorities • Identifies and communicates resource needs • Record keeping • Acquires, stores, and allocates materials • Meets deadlines
Functional	• Knowledge of basic work processes, procedures, customers, and products • Chooses right tool, procedures for job • Maintains, troubleshoots equipment & materials • Basic quality tools (SPC, data collection, etc.) • Basic financial understanding • Technical proficiency • Safety & environmentally aware
High-performance workstyle	• Self-motivated • Fast and willing to learn • Efficient • Resourceful • Results oriented • Collaborator • Conscientious • Flexible • Ethical
Information	• Acquires and uses available information • Collects, organizes, maintains, & reports data • Uses computers to process/acquire/communicate information • Obtains information via basic questioning • Uses data to solve problems

their employment agreement. Many of these workers were from diverse backgrounds and most were non–native English speakers.

During our meeting, Mr. Williams explained that Polaroid's executives and managers were committed to supporting the workers in this program. The $5,000 investment required for each employee, he shared, demonstrated the corporation's commitment to education. Polaroid also expressed its support for the program by having classes take place during the workday. Most learners were given paid release time while attending program classes. Polaroid was also committed to supporting learners through the completion of the program. Even though two employees, Veronica and Rita, were laid off from their positions at Polaroid during the second trimester of the program, Polaroid continued to financially support their participation in the diploma program.

About the Process of Applying to the Diploma Program

Shop-floor workers who had lower-level literacy skills or who were lacking in "core skills" were two groups of learners who could apply for admission to the CEI Adult Diploma Program. Another, much smaller group of workers who did not complete or start their high school education could also apply. Some learners told us that they approached their supervisors and requested support for application to the program, while others were encouraged to apply by their supervisors. All applicants had to be recommended by their supervisor as a good candidate for the program to participate.

Workers from Polaroid's Waltham and Norwood plants who wanted to enroll in the program also needed to take CEI's assessment tests (measuring skill levels in reading, writing, and math). To be accepted, workers had to be able to read at the sixth-grade level.

The Learners in the Polaroid Cohort

In February 1998, before the CEI program officially started, the research team met the courageous, motivated, and somewhat apprehensive adult learners who would eventually form a cohesive and closely bonded cohort. When we began our study, 19 adults had passed the CEI entry assessments in math, writing, and reading and had been accepted into the CEI Adult Diploma Program. Sixteen of these learners, for various reasons (mostly economic), had not attended high school in their native countries; one had earned a college degree in his home country; and two of them dropped out of high school in the United States. Several learners had gained experience as adults in skill-oriented workshops or trimester-long classes (ESOL classes or multiday workplace training programs). However, for the majority of the learners, this was their first experience in a formal classroom setting since elementary school.

Sixteen of these adults were Polaroid employees, and three worked at another nearby manufacturing company. Before the second trimester began, in September 1998, one Polaroid employee and two employees from the neighboring company had dropped out of the program.[2] Sixteen adults (eight women and eight men) completed the 14-month program and received high school diplomas. The learners who completed the program are introduced in Table 4.2.

The majority of the 16 Polaroid employees who enrolled in the diploma program were hired in the 1970s without high school diplomas. By 1998, when the program began, these employees held a variety of positions, ranging from working in the mailroom to designing filters for car and airplane windows to making film and checking it for defects. The average age of the learners was 42 years old, and the range was from 27 to 58. The majority of learners had children, and most were married. As was the case with participants at the other two study sites, the ethnic and racial backgrounds of this cohort were diverse. Two learners were born in the United States, ten in the same home country in West Africa, three in the Caribbean, and one in Asia. Only two of these adults (those born in the United States) spoke English as their first language. Although Tough had earned a college degree in his home country of Vietnam, the other adults in the class had, on average, attended school for only 9½ years. On average, the learners' mothers had about 4 years of schooling and their fathers about 7½ years in their home countries.

Many learners spoke with tremendous pride as they shared stories about what coming to the United States meant to them and their families. Their eyes filled with tears as they talked about the courage it took for them to leave their home countries and families of origin so that they could begin a "new life" here, in what they referred to as "the land of opportunity." Though their reasons for immigrating varied and their experiences since their arrival were quite diverse, it was their shared goal of earning a high school diploma that brought them together to form this learning cohort.

ABOUT CEI'S ADULT DIPLOMA PROGRAM

In January 1999, CEI's program was recognized in Vice President Al Gore's summit, "21st Century Skills for 21st Century Jobs," which focused on the importance of enhancing workplace knowledge and skills. According to

Dr. Lloyd David, executive director and founder of CEI, the program was recognized as "one of twenty model programs throughout the country selected as an exemplar of 'best practices' in workplace training and education."

After meeting with CEI staff and reviewing the institute's program design and curriculum, we decided that this program met our selection criteria: It was a long-term program (14 months); its approach to educating adult learners and its curricula appeared to be developmental in orientation; and it provided learners with multiple forms of support and challenge (in terms of teachers, tutors, program staff, curricula design, and program structure). The program's structure and curricula appeared to create a powerful learning environment for learners.

Hammer and Champy (1993) discuss how modern-day organizations devoted to best practices make use of benchmarking. "Essentially, *benchmarking* means looking for the companies that are doing something best and learning how they do it in order to emulate them" (p. 132). In their expansive review and analysis of best practice approaches in professional organizations, Harbison and Kegan (1999) discuss the process of benchmarking within the context of transformational learning. They explain that curiosity, an outward focus, and mindfulness characterize benchmarking for transformational learning, as opposed to a competitive stance focused on calculations of wins or losses.

Not only did the team believe that this site would be one at which we could deeply examine adults' learning experience, but we also believed that it was one from which other program designers and practitioners could learn and gain new insights.

Program Design

Since 1982, CEI has offered its Adult Diploma Program to adults who are at least 20 years old and who have not graduated from high school. Adults earn their high school diplomas from Cathedral High School, an accredited private high school in Boston.

Classes meet two or three afternoons each week for 10 to 15 months. Enrolled students take classes as a group; attendance is required (there is no open-entry-open-exit option). Most of CEI's teachers have been or continue to be K–12 educators. The Polaroid Adult Diploma Program classes were held at the Norwood plant for 2 hours on Tuesdays and Thursdays from March 1998 through June 1999. CEI also provides learners with tutorial and counseling services. Tutors are available to students after, and sometimes before, classes.

Table 4.2. Polaroid Learners' Descriptive Characteristics and Developmental Assessments

Name	Gender/Age at Program Start	Region of Origin[1]	Way of Knowing at Program Start and Finish	Characteristics of Learner
Bill	Male/ late 40s	United States	Instrumental 2 to 2(3) Δ[2]	Bill, born in the United States, dropped out of school after eighth grade. He later joined the military, where he "learned a lot about life." Bill was married and had four children (preteens to teenagers). He and his wife worked and shared child care. He struggled to find time to do his homework while balancing responsibilities as worker, parent, and spouse. Bill worked on shop floor at Polaroid and supervised others.
Renada	Female N/A	West Africa	Instrumental 2 to 2(3) Δ	Renada lived in the United States for 30 years. Several family members lived in Massachusetts. At home, Renada spoke Creole/ Portuguese. She was finalizing her divorce. She had two children in their mid-20s and one teenager. Renada wanted to earn a high school diploma and to improve her English. Renada worked in Polaroid's lab administering tests and processing film.
Sal	Male/ early 30s	West Africa	Instrumental/ socializing transition 2/3 to 3/2 Δ	Sal and his wife worked and had a child who was in grade school. He, his siblings and parents lived in the same town. His first language was Creole/ Portuguese. Sal wanted to earn his high school diploma and to increase his chances for promotions. Sal worked on the shop floor at Polaroid.

[1] All learners from West Africa are from the same home country. Pierre and Christopher are from the same Caribbean country. Hope is from another Caribbean country.

[2] The symbol Δ signifies a change in a participant's meaning system from program start to finish—what is referred to in the chapter as a *transformational change*. Where the symbol Δ does not appear, the research team's developmental assessments did not indicate this kind of change. In Chapter 2, I explain the notation system employed to describe ways of knowing (Lahey et al., 1988).

Hope	Female/ late 50s	Caribbean	Instrumental/ socializing transition 2/3 to 3/2 Δ	Hope was the oldest learner in the cohort. She had lived in the United States for 30 years, was married, and had two adult children. When she arrived in this country from the Caribbean she took the GED exam but did not pass. She was eager to earn her high school diploma. Hope was the class speaker at graduation. She worked for Polaroid for 10 years and was selected to go abroad to teach others how to work her machine. She worked several jobs at Polaroid.
Teresina	Female/ late 40s	West Africa	Instrumental/ socializing transition 2/3 – 2/3	Teresina had lived in the United States for 10 years and had a high school diploma from her home country. Before this program, she had attended high school in Massachusetts for 2 years but stopped because of child care responsibilities. Her first language was Creole. She had two toddlers. She was eager to earn her diploma and improve her English. She worked on a machine on the shop floor at Polaroid.
Angelina	Female/ mid-30s	West Africa	Instrumental/ socializing transition 3/2 – 3/2	Angelina had lived in the United States for 15 years and was married. Her husband also worked. She had two grade-school-age children and one teenager. Angelina wanted to earn her high school diploma and improve her English so that she could be a better team member at Polaroid and so that she could help her children with homework. Angelina worked with a team on the shop floor and wrote reports.
Helena	Female/ late 40s	West Africa	Instrumental/ socializing transition 3/2 – 3/2	Helena had lived in the United States for 30 years. She completed the eighth grade in her home country. She placed a high value on education and encouraged her children to attend college. Helena was recently divorced. She had family in the Boston area. Helena spoke Portuguese and Creole at home. She wanted to earn her high school diploma and to improve her English. She worked on computers doing film processing at Polaroid.

[continued]

Table 4.2. (continued)

NAME	GENDER/AGE AT PROGRAM START	REGION OF ORIGIN	WAY OF KNOWING AT PROGRAM START AND FINISH	CHARACTERISTICS OF LEARNER
Veronica	Female/ early 30s	West Africa	Instrumental/ socializing transition 3/2 – 3/2	Veronica had lived in the United States for 15 years. When she arrived she began working and going to school; however, she stopped going to school when she married her husband. She had two teenage children. Veronica enrolled in the program so that she could help her children with their homework, develop better work skills, and improve her English. Several family members lived nearby. She worked for Polaroid on the shop floor and was laid off during the second trimester.
Rita	Female/ early 40s	West Africa	Instrumental/ socializing transition to socializing 3/2 to 3 Δ	Rita had lived in the United States for 20 years. At home, she spoke Portuguese/ Creole with her husband and two teenage children. In her home country she did not complete elementary school because she needed to work to support her family. Rita believed a high school diploma would help her to learn skills needed for work and to improve her English. She worked in the camera division and then in the mailroom at Polaroid, until she was laid off during the second trimester.
Pierre	Male/ late 40s	Caribbean	Socializing 3 – 3	Pierre had lived in the United States for 15 years. He was divorced and had five children. Pierre's long-term hopes included helping children learn French and Creole (the languages he spoke at home) and returning to his home country to teach children. Pierre wanted to improve his English. He worked in quality control at Polaroid.
Tough	Male/ late 20s	Asia	Socializing 3 – 3	Tough had lived in the United States for 2 years and had an architecture degree from his home country. Tough had one sister who also lived in Massachusetts. Tough wanted to improve his English. He worked at the nearby manufacturing company since arriving in the U. S. At work, he was responsible for administrative tasks.

Name	Gender/Age	Origin	Stage	Description
Christopher	Male/late 30s	Caribbean	Socializing/self-authoring transition 3/4 – 3/4	Christopher had been living in the United States for 10 years. He lived with a family member whom he took care of. Earning a high school diploma was, for him, a key to survival and to moving ahead. He enjoyed learning with cohort members because they were polite and respectful of each other. Christopher had never been married and was the father of a teenager and an infant. He worked with a team and also independently making film on a machine at Polaroid.
Paulo	Male/early 40s	West Africa	Socializing/self-authoring transition 3(4) to 3/4 Δ	Paulo had lived in the United States for 10 years and worked at Polaroid since he arrived. He enrolled in the program to have "a better future," more knowledge, to be a better worker, to help his family, and to improve his English. Paulo also spoke Portuguese, Creole, and Spanish. He was married with two college-age children. He worked in dome lamination (writing reports, delivering presentations, and collaborating with supervisors and engineers).
Daniel	Male/early 50s	West Africa	Socializing/self-authoring transition 3/4 to 4/3 Δ	Daniel had lived in the United States for 20 years. He thought that this program would help him improve his work skills and his English. He was married with two adult children and two preschool children. Daniel spoke Creole, Portuguese, Spanish, and English. He was a lead technician at Polaroid, and taught those he supervised.
Magda	Female/early 50s	West Africa	Socializing/self-authoring transition 3/4 to 4/3 Δ	Magda had lived in the United States for 25 years. She was married and had four children (late teens to 20s). Magda believed earning a diploma would help to develop work skills and improve her English. At Polaroid, she worked on computers (taking measurements, analyzing data, and writing reports).
Jeff	Male/late 40s	United States	Self-authoring 4 – 4	Jeff was born in the South and dropped out of high school in the eleventh grade. He was very happy to be in the diploma program. Jeff spoke English. He was divorced and had two adult children. He made batteries.

Program Curriculum

All adults enrolled in CEI's Adult Diploma Program take five classes: mathematics, writing/English, U. S. history, science, and a life employment skills workshop. The workshop focuses on career exploration. In the 1998–1999 program, John taught math and Margaret taught writing/English during the first trimester. In the second trimester, John taught science, Kirk taught U. S. history, and Judith taught the life employment workshop. Many program classes focus on writing and the development of research skills, and the writing classes have a specific focus on work-related issues.

Every course in the program emphasizes what CEI refers to as its "pervasive standards" (L. David, personal communication, December 20, 2000). These standards are closely aligned with what our team's colleagues at Equipped for the Future refer to as EFF standards (Stein, 2000). Based on research of responsibilities in multiple realms of adult life, such as work and family, Stein describes the 16 EFF standards as the core skills that are necessary for effective performance as a parent, worker, and citizen.

Dr. David acknowledges EFF's critical influence on his thinking about how the CEI program can better support the acquisition and development of skills that adults need to meet their responsibilities as workers and learners. Communication, problem solving, presentation, and computer skills are among the predominant standards that infuse the CEI curriculum and program design. Each course emphasizes these standards as well as reading, writing, and critical thinking skills.

CEI customizes its curriculum in accordance with needs of participants at the individual workplace (Continuing Education Institute, 1992, 1997). For example, in the life employment workshop class workers have the opportunity to learn new skills (e.g., resume writing, interviewing skills) and to learn how to utilize and develop those skills.

Significantly, CEI classes are oriented toward reinforcing "teamwork concepts" (Continuing Education Institute, 1992, p. 4). Collaborative group learning is used in all classes to facilitate and enhance adult learning, and this, as well as other aspects of the CEI program design, seems to reinforce teamwork and various forms of adult collaboration.

THE 1998–1999 CEI PROGRAM AT POLAROID

All of the learners in the Polaroid program were working to earn their high school diploma. Importantly, and unlike the programs at the other two sites in the study, CEI'S Adult Diploma Program at Polaroid called for the same group of learners to work together within a set timeframe to meet all program requirements for earning their diplomas. Toward this end, a group of learners attended the same classes with the same teachers for 2 hours, 2 days a week, over a 14-month period. Also (and again unlike the programs at the other two sites), the CEI program did not give learners an open-entry/open-exit option. Learners were part of a stable group engaged in a shared learning experience that was directed toward accomplishing a common goal. This arrangement made for a powerful cohort, a term that has its roots in the ancient Roman military when it was defined as "a group of warriors or followers"—in short, a group whose members have strong ties (*Merriam-Webster's Dictionary*, 1974, p. 148).

Although CEI refers to these groups of learners as a *class*, the research team adopted the term *cohort* to describe participants' experiences in their learner groups in all three sites, and defines it as a tightly knit, common purpose group (Drago-Severson et al., 2001b; Kegan et al., 2001a, 2001b).

The learners in this program were a cohort not just because they were taking the same classes at the same time with the same teachers. They became—or transformed themselves into—a community of connection in which each member supported and was supported by every other member. These learners expressed a sense of belonging and a feeling that their fellow cohort members and teachers cared about them and their success. As many of the learners told us, the cohort was, to them, "like a family."

The research team had not set out to examine what influence a cohort might have on learners' experiences, but we came to understand that being part of a cohort mattered greatly, although in different ways, to participants at all three sites, and especially to learners in the Polaroid program. For these learners, membership in the cohort was one of the most critical supports to their learning. The study data show that sustained connection to fellow cohort members made a difference in at least three ways. Jennifer Garvey Berger and I developed the categories presented here related to the three ways that the cohort served as a support to learners at the Polaroid site (Drago-Severson & Berger, 2001). For discussions of the cohorts at the other two research sites see Helsing, Broderick, & Hammerman, 2001; and Portnow, Diamond, & Rimer, 2001.

The cohort made a difference to participants' *academic* learning, by which I mean the theoretical and/or organized, systematic study within the context of the academy. (By cognitive development, which I address in later chapters, I refer to development of the mind—the process of knowing.) It also made a difference in their emotional and psychological well-being, and in their ability to broaden their perspectives on themselves, each other, and their lives (Drago-Severson & Berger, 2001; Kegan et al., 2001a). This will be discussed in Chapter 5.

This central finding has important implications for both program design and teacher practice. It suggests how ABE teachers might structure classroom environments so that we can better support learners who make sense of their experience in qualitatively different ways. Some teachers of adult basic education (ABE) and English for speakers of other languages (ESOL) use group learning as a pedagogical approach to build classroom cohesion and/or facilitate learning (B. Garner, personal communication, January 11, 2001). Some program designers refrain from building stable cohorts because of funding requirements (Beder & Medina, 2001) or the need for an open-entry/open-exit policy given participants' life situations (the need to be at work, care for family, and so on at various times that conflict with the program schedule) (B. Bingman, personal communication, November 20, 2000). The work done at Polaroid suggests that the benefits of building cohorts, or variations of them, into ABE program design should be reconsidered.

Those who write about K–12 and university education stress how collaborative learning groups enhance learning and facilitate the development of critical-thinking skills (Bosworth & Hamilton, 1994; Pedersen & Digby, 1995). Now, in ABE and ESOL, researchers have begun to ask students what learning in the classroom means to them (Comings, Sum, & Uvin, 2000; Quigley, 1993, 1997). Employing a constructive-developmental lens to understand how the cohort supported adult learning is relevant to current concerns in the ABE field in three ways. First, Quigley (1997) and Gowen (1992) underscore the need to examine learners' experiences in ABE classrooms and present learners' voices, which have been absent from the literature. In focusing on how learners make sense of their learning experience, the research team's work addressed this concern. Second, in March 1999, the Task Force on Adult Education developed program standards aimed at creating more effective ABE programs. The group recommends instructional activities directed toward affording learners active roles in their learning by integrating group work and tasks that foster communication skills. At Polaroid, the research team documented the experience of adults who participated in a program that included these components. Third, Taylor (1996) emphasizes the value of using developmental theory to inform our understanding of adult learners' experiences. She maintains that knowledge of the qualitatively different ways in which learners make sense of their ABE/ESOL classroom experiences will strengthen classroom practice and program design. As will be discussed in the next chapter, the work of the research team shows how the supports offered by the cohort are experienced differently by learners across a wide range of ways of knowing.

COHORTS AND COLLABORATIVE LEARNING DEFINED

In this section I provide background from the literature on cohorts and collaborative learning before discussing them as part of this research in the next chapter.

Cohorts

While the practice of building educational cohorts in educational reform programs dates back to the 1940s, their use was restricted and by the 1980s they had all but disappeared from the mainstream (Basom, Yerkes, Norris, & Barnett, 1996). From 1940 to 1980, cohorts had varying degrees of success. Basom, Yerkes, Norris, and Barnett found that, during this time, cohorts were situated within an authoritarian style of school administration. Many educational administration programs included the cohort model in their design as a way to strengthen collegiality among class members and as a tool for selecting students into a class. Basom and colleagues (1996) contend that programs designed with the cohort model in mind contrasted sharply with the social surroundings of the times (1940s–1980s) and thus declined in number.

At the turn of the 21st century, however, societal shifts and changes in education brought about a reemergence of cohorts in university graduate programs (Barnett & Muse, 1993; Basom et al., 1996; Hill, 1995; Teitel, 1997). For instance, Basom and colleagues found that colleges and universities had begun to adopt the practice of using cohorts in graduate educational administration programs as a "fashionable" (p. 99) format in their preparation programs. In deciding on an educational administration graduate program, many students now choose programs that offer the support of membership in a cohort because they prefer to work collaboratively. In this context, groups set common goals, determine criteria for the initiatives they will engage in to achieve those goals, and establish their own criteria for assessing their success.

In discussing why educational leadership programs across the nation are resurrecting the use of cohorts, Marie Somers Hill (1995) argues that cohorts help educational leaders develop the skills they will need to work successfully in a changing and increasingly complex society. Hill writes that cohorts were intended for networking, in particular, such that graduate programs in educational leadership intentionally organized cohorts that would stay together for the duration of their graduate program.

While the Polaroid cohort learners were not preparing to be educational leaders, were not required to create their own criteria for assessing their success, and were assessed by program teachers as individuals and not as a group, they have a great deal in common with the cohorts in college and university settings. For example, researchers have found that university students find the greatest benefit of the cohort to be the support and belonging they derive from each other (Hill, 1995). Many members of the Polaroid cohort echoed this belief.

Collaborative Learning

During the past 3 decades, researchers have examined the increasing role and benefits of collaborative learning in higher education and K–12 contexts (Bosworth & Hamilton, 1994; Eble & Noonan, 1983; Pedersen & Digby, 1995). Learning is now understood to be a constructive process, and it is acknowledged that students benefit from opportunities for questioning and reflecting in dialogue with each other (Eble & Noonan, 1983).

Bosworth and Hamilton (1994), in *Collaborative Learning: Underlying Processes and Effective Techniques,* contend that interactive education has been a college mainstay, especially in medicine and the sciences. The interactions between colleagues who work together in learning groups not only serve a social function; the conversations and activities they share also promote active learning (Eble & Noonan, 1983). While some teachers rely on the informative lecture format of educating learners of all ages, many are including collaborative learning experiences in their day-to-day pedagogical practices with greater frequency. As Bosworth and Hamilton (1994) write, new features of modern life, such as the information revolution, have likewise revolutionized college education. By collaborating in the learning process, students are exploring their common disciplines and speaking the language of those disciplines with each other. Benefits of this approach have been students' increasing senses of social responsibility through learning cooperatively and a more comprehensive understanding of material, gleaned through joint thinking.

What, exactly, is collaborative learning? Gerlach (1994) explains it as a pedagogical tool that creates a mutual learning environment for a teacher and a group of students. In collaboration, the process of learning is focused on students' curiosity and meaning-making, rather than a didactic approach by which a teacher deposits information into students.

Gerlach's definition marks a substantial shift from Eble and Noonan's (1983) conception of cooperative group learning, which was defined by two central characteristics: a dialogical process for active learning, and a means for instructors to guide students and offer knowledge. In a lecture-transmission paradigm, the teacher is clearly "the locus of knowledge and authority" (Flannery, 1994, p. 16). Similarly, Flannery maintains that cooperative learning simply uses student groups within this traditional system of knowledge and authority. Flannery argues that a collaborative learning context, by contrast, is one in which students and teachers construct and share knowledge, at least in part. A social component and an orientation to generating—not just absorbing—knowledge are important distinctions in collaborative learning.

Hamilton (1994) offers a model for developing proficiency with collaborative learning methods. Her approach, which she presents as a developmental model, is based on her research in universities with college-age students. The five stages of developing proficiency with collaborative learning, according to Hamilton's model, are (1) understanding the rules and strategies, (2) applying the skills learned, (3) improving the learner's ability, (4) developing expertise, and (5) achieving mastery. Hamilton offers helpful suggestions to teachers who wish to establish a collaborative learning environment in their classrooms. They are based on three distinct models of collaborative learning identified by John Trimbur (1993). Hamilton recommends that teachers adopt the model that is best aligned with their teaching philosophy or personal style.

The first model, which Trimbur (1993) names the "postindustrialist model," is oriented around a collective effort to problem-solve in a context where the instructor regulates the composition of groups, the completion time, and possible answers (Hamilton, 1994). The second model, which Trimbur calls the "social constructionist model," permits students more active involvement in learning while fostering skills for negotiation and collaboration. Trimbur calls the third model the "popular democratic model." This model suggests that the learners' challenge is to employ their differences to find diverse and varied meanings for the concepts they discuss. Not only do these models have different goals, but each also allocates different types and levels of responsibility to teachers and learners. Furthermore, each model recommends different principles for designing classrooms and suggests alternative ways to structure authority.

How might learners, who make sense of their experience with different ways of knowing, respond to each of these models? What types of developmental supports and challenges might they need? How might learners benefit if teachers were to incorporate components of all three models into their classroom structure? How might ABE/ESOL teachers who include collaborative learning in their instructional practices benefit from understanding the different developmental levels of the adults in their classrooms? The next chapter should help readers begin to answer these questions.

SUMMARY

In this chapter I introduced the cohort of Polaroid learners, discussed key features of the Polaroid Corporation where they worked, and presented aspects of the Continuing Education Institute's Adult Diploma Program. I hope this information has helped readers to understand something of these learners and their experiences in the Adult Diploma Program. In addition, the chapter provided a history of cohort use and an introductory discussion of collaborative learning to better understand ideas that I present in the chapters that follow in this book.

As noted, approximately 5% to 10% of Polaroid's employees were hired with limited literacy skills or were lacking in the "core skills" as detailed in Polaroid's competency Star Model. The Polaroid Corporation demonstrated both a value for education and a belief that employees can grow by bringing the Adult Diploma Program in-house and granting paid release time to workers who participate.

As discussed, the group of learners who participated in the Polaroid-sponsored Adult Diploma Program (most of whom had been employed by the company since the 1970s) was diverse with respect to age, race, ethnicity, and prior educational experience. I discussed demographic characteristics of this sample and the variety of positions held by these Polaroid employees. Though their reasons for immigrating varied and their experiences since coming to the United States differed, it was their shared goal of earning a high school diploma that brought them together in a way that formed this learning cohort.

I emphasized our team's reasoning for selecting CEI's Adult Diploma Program, and highlighted important characteristics of its curricular designs and program structure that appeared to create a powerful learning environment for participants. More specifically, CEI's curricula and approach to educating adult learners seemed to be developmental in nature, and the program provided learners with multiple forms of support (teachers, tutors, program staff, curricular designs, and program structure). CEI's dedication to customizing curricula to individual needs and reinforcing teamwork concepts through collaborative group learning were two additional features of the program that were seen as particularly important.

In math classes, for example, I observed that adult learners often worked to solve more challenging math problems in collaborative groups of four or five people. In writing/English class, learners regularly worked in small groups to draft essays before sharing them with the entire class to learn from constructive feedback. I also observed learners working in pairs on certain science projects to develop ideas, search the Internet for information, or critique one another's work. This kind of collaborative learning appeared in every class of the CEI program. Not only did our team believe that the CEI program at Polaroid would be one within which we could deeply examine adults' learning experiences, but we also believed that it was a program from which other designers and practitioners of adult learning could gain new and important insights.

Our team did not set out to examine the influence a cohort might have on the experiences of learners. However, we came to understand that being part of a learning cohort mattered greatly, although in different ways to participants, and especially to learners at the Polaroid site. In the next chapter I present the learners' experiences of both the cohort and collaborative learning. I also demonstrate how they experienced participation in the cohort as a critical support to their academic learning, emotional well-being, and cognitive development.

This core finding has vital implications for both program design and teacher practice. It suggests how teachers might structure classroom environments so that we can better support learners who make sense of their experiences in qualitatively different ways. Importantly, learners in the Polaroid program were a cohort not simply because they were enrolled in the same classes at the same time with the same teachers. They became what I call *a community of connection* in which each member supported and was supported by every other member. The cohort was, as many learners referred to it, "like a family."

This concludes the part of the book that provides readers with the background needed in order to better appreciate what follows: the stories of learners and how they made their way through the diploma program. As the narrator, Rose, of the 1999 film *Titanic* says near the beginning of the film, it's time to "let the story in."

CHAPTER 5

"Not I Alone": The Power of the Cohort and Collaborative Learning

IN THIS CHAPTER, I focus on one of the study's core findings: the importance of the cohort and collaborative learning as key supports for adult learning. I would like to acknowledge Hope, a learner in the Polaroid cohort, for my use of the phrase "Not I Alone" in the chapter title. She used it repeatedly when referring to her cohort experience. It eloquently captures an important aspect of what she and the other adult learners experienced in this group. For these learners, belonging to a cohort, a tightly knit group with a common purpose, proved important to supporting skill development and transformational learning. Here I present the Polaroid learners' descriptions of what it was like to be part of such a cohort and why it was so valuable to them.[1]

The adult learning literature generally asserts that the need for close connection to a group of colleagues is less important for adults than it is for adolescents, who are in the midst of developing their identities and separating from their families and have not yet created their own, new community of affiliation (Drago-Severson et al., 2001b; Kegan et al., 2001b). This literature often maintains that adults who have already formed social support networks with their families, friends, and coworkers are less in need of such community (Aslanian & Brickell, 1980; Cross, 1971, 1981; Drago-Severson et al., 2001b; Kegan et al., 2001b; Knowles, 1970, 1975). This "common knowledge" notwithstanding, the research team found that the interpersonal relationships that learners in the Polaroid cohort developed made a critical difference not only to their learning experience but to their emotional and psychological experience (Drago-Severson et al., 2001b; Kegan et al., 2001b).

As discussed in Chapter 2, a "holding environment" is a context that provides both developmentally appropriate supports *and* challenges that can help learners—who make sense of their experiences in qualitatively different ways—grow. Here, I will show how the Polaroid cohort provided just such an environment. I illuminate how learners with different ways of knowing experienced the cohort and collaborative learning as a support to their academic learning, their emotional and psychological well-being, and their ability to broaden their perspectives on themselves, each other, and their lives.

To review the ways of knowing that are described in Chapter 2 and are relevant to this cohort, there were three epistemologies evident within this group: instrumental, socializing, and self-authoring. Those who maintain an instrumental way of knowing tend to view the world concretely and dualistically; they do not yet have the capacity to think abstractly. Socializing knowers have grown to be able to comprehend abstractions, including the vantages of others (in fact, they are identified with and cannot take a perspective on others' perspectives of them). Other people's expectations of them become their own expectations of themselves. Adults who are self-authoring knowers, however, have grown to have the capacity to take a perspective on interpersonal relationships; they are able to refer to an internal authority and reflect on others' perspectives, weighing the merits of both and realizing that both can represent reality. Self-authoring knowers have an internally generated value system to which they appeal to when making decisions.

"EVERYBODY THINKS DIFFERENTLY": THE COHORT AS A HOLDING ENVIRONMENT FOR LEARNING AND TEACHING

While the great majority of the Polaroid learners valued the opportunity to work with colleagues in pairs, small groups (four or five people), and large groups (the whole class), they made sense of these experiences in developmentally different ways. In this section I present one case representative of each way of knowing to illustrate the qualitative distinctions in how learners understood the cohort and their collaborative work with cohort members. See Table 5.1 for a summary of the cases presented in this chapter as examples to show the power of this holding environment as a medium for teaching and learning.

The Instrumental Way of Knowing: Bill

Bill was one of two cohort learners who made sense of his experience at the fully instrumental meaning-making stage at program start. At program completion, the team observed the emergence of a socializing way of knowing.

Bill is a gregarious, American-born, married man in his late 40s. He has four children who, at the time of the program, were in their preteens or teens. He worked in the film department at Polaroid. One of the two native English speakers in the program, Bill dropped out of school after

Table 5.1. Participant Cases Selected to Illustrate the Cohort as a Holding Environment for Learning and Teaching

NAME	AGE AT PROGRAM START	REGION OF ORIGIN	WAY OF KNOWING AT PROGRAM START AND FINISH
Bill	late 40s	United States	Instrumental [2 to 2(3)] Δ [1]
Hope	late 50s	Caribbean	Instrumental/socializing transition [2/3 to 3/2] Δ
Pierre	late 40s	Caribbean	Socializing [3]
Paulo	early 40s	West Africa	Socializing/self-authoring transition [3(4) to 3/4] Δ
Jeff	late 40s	United States	Self-authoring [4]

[1] The symbol Δ signifies a change in a participant's meaning system from program start to finish. Where Δ does not appear, the research team's developmental assessments did not indicate this kind of change. In Chapter 2, I fully explain the notation system employed to describe ways of knowing (Lahey et al., 1988). For example, at program start, Bill demonstrated a singularly operating instrumental way of knowing, "2," and at program completion he demonstrated the emergence of a socializing way of knowing operating alongside of an instrumental way of knowing, "2(3)."

completing eighth grade. After leaving school, Bill eventually decided to serve in the United States Marines, a place where he felt he learned much about life.

Although Bill's previous experiences in school had not been positive, he was highly motivated to earn his diploma. He spoke softly as he said that his oldest son had "dropped out of the eleventh grade" and that part of his motivation for wanting to complete the program was to be a "good role model" for his children.

In April 1998, before beginning the diploma program, Bill's preferred way to learn was "on the job." Before entering the program, when Bill needed to learn something new at work he would most often remember it after hearing it "once or twice." If that did not work, he would write it down so that he had a better chance of getting it "locked in." Although he expressed regret about not having earned his high school diploma earlier, he was confident in his ability to learn in this program. "Anything I really put my mind to," he said, he eventually would be able to learn. "It ain't nothing I can't accomplish."

At work, Bill learned mainly by himself, in isolation. After gaining experience in collaborative work during his first trimester in the diploma program, however, he began to discuss a new and powerful way to learn. When asked what had been most helpful about his classes, he happily shared:

> I think when we had group sessions, you know? Even in math and writing. . . . We'd get together, and we'd all talk about [ideas]. . . . It was more thoughtful a process of him [the math teacher, John] and everybody else's ideas, then saying what your ideas were. You know, one-on-one-on-one is kind of blah, blah, blah, but when you get in the groups it was a little more helpful.[2]

Working with smaller groups of four or five of his classmates helped Bill to learn mathematical concepts and to improve his writing because he was able to talk and to share his ideas. Sharing his thinking and asking questions helped him to clarify his own ideas, to learn about other people's ideas, and to get answers to questions he might have. Despite the fact that he had a history of learning independently at work, doing so in class, or solely by means of listening to the teacher lecture, proved challenging. He found it difficult to focus when the teacher presented ideas on the blackboard. Being in a group allowed him to focus on what others were saying so that their ideas could help him to reflect on and express his own. Working with classmates in a small group seemed to facilitate Bill's learning in another way—it almost forced him to pay attention. When someone talked in front of the room, outside of a group context, Bill was more inclined to "daydream" and "drift away," he said.

Bill did not like to do things alone that required him to focus inwardly, such as reading books. He preferred to direct his attention outward, and he liked to talk. This helped him learn. While learners making meaning in a variety of ways of knowing might have a preference for group learning over individual learning, the *way* that Bill made meaning of group learning was through his instrumental way of knowing.

Adults with an instrumental way of knowing have clear knowledge of their own enduring traits. In Bill's case, it was apparent to him that book learning was not his preferred way of acquiring information. Bill was oriented almost exclusively to the concrete outcomes and hopes for his learning (demonstrating an instrumental way of knowing). Similarly, when he worked in a group, it was effective for him for other external reasons. He felt he had "to listen to everyone" and stated that he had "no choice" other than to learn when he was in a group. He described this orientation as *external* to him, and therefore the solutions to this learning problem were also external.

Another important aspect of Bill's learning is that he constructed knowledge as being right or wrong. As an instrumental knower, he did not yet understand that there might be many right answers to one question. Bill saw knowledge as external to himself, something that others had and that he could acquire from them. He had a desire to improve; Bill wanted to know the right answers and the correct way to get those answers. Working in a group, Bill said, was more helpful than working one-on-one because he had a better chance of learning the right answers. Group members also helped him to correct his mistakes. Collaborating with cohort members served a practical and functional purpose; Bill utilized group learning as an occasion to get answers, improve his skills, raise questions, and encourage others to speak up. Bill demonstrated the strength of the instrumental way of knowing, emphasizing the concrete outcomes and tangible benefits he derived from working collaboratively with cohort members.

As an instrumental knower, Bill found that the cohort served a functional, pragmatic purpose for him; his classmates were useful in that they helped him meet his own specific concrete needs and goals. Other adults supported Bill by helping him obtain the needed outcomes for program success (the right answers, right skills, and facts). Bill did not, yet, orient to the internal emotional or psychological aspects of his experience. He, like others with this way of knowing, valued the cohort and collaborative learning for instrumental reasons that seem to align with Hamilton's (1994) articulation of the goals for the "postindustrial model" (Trimbur, 1993) of collaborative learning. Not only did group members sometimes help him acquire the required and correct "answers," but they also listened as Bill shared his thoughts. Having the opportunity to speak his thoughts and ideas seemed to support Bill's learning. Group learning experiences created a safe holding environment in which Bill was able to experience himself *as a learner*. The small cohort groups were where Bill could learn new ideas and use them to add to his own learning.

Transitioning from the Instrumental to the Socializing Way of Knowing: Hope

Hope constructed her experience in the transition between the instrumental and the socializing way of knowing (2/3 at program start and 3/2 upon completion. This type of evolution in meaning system is discussed in Chapter 2.). During this transition, both ways of knowing are fully operating, and a person has an increasing capacity for internalizing the perspectives of others. Seven of the 16 learners made sense of their experience in this way; however, some had an instrumental way of knowing leading (or primarily organizing) their meaning making while others had a socializing structure leading.

Hope, in her late 50s when I met her in February 1998, was the oldest learner in the cohort. She was born in the Caribbean, made her way to the United States in the early 1970s, and began sending money home. Hope attended school only up to the seventh grade in her home country and spoke with pride when she told me that she "made a promise" to her mother that she would help finance her younger siblings' education. In her words, "I told my mother that I want them [her siblings] to do more than [me], don't work as hard as I do. They're still working hard." After many years of sacrificing for and supporting her younger siblings, Hope now felt it was her time to earn her diploma.

Hope's generosity of heart, spirit, and mind were apparent as I listened to her discuss her relationships with family members, friends outside the program, colleagues at Polaroid, and peers in the diploma program. She was very much oriented toward helping others; in fact, she said that it gave her a sense of satisfaction. Like Bill, Hope also valued the smaller cohort groups for the practical purpose of helping her learn the correct answers. However, unlike Bill, she derived enormous satisfaction from the process of giving help to others and receiving emotional as well as practical help from them.

> We try to help each other . . . to explain *the best way*. Suppose you are a bit more far ahead than the other person. You try to help the other one [in the group who is] slow[er].

Hope's socializing way of knowing was apparent in her ability to see the connections between her words and feelings when she described her relationships with cohort members. At the same time, she evidenced an instrumental way of knowing by describing her feelings in very concrete terms (focusing, e.g., on things happening to her, what a diploma meant to her in terms of getting a job), with only momentary references to emotion that did not fully describe an internal psychological experience but only suggested one.

When I spoke with Hope before the start of the program, she felt apprehensive about her ability to learn independently (by reading) but confident in her capacity to learn in a "hands-on" manner. Hope "prayed" that she would have the confidence to ask questions of the teachers and her classmates when she needed help and that she would not "be afraid" of other people's reactions to her questions and her accent. Hope admitted that in her prior work and learning experiences in the United States, she sometimes withheld questions for fear that others would either make fun of her accent or not understand her questions. But she understood the importance of asking questions: "You have to be truthful with yourself, and don't say you understand when you don't. . . . Cause if you're not truthful with the person who's teaching you, you're not going to get anything out of it."

Hope repeatedly voiced concern about how she was being perceived by her classmates and, especially, by her teachers, whom she called "the people in charge." This orientation reflects a socializing way of knowing, indicating that she identified with and defined her own sense of self-worth on the basis of other people's opinions and evaluations of her. At the same time, Hope demonstrated an instrumental way of knowing through her focus on the concrete consequences that would follow were she not able to ask questions. Her goal in the diploma program was to develop a trusting relationship with the teacher so that she could feel safe asking questions that would help her to learn.

> I hope the person who's in charge of the class don't get aggravated because you ask the same question over and over again because you don't understand. There got to be a trust that . . . you don't understand and you ask the question, that he or she [the teacher] doesn't get upset. You have to have patience, and the teacher has to have patience. And if you earn that trust between the both of you, things will work out.

Speaking about the trust that can develop between herself and her teachers and hoping that it is not betrayed requires at least a socializing way of knowing. Hope focused on the quality of her relationship with her teachers, and thought about how it could facilitate her learning. At the same time, the way she described the value of a trusting relationship between student and teacher was concrete. Hope emphasized how a teacher and student should interact in their social roles: the student has to "have patience" and the teacher "has to have patience."

While Hope initially focused on her teachers as the primary support for her learning, after one trimester she began to include her cohort colleagues as another key source of support. In September 1998, she spoke about the importance of the cohort in terms of practical support.

> Especially when we . . . get into a group. Like, sometime[s] we go in [a] group of four, and each person would add a subject to write about . . . and then talk about. Then we'd get up and explain what . . . the topic was, and what is your conclusion. So, that was . . . a

good experience for me, because if I make a mistake, the other person would be [there] . . . to back me up.

For Hope, learners supported one another by sharing their knowledge, expertise, and understanding. If one person needed help applying a formula to get to an answer in math or checking subject-verb agreement to craft an essay in English, someone else who understood was available to help.

Cohort members helped each other to learn the "best way," or the correct way, in Hope's view. She valued being able to depend on her peers to help her with concrete outcomes ("right answers"), such as when they helped her to find and correct her mistakes (concrete consequences). At the same time, she also had a sincere interest in helping others when they struggled with their learning. Significantly, she connected her increased self-confidence in voicing her opinions and sharing her questions to the work she had been doing in collaborative groups.

In June 1999, Hope recalled her experience of learning the value of x in math. Despite the challenges in math class, given Hope's lack of experience with algebra, she recounted, "But gradually I learned, and I think everybody learned. And we help each other." Not feeling alone, realizing that she and others in the cohort were united in trying to figure out how to understand this concept, was a source of comfort and thereby also a source of support. She mentioned one student who always offered encouragement, saying, "Hope, don't get so mad with yourself."

There is evidence of a socializing way of knowing in Hope's focus on the emotional nature of learning together with other colleagues. Although she valued the usefulness of being able to depend on her peers to help her get the "right answers," she also showed loyalty to and an interest in helping them.

Hope emblematizes how learners with this way of knowing experienced the cohort as a source of support for their academic efforts. While Hope valued collaborative learning for instrumental reasons (getting "the right answer"), which align with Hamilton's (1994) description of the goals for the "postindustrial model" (Trimbur, 1993), she and other learners with this way of knowing also appreciated the emotional and psychological supports the cohort and collaborative learning provided. This reasoning seems to mirror Hamilton's goals for what Trimbur calls the "social constructionist" model of collaborative learning.

The Socializing Way of Knowing: Pierre

While 11 cohort learners demonstrated a socializing way of knowing operating in combination with other fully operating structures (instrumental or self-authoring), Pierre demonstrated a singly operating socializing way of knowing at program start and finish. With a socializing way of knowing, a person's internal experience becomes the focus of his or her orientation. One of the strengths of this meaning system is a capacity to internalize the perspectives of others; in fact, a person with this way of knowing derives his sense of self from others.

Kegan (1982) discusses the way in which a person with this meaning system conceives of the relationship between self and other. He writes: "You are the other by whom I complete myself, the other whom I need to create the context out of which I define and know myself and the world" (p. 100).

Pierre was embedded in, or identified with, his relationship with his teachers, deriving his sense of worthiness from their evaluations of him. He was not, however, identified in this way with his fellow students. Pierre preferred to work alone rather than with cohort members, and he did not seem to value or enjoy interacting with them. Unlike other socializing knowers, Pierre did not seek approval from or look to fellow cohort members for help in making decisions or formulating his opinions. Instead, he seemed to define himself and draw self-confidence from his teachers' opinions of him only.

Pierre, who was in his late 40s when I met him, worked full time during the day at Polaroid and worked at night as a taxi driver. He left his Caribbean home country and immigrated to the United States early in the 1980s. Unlike most of the cohort learners, Pierre had attended high school for 4 years in his home country. Like many of the women in the cohort, Pierre had been unable to continue in school because he had to work to support his family. He had five children from different marriages, ranging in age from mid-teens to mid-20s. At home, Pierre spoke English, French, and Creole. Although he had relatives living in the Boston area, he did not tell them about his decision to enroll in the program. Unlike many of the other learners, he did not mention a fear of being laid off; to the contrary, he seemed confident in his abilities as a learner and worker.

In March 1998, Pierre said that he faced a learning barrier in the program because he was not able to express his thinking clearly in English. Like Hope, he wanted to grow more "comfortable" speaking English. He explained: "A lot of time it gets me *frustrated* because the way I can explain . . . don't seem like clear enough to me, and I can feel the lack in myself. . . . I don't feel comfortable." Pierre recognized this internal feeling as frustration; he was aware of how his accent influenced the way others responded to him. Pierre demonstrates a socializing way of knowing in his concern about how others see him. It was a source of pride for him to be able to convey his fullest self to others. Pierre made an important distinction between what he was able to *say* (given his expressive language skills) and what he *knew*. This does not seem to be about experiencing himself as a generator of knowledge (which would be a self-authoring construction) but about expressing the knowledge he had already learned, which was contingent upon having the vocabulary and language skills needed to communicate.

During the second interview with Pierre in September 1998, he provided more details about what it would mean for him to feel "comfortable" in his learning. He said that comfort came from "knowing more words," being able to "see more, understand more," and not taking much "time to answer" a question directed at him. After attending the program for one trimester, he felt more "comfortable" because he was "able to understand more now." He further stated: "A lot of thing(s) I used to hear on the street, [I] never know the meaning of it, I just say the word, doesn't know what it mean. And I can say a lot of them, I feel comfortable with them now."

He contrasted this feeling of confidence with the "nightmare" of not knowing the words. Pierre connected his comfort with learning with his confidence, which had grown alongside his language skills as a result of his participation in the program:

> I'm willing to learn because it was a nightmare a lot of time. And just the words you don't know. . . . you don't know what it's meaning. And it's an embarrassing moment for me. But now I feel pretty confident. . . . It's really important to me. . . . I'm still in the learning process. My mind is open to learn. I'm going to see more because it's really important to me. And they [*the teachers*] really give me . . . myself. They put me on the self-confident, I can learn.

Note that he believes it is the teachers who "give" Pierre his self-confidence. Pierre wanted to understand the meaning of words rather than learning for the sake of getting the "right answer," which would be typical of the instrumental way of knowing.

The manner in which Pierre preferred to learn, however—by himself or with the teacher's help—contrasts sharply with the majority of the learners in his cohort who experienced fellow cohort members as sources of academic support. Unlike most program participants, Pierre did not like working in small learning groups. In his words, "Thinking alone I'm doing my best." He reported that when he disagreed with what was being said, he would "go along with it" because he did not want to disappoint anyone. He explained, "If that's what [people in the group] want, that's what you want. I know to me, that's what I want." In the way he treated and dealt with others, both within group learning situations and at work, Pierre seemed to look to a set of socially defined rules of appropriate behavior that were based on a strong sense of wanting to treat others the way he would like to be treated.

Pierre took pride in being sensitive not to impose his questions on fellow classmates, which may be another example of his interest in abiding by what he considered to be socially appropriate norms of behavior. Rather than soliciting help from a classmate when he was "struggling" with an assignment (as many other socializing knowers might do), Pierre preferred to ask the teacher: "Okay, here's where I am, what should I do?" It may be that Pierre viewed the teacher as the only source of authoritative knowledge. Alternatively, Pierre may have been thinking that he would rather not impose his question on a classmate, given his desire to follow what he considered to be appropriate rules of social behavior.

In the last interview, just before graduation, Pierre felt far more certain about his English skills and also began to align himself with cohort peers in small but significant ways. Pierre likened himself to cohort peers in that they were also "foreigners" and working toward a common goal. In his view, all members of the cohort had their strengths and weaknesses: "We all got our strengths. We all have our weaknesses. Maybe what I, what I am good at, maybe they lack of it. What they are good at, maybe I lack at it."

The way Pierre understood the fact that everyone was both different from and the same as him demonstrates a socializing way of knowing. For Pierre, difference is made okay because everyone is still connected and basically the same, which preserves the relationships. Even at the end of the program, in June 1999, Pierre continued to prefer learning on his own. When asked if his relationships with cohort members had changed, Pierre said no, adding that he did not "pay attention too much" to the other adults in his cohort. In contrast with Hope, who appreciated the opportunity to work with cohort members for academic and emotional reasons, Pierre mostly thought that his classmates distracted him from his real goal of listening to what the teacher had to say.

Pierre viewed the teacher as the person responsible for supporting his learning. While other learners also saw the teacher as a key support, none of them saw the teacher as their *only* support. All of them, except for Pierre, viewed their classmates as supports. It is important to note that although Pierre was a socializing knower who needed validation and acceptance from important others in his life, in interviews he said he did not have a close relationship with any of the members of his cohort. In addition to orienting to what he considered to be societial rules and norms, Pierre may have looked to a different set of important others for his sense of belonging.

Transitioning from the Socializing to the Self-Authoring Way of Knowing: Paulo

Paulo made meaning of his learning experience in transition between the socializing and self-authoring ways of knowing. A person with this way of knowing has the capacity to stand back and can reflect on his or her interpersonal relationships and shared loyalties.

Paulo, born in West Africa, was in his early 40s when we met him. Almost immediately, he told us how proud he was that he was now "an American citizen." Although he spoke four languages (Creole, Spanish, Portuguese, and English), one of his hopes for learning in the program was to improve his English. He was married, with four children.

When he joined Polaroid in the mid-1980s, just after immigrating to the United States, he needed to learn English so that he could communicate with coworkers and supervisors. He had been very successful at Polaroid, so much so that while participating in the diploma program Paulo was promoted at least twice, an achievement he attributed to improved skills in math, writing, and communication. Paulo was one of only two adult learners in the diploma program who held an official leadership position at Polaroid. Paulo was "very proud and happy" about his accomplishments at work and in the program; he frequently stated that he was feeling "very, very strong" because of all that he was learning. Paulo attached great value to the recognition he had received from his plant manager and the Polaroid engineers for his performance on the job; making these important others happy made him happy.

During his first interview Paulo emphasized the importance of having teachers who understood "who he was" and "where he came from" if they were to be good teachers for him. He wanted to make sure that both the teachers and the other learners understood that he was "not stupid" and that he might need additional help learning because he spoke English as a second language. If the teacher understood his "background," he explained, then learning would be "more easy" for him. This meant that if teachers and other adult learners knew that he was born in West Africa and was not a native English speaker, it would it be easier for him to ask for and receive help from them. Paulo's experience of this kind of mutual respect between teacher and learners made the cohort a safe holding environment for him.

Paulo possessed a lovely gentleness and generosity of heart that was reflected in his relationships with other cohort members. For example, Paulo's teacher, John, recognized Paulo's ability to teach others and told me that Paulo was one of his "best helpers" in math and science classes.

In Paulo's view, both the teachers and the students were responsible for supporting students' learning (quite different from an instrumental construction of group work, which gives the teacher full responsibility). Paulo believed that it was important when working in groups to share knowledge with others if you were the person who knew something "a little better." In his view, all of the adult learners were "go[ing] in the same direction." At this point in the program (September 1998), Paulo believed that working alone or in groups of two was the most effective way for him to learn. He preferred to avoid larger groups, since they invite conflict. He explained,

> Me and one person together, I think it's more helpful to me than group. Because sometime one person in a group disagree with you so then start a lot of talk, until you finish, you don't put together to understand. . . . But when myself and somebody else, we can put together easily. If I say something wrong [the other person helps and says] "Maybe it's supposed to be like that."

Paulo demonstrated a self-authoring way of knowing when he took responsibility for his learning and reflected on what it would take for him to facilitate his own learning. Although he understood that disagreements within groups were moving toward a larger goal (that is, learning), he preferred the pair work that felt more conducive to his learning.

While it was important to him that group members respect him and one another, he was concerned about others' opinions of him. Paulo did not appreciate other people thinking that he was inadequate or that his opinions were wrong (demonstrating a socializing way of knowing). While adults at all developmental stages may dislike conflict, those with a socializing way of knowing often find conflict with others to be threatening, since it can be experienced as a breach in the relationships that make the self cohere. Kegan (1982) eloquently illuminates how socializing knowers experience conflict. For these knowers, conflicts are not about deciding between one's own and another person's desires; rather, they are conflicts between

> what I want to do as a part of this shared reality and what I want to do as part of that shared reality. To ask someone to resolve such a conflict by bringing both shared realities before herself is to name precisely the limits of this way of making meaning. (Kegan, 1982, p. 96)

When a learner is growing toward a self-authoring way of knowing, there is a capacity to recognize that conflict can be a way to learn more and that agreement is not an end in itself but a means toward some greater end—an opportunity for growth. While Paulo understood that cohort members were working toward a common goal, he preferred that there be less conflict in learning situations because it interfered with his learning.

But Paulo's thinking about his relationship to the cohort and his experience in small group learning changed remarkably over time. Contrary to his earlier opinion that people learned the most alone or in pairs, by the third interview, in February 1999, Paulo had come to believe that a person learns more in a group. At this point, Paulo reported feeling more "comfortable" with other cohort members, meaning that others understood him, which was critical to his learning. Moreover, Paulo no longer felt badly or inadequate if, for example, he made a mistake pronouncing a word when working with others in small groups. When asked what helped to make group learning good for him, he said:

> [The group is] a good way to learn, because if you see anything, you see wrong pronunciation, so anybody can help you, or the pronunciation is supposed to [be] this way, or math if you know, you can help work together, work in team. The same on homework. If you work together, everything is be easy. . . . You learn more working together.

Paulo's thinking about the value of group work and his relationship to the cohort changed during the program. This change was likely not the result of his growing more comfortable in groups simply because he became accustomed to it; it seemed that he grew more comfortable in groups because he had become less concerned about (or identified with) the group members' opinions of him. At the socializing way of knowing, it can be very painful to have others disagree with you. As Paulo became more self-authoring, he developed a perspective on his cohort relationships such that he no longer needed them to define him. He was able to give and accept help and to disagree on occasion without feeling that he was damaging the fabric of the relationship. This change also freed him to have a new relationship with collaborative learning. Kegan (1982) describes the movement from a socializing to a self-authoring way of knowing as a movement from *being* one's relationships to *having* them. In other words, a person grows from being identified with his or her relationships to being able to reflect on them.

The program cohort, a holding environment in which Paulo and other learners knew and understood one another and their teachers, helped Paulo to feel safe in expressing himself, in making mistakes, and in giving and receiving help. In this way, the consistent and enduring nature of the cohort was a holding environment that both supported and challenged Paulo's learning and growth.

The Self-Authoring Way of Knowing: Jeff

Only one member of the cohort, Jeff, made sense of his experience in a way that solely reflected a self-authoring way of knowing. One of the two U. S.-born adult learners in the Polaroid cohort, Jeff was in his late 40s when he began the program. During high school, Jeff continued to have "a hard transition" in terms of adjusting to the demands of school. In eleventh grade, he told his mother that he couldn't "cut it" and decided to enroll in trade school. After 2 years of trade school, he returned to high school but left before completing 11th grade. He then enlisted in the United States Army. When we met Jeff, he lived alone and had two children from his previous marriage.

Jeff worked the C shift, 11 p.m. to 7 a.m., at Polaroid, where he made batteries. He told us the machines he operated fascinated him. Whereas most of the other adult learners solved work problems by asking a supervisor or turning to a computer for instructions, Jeff preferred "figuring things out" on his own. Jeff described himself as someone who feels in charge of himself, his profession, his work, and his interests.

Initially, Jeff expected that sharing a class with other adults who had different academic needs (e.g., learning to express themselves better in English) would prove challenging. Yet over time Jeff cultivated an appreciation for working with his peers. Jeff's thinking about how and why it was helpful to learn with other people differs significantly from others whose stories I have presented. His reasons for valuing group work were rooted in the *process* of collaboration itself rather than in the opportunity to give and receive practical or emotional support around learning. Furthermore, Jeff recognized right away that he would be able to learn through group work and that other adults' processes of learning had value.

Jeff also told us that helping others is a way to help himself learn about their thinking processes. If the act of being able to help others had been the source of his sense of self-worth, he would have been demonstrating a socializing way of knowing. Instead, while Jeff enjoyed the process of helping his colleagues, he was also able to hold a perspective on his own and other cohort members' learning experiences.

Jeff possessed the capacity to take a larger perspective on the group's learning and to share his internal reflections about how and why he valued group work.

> [In groups,] it was like, you might get stuck here, on say [number] four and five. [I'd say] "Well, you did this, how about trying this?" and kinda explain. And then once they [people in his group] finished, we took our papers, and showed it to them [other people in his

group], which they came up with the same answers we did. I think it was just the process of helping them . . . get over that . . . made it easier, I guess for them and me.

It was the "process" of joining together in true collaboration that made group learning so meaningful for Jeff. He took pleasure in being able to help cohort members experience academic success, and he also found fulfillment in his own achievements. His reasoning about why group learning with cohort members was beneficial came from his own standards (demonstration of a self-authoring way of knowing) and was not influenced by an external authority (which would indicate a socializing way of knowing). Jeff could critique his own competence and limitations as a learner, which is also reflective of a self-authoring way of knowing.

In developing his own perspective about the value of groups in the larger enterprise of learning, Jeff demonstrated remarkable capacities for perspective taking and self-authorization. These ideas were echoed in the last interview with Jeff, in June 1999, when he explained how learning worked for him. Through his work with other cohort members, he felt that he had been able to discover his own capabilities: "I realized that I know more than I thought I did." Particularly striking is how he used this newfound awareness to push himself toward deeper understanding. The act of doing, of writing, and of working in cohort learning groups with others facilitated his learning. The group was helpful to Jeff because, he said, "It helps when other people see your mistake. And other people can show you." Jeff continued by telling us how this worked for him:

We were given homework, and, you go home, and you do it. And some of the things, you were able to do 'em all, but then, one or two problems, you always run into that one that you can't. . . . We'd come back the next Tuesday . . . and we'd review what we'd done. And John [the teacher] would ask, "Well, did anybody run into any problems that they couldn't solve?" . . . And we all . . . had problems that . . . we got stumped on. And by putting it up on the board and . . . going from step to step, things that I missed on it, somebody else says, "Oh. You forgot this, this, and this." Which, when you look, you realize what it was you've done. But yourself, you can't pick it up. . . . You can't see no further or no other way. . . . You might have forgot a number, you might have put a decimal in the wrong place, or something like that.

Jeff demonstrates his self-authoring capacity to take a perspective on his own and other cohort members' learning experiences. Jeff appreciated the complexity of other people's learning experiences while also having a perspective on his own experience and how it was similar to and different from that of his colleagues.

As a member of the cohort, Jeff often played the role of shepherd, or protector. One of the ways in which he did this was by looking out for their learning needs—especially those of cohort members for whom English was a second language—and by taking a stand with John, the math teacher, on behalf of others, thus demonstrating a self-authoring way of knowing.

In February 1999, Jeff shared an example from the prior trimester when he needed, for the good of the class and himself, to tell John that John was "losing" the class because he was teaching too fast. In Jeff's view, many cohort members were not able to absorb the concept of using a variable, x, to solve an equation. Jeff, at this time, admitted that he himself was also a bit "lost." Jeff told John to slow down so that his classmates could understand the material.

In his last interview, Jeff revisited his intervention in math class, proud that he had acted on his own instincts to take a stand with John on behalf of—as he remembered it—the learning needs of the cohort.

> After everybody left, I had said to John, "You know, I understand. I hear what you're saying," but . . . "You're losing that part of the class." I says, "You only have [two] people who speak English [as a first language]. . . . The other ninety percent of the class, they're all from other countries, and it's harder for them to understand what you're saying. You have to explain yourself. You have to show them more details." Once he [John] started putting stuff down, and going around to each one of 'em and showing and explaining, they understood more and better, which helped turn that class around, and made all of them feel more comfortable.

In his reflections, Jeff was able to hold the multiple views of himself, the ESOL learners in the cohort, and his teacher. When recommending a change in his teacher's instruction, Jeff used his own judgment and acted on his own internally generated value system. His decision to talk with John on behalf of the cohort demonstrated his capacity to have a perspective on the larger context, to take a stand for his own beliefs or on behalf of others' interests, and to take responsibility for his own decisions. This example also illustrates Jeff's capacity to understand the group's experience. Jeff showed his caring nature and concern for the common goal of the cohort, and he had the capacity to turn inward toward his value system to decide what he needed to do, demonstrating his self-authoring way of knowing.

Summary of the Cohort as a Holding Environment for Learning and Teaching

I have shown how the cohort at Polaroid served as a holding environment: spacious enough to support and challenge learners with different ways of knowing. Specifically, I have illustrated how learners had different experiences of the cohort as a support to their academic learning and how, with their unique ways of knowing, they made sense of their collaborative learning experiences in different ways, depending on their meaning system.

Pierre, a socializing knower, preferred to either work on his own or work with the teacher. He is the only learner in this sample who did not experience his classmates as an additional source of support. However, toward the end of the program, Pierre aligned himself, for the first time, with cohort members in that he had a newly developed appreciation for other people's struggles to learn English.

Significantly, I have shown how learners, across ways of knowing, valued the cohort for *instrumental* reasons (i.e., it helped them achieve "concrete goals," help with completing coursework, doing homework) closely aligned with Hamilton's (1994) conceptualization of Trimbur's (1993) "postindustrial model". However, instrumental knowers valued the cohort for these concrete reasons *only*. Socializing knowers, while valuing the instrumental supports provided by working with cohort members, also appreciated collaborating with cohort members for the emotional and psychological support they provided as they pursued their academic learning goals (i.e., for reasons that align with Hamilton's stated goals for Trimbur's social constructionist model). Finally, self-authoring knowers not only named the instrumental and emotional supports as important; they also focused on the ways in which working with others helped them to broaden their perspectives on themselves, others, and their learning as they pursued their academic goals (i.e., for reasons that align with Hamilton's goals for Trimbur's "popular democratic" model).

Feeling recognized by one another and by their teachers for the selves they were and the selves they were becoming helped these learners to feel "held," in the psychological sense, and supported. As Bosworth and Hamilton (1994) point out, a collaborative learning context is one in which "at least some aspects of classroom knowledge and authority can be developed or created by both students and teacher" (p. 18). These stories illuminate how CEI teachers worked with learners to share authority and enhance learning. The idea of the cohort as a holding environment that gently challenges learners, and thereby broadens their perspectives, is an important one that will be discussed again later in the book.

"LIKE A FAMILY": THE COHORT AS A HOLDING ENVIRONMENT FOR EMOTIONAL SUPPORT

While the literature on group learning suggests that collaborative learning can serve as a social and emotional support (Bosworth & Hamilton, 1994; Pedersen & Digby, 1995), this study offers a new perspective on *how* learners experience this sense of well-being in qualitatively different ways.[3] I will show that this emotional support is experienced differently by learners who make meaning in different ways. While for many participants the cohort became, as Hope and others said, "like a family," what "family" meant to each of the learners was different depending on his or her way of knowing. Although the majority of learners credited their colleagues with contributing to their success, I focus on three adults at different developmental places to illustrate how the cohort provided them with emotional support.

Notably, Bill—and Renada, the other participant making meaning with an instrumental way of knowing—did not talk very much about feeling *emotionally* supported by the cohort. They perceived the support they got from the cohort in more practical and concrete terms: help with homework, friendly encouragement, and help pronouncing words correctly.

Transitioning from the Instrumental to the Socializing Way of Knowing: Helena

Learners making meaning in this transition often have an orientation toward both the concrete understanding of the instrumental way of knowing and the internalization of others' perspectives of the socializing way of knowing.

Helena, who was in her late 40s when the research team met her, emigrated from West Africa in the late 1960s. She had two children, both in their early 20s. Her first language was Portuguese. Helena talked about the cohort without prompting during her last interview, mentioning the group as a contributor to the "good time" she had in class: "I tell you, we had a good time, and we very good group people, too . . . because we learn. Like if I don't understand something, if that person know, they told me, or if I know, I told them. So we work together." Here Helena is not reflecting on the emotional support she and her classmates gave one another; rather, she is stating as a fact that they are "very good group people," explaining that being in a good group of people involves a positive mutual exchange in which whoever holds the information shares it. This orientation might be primarily instrumental (as the relationships in the group are used for specific, practical purposes), but Helena's understanding of the group process goes beyond her expectation of obtaining information. Helena was also interested in offering forms of emotional support to her colleagues.

Helena demonstrated a socializing way of knowing in noticing connections between herself and others, caring about those connections, and offering them as important factors in her life in a way that Bill and Renada, who were instrumental knowers, did not. By the end of the program, Helena described the support of her colleagues as vital to her success:

> Because we here like family. Especially me, I am very close to my family, very close to my family, so here everybody friend. I think because we got along good. We got along very, very good. So, we never have any problem, like upset somebody, or talk about somebody.

Helena's orientation to the group as a family suggests her socializing way of knowing. The fact that she described what she meant by "family" ("here everybody friend," everyone "got along good," people didn't talk badly of one another) demonstrates a more advanced capacity for reflection (e.g., about what it means to be family). Yet the features she describes to define "family" still seem to be fairly concrete—people get along well and do not upset one another. The cohort met these needs for Helena and increased her comfort level and her ability to accomplish her goals. As a holding environment, the cohort became a place where people were kind to one another and encouraged one another through the many difficulties of the program and the challenges of balancing the multiple responsibilities of their adult lives.

The Socializing Way of Knowing: Christopher

People who are socializing knowers are less oriented toward the external facts of a situation than toward their internal sense of things, an internal experience of the thoughts and ideas of others.

Originally from the Caribbean, Christopher was in his late 30s and had been in the United States for more than 10 years when the research team met him. He was highly motivated to get his diploma; Christopher saw education as "more important than money. . . . It's like a key, I can open the door, with a diploma. . . . After I get it, I can decide what to do."

While Helena spoke mostly about how her cohort colleagues encouraged her by telling her to stay in the program, Christopher, when talking about how helpful the cohort was to him, spoke mostly about *the way* the members of the cohort interacted:

> We've been very respectful . . . So, we not make fun of people by saying stuff like if they don't know what to say, we polite. We do appreciate each other. I will miss everybody after the class. And then I will hope, I really hope . . . we can still keep in contact. . . . Calling each other . . . things like that.

For Christopher, the cohort was not a group of people who might offer one another particular, concrete supports (such as advice about staying in the program). The cohort was about a way of being in a relationship with one another, a way of giving an abstract level of support, of accepting one another. Together cohort members created a safe place where no one would "make fun of people."

Wanting to explain that this was not just a serious group, though, in February 1999, Christopher said, "But we are having fun. People are teasing a little bit, but with respect, you know what I mean. So, there wasn't any confusion about that." For Christopher it is the atmosphere of the group, rather than a single element of it that felt supportive: they learned together, they had fun together, and they were polite to one another. If Christopher had been further along in the transition to the self-authoring way of knowing, he might have been able to step back from this perspective and look at the larger learning enterprise in which they were all engaged.

The Self-Authoring Way of Knowing: Jeff

Jeff, the only person in the cohort with a fully self-authoring way of knowing, experienced the supportive and challenging "push" from working with other cohort members. He elaborated on how it was the "process" of learning with others that was a source of encouragement for him.

Jeff was oriented to the more abstract, psychological supports to be derived from the cohort. Like Helena, Jeff noticed connections between himself and others, cared about those connections, and offered them as important factors in his learning. However, unlike Helena, Jeff reflected on what these relationships meant to him in a more abstract way. His self-authoring capacity enabled him to have a wider perspective on the complexity of the larger learning enterprise in which all cohort members were engaged. Jeff reflected on his feelings and examined the roots and importance of those feelings. He did not experience conflict as a threat to his sense of cohesion with the group. It was clear, however, that he took joy in the successes of his classmates, just as he took pleasure in his own successes. In the team's last meeting with Jeff in June 1999, he explained,

> Being in the class environment . . . it makes you feel better. You get the reward. You're able to see other . . . people's faces when you've done something, and you've got it right. Same with them, when they've done something. They got it right, you know. You can see other people, and you know that—hey, yeah, we're doing it. We're getting it down. . . . It gives you that little push, when you got other people working with you and around you.

When Jeff discussed how "being in the class environment makes you feel better," he was referring to his ability to experience "the reward" not only of "seeing other people's faces" when *he* did something "right" but of sharing in the joy when they did something well. Both feelings gave Jeff a sense of satisfaction. Rather than constructing doing something right in terms of "the right answer," Jeff was referring to being "right" in terms of demonstrating an understanding of a concept and understanding the *process* in contrast to following a rule.

Although it made him "feel better" to be in a classroom environment, and he admitted that this was a motivator, it was not *the* main source of Jeff's motivation (as it might be if he were a socializing knower). Jeff demonstrated a self-authoring meaning system in that he was internally motivated by his own values and beliefs.

Jeff had sophisticated and complex ideas about how and why the process of working in a group was helpful and supportive: "It give[s] you that little push, when you got other people working with you and around you." Although the group gave Jeff the "push," he seemed to experience it internally. This comment demonstrates Jeff's understanding of how the cohort encouraged him, and it also shows his capacity to have a perspective on the process of group work. He *knew* what he thought about group work; he could reflect on his own perspective about this and consider why he thought it was effective and supportive to his own and other people's learning. For Jeff, it was the *process* of working with others that was supportive and encouraging. He valued it because of its benefits for himself *and* other members of the cohort.

Jeff's reasoning was not influenced by an external authority, as it would be if he had been a socializing knower. His focus was on the common goals that the cohort shared. As a self-authoring knower, Jeff constructed conflict as a natural part of learning from and working with others rather than as a personal threat. Working with other cohort members created a supportive holding environment for Jeff in which he received and gave support.

Summary of the Cohort as a Holding Environment for Emotional Support

I have examined how adults with different developmental levels experienced the cohort as a supportive and encouraging holding environment. For example, Helena noted and cared about her connections with cohort members ("everybody get along good," "we are a family") and defined her relationships with others in concrete ways. Christopher oriented to the more abstract forms of emotional support (the way these relationships worked) that he derived from cohort colleagues. Jeff was able to reflect on his feelings about the interpersonal supports he appreciated and was able to reflect on the process of working with others, including working through conflict, as a natural part of interpersonal relationships. This cohort was a strong holding environment for learners, by meeting their different needs for support and challenge. It created an environment where people with different ways of knowing could be well held and encouraged.

"I HAVE A BETTER APPRECIATION FOR PEOPLE": THE COHORT AS A HOLDING ENVIRONMENT FOR PERSPECTIVE BROADENING

In addition to supporting academic learning and providing emotional sustenance, the cohort also provided members with the means for broadening their perspectives on themselves, each other, learning, and life. Collaboration with cohort members often became a catalyst for learners' personal growth, as they were encouraged to share and become more aware of their own perspectives, to listen to others' perspectives, and thereby broaden their own.

This capacity for personal growth and transformation was evident no matter what the cohort member's meaning-making system was. Here I focus on how three learners—Bill, Hope, and Jeff—responded to the life stories exercise. While all three learners found this to be a powerful learning experience that broadened their perspectives, each made sense of the experience differently, depending on their meaning system.

The Instrumental Way of Knowing: Bill

When Bill began the diploma program, he said remarkably little about his fellow students, except to speculate that the "foreigners" might struggle with learning given their limited English proficiency. Bill's perspective on other cohort members shifted radically during the program. He connected this change to the experience of hearing other people's "life stories" presented as part of an assignment for the life employment workshop held during the final trimester.

For the life stories exercise, learners invested considerable time conceptualizing and writing personal narratives, which they then shared during the final weeks of the trimester with the entire cohort through oral presentations. Cohort members worked independently at home and in class and in small writing groups, where they shared ideas about their writing and received feedback from one another and from their teacher, Judith. Many of Bill's colleagues recounted the experience of immigration, telling stories of what it was like to leave their families behind with the hope of finding a richer life in the United States. Several presenters, and many of us in the room, were moved to tears as we listened to heartfelt accounts of new beginnings and the pursuit of "golden opportunities" that would bring rewards to themselves and their families. Bill was so deeply affected by these stories that he identified the experience as the most meaningful for his learning, saying that it "tugged at his heartstrings" and compelled him to see his classmates differently.

Bill was beginning to recognize the limitations of his former perspective, admitting, "I never thought about foreigners." What he learned from his foreign-born classmates transformed his thinking about himself and people from other countries. He explained:

> I just know I see them in a different light, people from other countries, than I did before. To me, they were just invaders. Not invaders, I shouldn't have said that. You know, I don't know what I mean. Just to see them and . . . actually talk to them and hear their life stories, and most of them struggling coming up. . . . I'm just trying, I ain't got the right words. . . . I have a better appreciation for people who come from poor countries and Third World countries.

Toward the end of the program, Bill realized that many cohort members came from "poor countries, these ain't big money countries, and these people grew up on farms and barefoot." With this newfound understanding of the hardship in his classmates' lives, Bill was able to recognize and applaud their accomplishments: "They're successful now, just maintaining jobs in America for all these years." This passage marks a profound shift in perspective for Bill. He began to empathize with people whom he had assumed were different from him and to see the ways in which they were alike. Instead of seeing those who were different from him as completely "other," completely separate from himself (as he did in early interviews), Bill now respected them for their accomplishments and put himself in their shoes, demonstrating a newly evolving sense of empathy for and identification with others. Notably, Bill felt "grateful" to cohort members for helping him learn about their lives and challenge his thinking.

While Bill noted a shift in his thinking about his classmates in particular and immigrants in general, he was not yet able to express what this broadening of perspective *felt* like. Bill struggled to find words to convey his experience, sometimes revising his own statements, restarting sentences, or uttering "I don't know"; these speech patterns were virtually absent when Bill discussed other topics. I interpret this stumbling in Bill's speech as evidence that he was trying to come to terms with his newfound understanding and reflect on his emotions. With continued support and challenge, Bill would likely grow into this capacity as well.

Transitioning from the Instrumental to the Socializing Way of Knowing: Hope

Like Bill, Hope described the exercise of sharing life stories as a powerful learning experience, one that broadened her perspective in lasting ways. Hope made sense of this learning differently, however, in part because she had a socializing and instrumental way of knowing.

Hearing other people's life stories challenged Hope's assumption that cultural differences separated her cohort colleagues from her. Hope demonstrated a capacity for abstract thinking, a strength of the socializing way of knowing, when she reflected on shared "values" among members of the cohort. Hope was able to attend to underlying messages in the life stories:

> We wrote about our parents, what . . . values that they taught us. . . . There were things that the group said that . . . although they were from different, other countries, you could see that they were the same values. They may speak a different language, but you could see that it was the same values. . . . Although . . . the parents never knew each other, we have some of the same values.

Despite obvious differences in their life histories, Hope now understood that she and many other members of the cohort were united by the core values instilled in them by their parents. While members of the group spoke different languages and came from very different cultures, they shared fundamental beliefs about how to live. She had a newly developed respect for what she had in common with her classmates. Hope's ability to recognize commonalties across the group enabled her to manage their differences rather than feel threatened by them.

Remarkably, Hope was able to generalize and apply her enhanced capacity for perspective-taking beyond the classroom and into other domains of her life. She explained how the learning made possible in the cohort was helping her at work:

> [Working with the cohort] made me understand people who I work with. Cause they're people I work with that's dyslexic. And make me think back. I wasn't dyslexic, but it make me think back. If I didn't go to this class, I wouldn't have the opportunity of helping them in some of the things they are, and a little bit more patience.

Through the supportive holding environment of the cohort, Hope was increasingly able to take on other peoples' perspectives, to see the world through their eyes. This ability to see a bigger world helped her in her work life. For Hope, difference was made okay by the fact that everyone was still connected and basically the same (a socializing construction). She discussed all of this in a concrete context (an instrumental construction).

The Self-Authoring Way of Knowing: Jeff

While Jeff enrolled in the program to earn a high school diploma, he came to appreciate the value of his "multicultural" class. Jeff reflected sensitively on the ways in which working with other cohort members of different ethnicities, cultures, and family backgrounds helped him to develop a broader perspective on himself and others. The life stories exercise helped him with this.

Jeff realized, through his work in small and large learning groups in the program and in particular the life stories exercise, that "everybody's learning is different," and he demonstrated the capacity to see that the entire cohort shared a common purpose. He understood that the group was effective not only for his own learning but also for other people's learning. Jeff's thinking about why the process of working in a group was helpful and how his perspective broadened over time illustrate his self-authoring way of knowing.

In the third interview (in February 1999), Jeff explained that at the start of the program he had worried that most of the other learners, who were immigrants, would slow his progress because they would need help with grammar and pronunciation. But his view of these learners changed with program participation and learning from the "life stories exercise." He soon came to understand their struggles with English as a learning need rather than a liability to his own learning. After engaging in the life stories exercise and the program, in general, Jeff began to recognize the implications of his classmates' prior learning experiences in a different educational system:

> I think for me it was like he [the science teacher] gave us the things to do [in the science research project]. We all selected a title, a topic [to investigate on the Internet for the science project]. And then he'd [the teacher, John] give us directions on how to do it. . . . Most of the people in the class didn't understand [John's directions]. That was because they are from another country. And the two [educational systems are] different, maybe the schoolings are different. Maybe because they are from another country. They don't grasp or understand the English language, so therefore, they can't [understand], as fast.

To complete work, like the research for the above-mentioned science project, each learner had to understand the teacher's directions, work independently, and work collaboratively. Jeff thought that those members of the cohort who were born outside the United States looked to him and Bill, the only two "Americans," to see if they found the instructions easier to follow.

> Now, we all worked in singles. But . . . myself and Bill in the class, were the only two Americans. Everybody else was multicultural. So it's almost like I got the feeling that they were kind of looking at us: "How much [do] they know?" I know no more than the rest of them do. But I kind of got the feeling that they expected us to know just a little bit more than they did. But when it comes down to it, we didn't know no more than the other person did.

Jeff had the capacity to see that others had different experiences and expectations of him than he did of himself. He also discussed that the other cohort members had important knowledge, ideas, and experiences to share.

Jeff reflected on the life stories exercise and explained more about how his perspective was broadened after being part of a multicultural class. As shown, these experiences provided Jeff with opportunities to challenge his own assumptions about his own and other people's learning and experiences and to reflect on his values. He had new appreciation for how his nonnative-born classmates must have "struggled." The cohort served as a holding environment for Jeff—supporting him while at the same time challenging him to broaden his perspective.

Summary of the Cohort as a Holding Environment
for Perspective Broadening

These cases show how the experience of the cohort made it possible for learners to broaden their perspective. Working closely with one another in the classroom in general and especially in the life stories exercise created the context for reflection. Engaging with others in the life stories exercise led learners to become more aware of the thinking that guided both their own behavior and that of others. The cohort served as a holding environment for learners that gently challenged and supported their capacity to change and broaden their perspective. In short, the experience of working with the cohort served as a catalyst for learners' growth.

While Bill, Hope, and Jeff found the life stories exercise to be a powerful learning experience that broadened their perspectives, each made sense of the experience differently, filtering it through their individual meaning system. This is a compelling example of how learning activities such as the life stories exercise can be made sufficiently roomy to accommodate learners with different ways of knowing. Bill, Hope, and Jeff show us that the life stories curriculum was transformational across gender, racial background, and way of knowing.

CONCLUSION

The cases presented in this chapter illustrate how learners experienced the cohort (a program design feature) and collaborative learning (a teacher practice). They show how sustained connection to fellow cohort members and work in collaborative learning groups provided a robust holding environment that supported learners' academic development, emotional well-being, and cognitive development. Furthermore, the cases illustrate how learners with different ways of knowing experienced collaborative group learning; the experiences of these learners seem to mirror the goals Hamilton (1994) articulates for Trimbur's (1993) three models of collaborative learning (discussed in Chapter 4).

The interplay between the diploma program's structure and the teacher practice of using collaborative learning created opportunities for learners to share experiences, form interpersonal relationships, and support one another's learning. The variety and forms of support and challenge offered to and given by these learners worked to transform this group of adult workers into a *cohort of learners*. Learners experienced their relationship to the cohort differently, depending on their way of knowing. Engaging in common learning experiences over an extended period of time in which learners worked *together* toward the same goal contributed importantly to the formation of a caring learning community. For many learners this cohort was "like a family," a fact that emphasizes the idea of the cohort as a "holding environment" for adult learning that both supports and challenges learners, leading to important implications for both adult education program design and teacher practice.

Learners in this cohort who were instrumental knowers primarily valued opportunities to work collaboratively for instrumental reasons. These learners appreciated working with cohort members because it helped them achieve their specific, concrete, behavioral goals. Their reasoning aligns with the goals Hamilton (1994) articulates for Trimbur's (1993) "postindustrial model." They reported that cohort collaboration helped them to:

- "find the right answers" in math and the correct sentence structure when writing.
- learn how to use the right words to better express themselves in English and improve their vocabulary.
- learn how to communicate better with other people at work, at home, and in other daily interactions (such as with school officials and their children's teachers).
- see classmates and even themselves as holders of knowledge (constructed as an accumulation of facts).
- understand the meaning of words and concepts.
- learn how to learn on their own (as evidenced by demonstrating a behavior).

The socializing knowers valued the instrumental supports named by instrumental knowers, and they also spoke about appreciating the encouragement they received from fellow cohort members. Socializing knowers especially valued the cohort and collaborative work for the important emotional and psychological support it offered as they balanced the multiple demands of work, family, and school. Their experience mirrors the goals Hamilton (1994) names for Trimbur's (1993) "social constructionist model" of collaborative learning. It helped them to:

- feel "comfortable" asking questions when they did not know the answer or did not know what do to in particular situations.
- learn to "socialize with other people."
- feel less "afraid when speaking English" in front of others (both within and outside of the classroom).

Although self-authoring knowers mentioned the instrumental and emotional supports of working with cohort members, they focused on their appreciation of the different perspectives that members of the cohort brought to any particular learning activity and the ways in which this helped them broaden their own perspective. Their experience aligns closely with the "popular democratic model" (Trimbur, 1993, as cited in Hamilton, 1994) of collaborative learning. Self-authoring knowers reported that working with cohort members helped them to:

- enhance their learning and teaching *processes* because they were exposed to varying perspectives (points of view) on issues.
- better understand and appreciate their own and other learners' academic and life experiences.
- recognize, and at times appreciate forms of difference and commonality both within and beyond the cohort.

The cohort and the collaborative learning groups in the CEI Adult Diploma Program classes served as contexts in which adults were often encouraged by each other, and by teachers, to challenge the assumptions that deeply influenced the ways in which they thought and behaved. The cohort and collaborative learning groups thus served as holding environments for growth. During the first and second round of interviews, two learners, Renada and Teresina, did not talk about the experience of group learning. However, as their expressive language skills seemed to improve (based on learnings from interviews and classroom observations), they talked about more fully participating in small cohort groups, and they spoke more often about valuing group work with cohort members. Thus, even for those members who initially did not seem as connected to the cohort as the others, the experience of this learning community apparently had a powerful effect.

Significantly, the three ways of knowing used to characterize learners' experience in the cohort closely match those described in the literature. While Hamilton (1994) presents these models as a kind of a hierarchy of use, it is important for teachers to consider that (1) not all learners can take advantage of the entire hierarchy, (2) some learners will find their highest level of use in one of the models, and (3) there is a need to create classrooms in which all models are working synergistically. As mentioned in Chapter 4, Hamilton (1994) suggests that a teacher can benefit from selecting and implementing one particular model *for any one class* that suits his or her teaching philosophy or personal style. However, because learners make sense of the same process, collaborative learning, in qualitatively different ways, selecting and implementing only one model would in fact support learners with one way of knowing better than it would others. Learners with different ways of knowing utilized several model types—to varying degrees and depending on their way of knowing—and they needed different supports and challenges to benefit from these experiences. It seems reasonable to suggest, then, that teachers adopt a plurality of approaches, flexibly incorporating components of all three models in any one classroom to attend to the wide range of learners' ways of knowing and their diverse learning needs.

"Good Teachers Understand Their Students": A Developmental View of Learners' Expectations of Their Teachers

> The literacy teaching-learning process is many things, but in the final analysis, it is an interpersonal relationship charged with emotion.
> —R. Quigley, *Rethinking Literacy Education*, 1997

MY PRIMARY PURPOSE in Chapter 5 was to illustrate how the interpersonal relationships formed in a cohort can support learners' development. In this chapter I explore the ways in which learners conceive of the teacher-learner relationship. In many cases, their perspective changed during the course of the program.

While the goals of adult basic education (ABE) programs range from helping adults become better prepared to participate in the workforce to developing skills to encouraging them to engage in social and political change (Evers, Rush, & Berdrow, 1998), the study of the Polaroid cohort and the learners at the other two sites infuses these goals with a different kind of understanding. While each of these goals is valuable in its own right, the research team found that it is also important to consider how learners make sense of their relationships with teachers in order to better support them as they reach for these goals. Like our colleagues at the National Institute for Literacy's Equipped for the Future (Stein, 2000), the research team believes that this kind of understanding will promote more effective teaching and learning, allowing educators to better meet the diverse learning needs of adults in ABE programs (Stein).

It is widely known that one of the most prevalent problems facing the ABE field is learner retention (Beder, 1994; Horsman, 1991; Quigley, 1997). For example, Quigley cites a federal study (conducted from July 1993 through June 1994) that showed the dropout, or attrition, rate in federally funded basic literacy and General Educational Development

(GED) programs to be close to 74%. Recently, ABE program directors across the nation have been asked to improve their program retention rates, but there is a lack of research investigating this problem (Beder, Medina, & Eberly, 2000; Quigley, 1997).

Researchers and practitioners alike acknowledge that adults who enroll in ABE and English for speakers of other languages (ESOL) programs come from diverse cultures and countries, vary in their expressive English skills and in their educational backgrounds, and have diverse reasons for enrolling, and multifaceted goals (Brod, 1995; Comings, Sum, & Uvin, 2000; Quigley, 1997; Valentine, 1990). A recent study conducted by Comings, Parrella, and Cuban (2001) investigated learner persistence in pre-GED programs to better understand how to help students persist in these programs. Through this investigation, the authors found that those students who were more likely to persist in these programs:

- Were more than 30 years old.
- Were immigrants.
- Were parents of teenage or grown children.
- Had a history of prior self-study.

Importantly, the authors discovered that previous negative school experience did not appear to affect persistence.

ABE scholars (Beder, Medina, & Eberly, 2000; Brod, 1995; Quigley, 1997) are appealing to researchers and practitioners, asking them to learn how to improve retention rates in ABE programs by focusing on what seems to work for learners who persist, referring to persisters who have completed programs as "successful learners." They see these learners as a rich source from whom to learn how to improve retention rates. Quigley makes a plea for researchers to focus on how learners make sense of their experiences in ABE programs so as to improve policy and practice. He asserts that the "voice consistently absent in many policy and practice decisions is the voice of the learner" (p. 193). Gowen (1992) echoes Quigley's call and urges researchers to listen carefully to learners' voices as a way to improve classroom practice. More specifically, Quigley recommends using qualitative methods to better understand the complex life experiences of those learners who resist dropping out.

One way the research team's study responds to these calls was to investigate how learners make sense of their relationships with their teachers. Given the longitudinal nature of our study, we were able to ask learners about their relationships with their teachers at four points during the 14-month program, which enabled us to understand their perceptions of these—and how, if at all, they changed—over time.

HOW LEARNERS CONCEPTUALIZED
TEACHER-LEARNER RELATIONSHIPS

What were these learners' expectations for how their teachers could support their efforts to learn? How, if at all, did their conceptions of what makes for a good teacher change over time? These are the questions I address in this chapter, focusing on how learners understand the teacher's role in their learning process.

In our research with this diverse group of learners from different cultures, with different levels of English proficiency, with different familial backgrounds and values for education, the team often wondered about the influence that cultural expectations of a teacher's role might play in their understanding of their relationships with teachers and of the teachers' authority. For example, some of these participants came from countries where teachers were highly respected and viewed as the ultimate source of knowledge. We wondered how, and whether, cultural expectations might factor into what learners would be able and willing to share with us. We also wondered how learners' previous educational and school experiences, both in the United States and in their home countries, might shape their experiences in the diploma program.

Recent research highlights the need to examine the teacher-learner relationship by focusing on learners' perspectives so that we can better understand the assumptions and expectations they bring to their learning experiences in ABE classrooms (Quigley, 1997; Taylor, 1996). The work of the research team responded to this call. There are important implications for understanding not only learners' expectations for their teachers but also how learners *make sense* of their expectations and their relationships with their teachers. In other words, what constitutes support for a learner with one way of knowing may be experienced as a challenge to a learner employing a different way of knowing.

Another important aspect of the research is what it revealed about how learners' conceptions of their relationship with teachers changed over time. As Tinberg and Weisberger (1997) remind us: "Our job as instructors is to both gain a 'reading' of where our students are and then to reach out to them in a way that helps them move beyond where they are to where they need to be" (p. 46). While Tinberg and Weisberger emphasize the benefits of employing constructive-developmental theory to better understand learners' experiences in community colleges, I suggest that this lens is equally valuable for understanding learners' experiences in ABE programs. This theory helps us to think about how to create learning programs that are dynamic holding environments for supporting learners as they grow from one way of knowing to another.

Most learners, no matter what their way of knowing, entered the program expressing worries about whether they would feel "comfortable" in the classroom context. Some were "scared" that they would not be able to achieve their goal of earning a high school diploma, while others voiced a longing to feel comfortable asking questions when they did not understand something the teacher said. Many learners expressed a hopefulness that their teachers would not consider them to be "stupid" because they could not express themselves well in English (when they entered the program). During the program, participants reported feeling "more confident" in their abilities to ask questions, to speak in front of classmates, and to complete program requirements. All learners entered the program with hopes and expectations about how the four program teachers would support them in their learning. Table 6.1 illustrates the ways in which participants, across ways of knowing, understood the teacher-learner relationship.

Whatever their individual way of knowing, students did voice some common expectations as to how they wanted their teachers to support them in their learning. For example, the majority of learners at the Polaroid site (as well as most learners in the other two sites) thought it was important for teachers to "be on time to class" and to "speak slowly," so that learners could understand. However, as we will see, adults made sense of these experiences differently, depending on their way of knowing.

The Instrumental Way of Knowing

The instrumental knowers thought it was the teacher's job to give learners what they need to learn to master academic content. They understood the teacher to be the central authority in the learning process. It was also the teacher's responsibility, to them, to teach learners the appropriate directions they needed to follow in order to succeed in learning. They considered good teachers to be those who give clear and explicit, step-by-step instructions on how to proceed with in-class or homework assignments.

Bill and Renada: Growing from Instrumental to Socializing. Both Bill, a native speaker of English, and Renada, a nonnative English speaker, made sense of their experience with an instrumental way of knowing at program start, and upon program completion, both learners demonstrated an emerging socializing way of knowing. For Bill and Renada, good teachers were willing to take time to "explain" and reexplain, if needed (even if it took several different types of explanations). They felt best supported in their learning when teachers used direct, concrete teaching approaches and then gave them multiple opportunities to apply their learning. These learners were preoccupied with learning the rules they needed to follow to dem-

onstrate skills that they had learned. Good teachers, they told the research team, are those who can give them the right skills, facts, and ways of solving problems so that they can, in turn, "get the right answers." With the instrumental way of knowing, a person constructs knowledge as something that is right or wrong. Teachers give learners knowledge (which is understood as an accumulation of skills and facts, such that more skills and more information equal more knowledge). Knowing the "right way" to complete academic tasks, for these learners, yields learning.

Bill and Renada assessed their success by grades and test scores assigned by the teacher. They knew they had learned something when they were able to perform a task on their own (learning is defined by demonstrating) and when the teacher, an external authority, gave them a good grade. As authorities, teachers evaluate learners' work. It is their job to "correct" learners' mistakes; help them to pronounce words; fix their spelling, grammar, and sentence structure; and teach them the rules they need to know to solve academic problems. Instrumental knowers believe that if they follow the teacher's rules or directions and do what they are "supposed to do," then they should get a good grade (the external reward). Learners with this way of knowing told our research team that if they put the time into their studies, the direct result would be that they learned the skills that had been taught.

This is how Bill responded when I asked him during his first interview what he thought made a good teacher:

> A real good teacher would, given the time, explain something to somebody completely. . . . I know, like in school right now, you've got a teacher, she's got forty kids, she can't go to everyone individually and do it, boom, boom, boom. And this teacher here is gonna have what, seventeen of us? . . . I know she can't come and say, "Sit down with some of the people who can't speak English and explain things to 'em a hundred percent," because it will make everybody start getting bored, waiting. But a good teacher will be able to either take that person aside at the end of class [and] talk to them or give them that extra couple of minutes to explain that one thing that they don't get. . . . Some people need extra help, of course. Especially the people who don't speak English. Cause that's the only problem that I see with it, as far as "I don't understand." Like if I went to [another country], I wouldn't understand either. So I understand that they don't understand a lot.

For Bill, good teachers are those who are able to "explain" concepts very well to their students. Although he realized that nonnative speakers of En-

Table 6.1. Learners' Constructions of the Teacher-Learner Relationship

WAY OF KNOWING	LEARNER EXPECTATIONS FOR A GOOD TEACHER	SAMPLE OF LEARNERS' COMMENTS
Instrumental knowers	For these learners, good teachers are those who: • show them how to learn. • *give* them their knowledge and the rules they need to follow to get the right answers. They know they have learned something when they can "do it" (demonstrate a behavior) and when they get a good grade (a consequence).	Good teachers "give you that little push," "make me learn," and "explain how to do it, ask you write it down, and you write down exactly how to do it. Then we'd do it."
Instrumental/ socializing knowers	For these participants, good teachers: • explain things to help them understand. • help them learn by showing them how to do things. • give them rules to follow so they can do things the right way. • give them their knowledge and tell them what they *should* know. They know they have learned when they are able to do something and because the teacher tells them so.	Good teachers "teach me all the time," and "show me the correct way to speak so that others will listen." They "make you understand, like if I don't know something, I ask her, 'Can you repeat it?' Then she explains again." Good teachers say "I have to do it this way because if I don't it's no good." They "make me do writing, speaking. She's good, she's always there."
Socializing knowers	For these learners, good teachers: • care about them. • explain things to help them understand. • really listen and support them. • *know* what is good for them to know, and they tell them what they *should* know. • have certain human qualities; they are described as kind, patient, and encouraging. These adults can feel, inside, when they have learned something and the teacher acknowledges them in that.	"If you don't have a good teacher, you're not going to be self-confident." "If [the teacher] doesn't teach you the way you learn good, that doesn't help you." "I ask the teacher to explain to me how I'm going to do it."

Table 6.1. (continued)

WAY OF KNOWING	LEARNER EXPECTATIONS FOR A GOOD TEACHER	SAMPLE OF LEARNERS' COMMENTS
Socializing/ self-authoring knowers	These participants think that good teachers: • explain things well and help them understand. • care about students as people; • understand participants' background, and that helps when they are learning. • listen well and are knowledgeable. • know what these adults need to learn, and these adults, themselves, know what they want to learn (they feel that they, too, have knowledge). • are described as polite and patient. • help them learn what they need to know so that they can pursue their own goals. • listen to their feedback so that they can improve their teaching.	"I like a soft person . . . who considers when you are asking a question, they answer you, they don't ignore you. That's the kind of person I like to be a good teacher. So they really understand people. They care for their students." Good teachers "keep explaining things in different ways, they show you different ways to learn. I like that technique." I can ask a good teacher "for help with what I know I do and do not understand." "I think it's very tough for a teacher to teach and listen and explain all the time." Good teachers "do their jobs and help me to do better, I'm proud of that."
Self-authoring knowers	For these learners, good teachers: • are one source of knowledge, and they see themselves and their classmates as other sources. • are open to students' feedback to help improve teaching practices and they expect good teachers to listen to that feedback. • use a variety of teaching strategies. • help learners meet their own internally generated goals. These participants know internally when they have learned something, and when they have, they can then think of multiple ways to teach what they know to others.	Good teachers "understand their students." "No matter how good a teacher you have, if you don't really want to learn, you're not going to learn nothing." Good teachers "make learning interesting. It has to be interesting to the student." "What you do with knowledge after it's given to you is of your own choosing."

Adapted from Drago-Severson, E. (August 2001, p. 529).

glish had different learning needs, Bill wanted the teacher to attend to *his* learning needs. He was not yet oriented to an inner or abstract experience of what makes a good teacher (evidence for this is the absence of such language).

For Renada, good teachers are those who "try to give" her the information she needs to be able to demonstrate a particular skill. During the first interview, she told us that "good teachers" make "good students," indicating that she understood the teacher-learner relationship in a cause-and-effect way. In other words, she thought that it is the teacher's responsibility to transmit, or "give," information to the learners so that they can then demonstrate their ability to complete the academic task or demonstrate the behavior on their own. For both Bill and Renada, teachers who "explained" a concept well and repeatedly, and those who gave clear and explicit instructions as to how to accomplish tasks, were the best kind of teachers—the kind that made them learn.

The second series of interviews took place after learners had completed their first trimester in the program. At that time, our research team invited Bill to tell us how the teachers in the program were supporting his learning. Bill shared a story about how John, the math teacher during the first trimester, had "made learning fun" by both bringing things in that helped learners grasp mathematical concepts and by having a lot of "energy." As part of a math lesson (which I observed), John gave groups of learners bags of M&M's and invited them to calculate the percentage of differently colored M&M's in the bags. After the groups finished doing the calculations, learners ate the candy—a reward that also made learning fun, from Bill's perspective. Bill spoke about the ways John supported his learning:

> He brought in the M&M's. He . . . brought in things, you know, it wasn't just all the same—it wasn't just, "Okay, here's the math. Go ahead and do it." . . . He'd explain things, and John was good. He'd talk to you, *and he'd give you the individual attention if you needed it*. . . . and he'd run around that room—John had a lot of energy, you could feel him. He'd run,—he'd go from every person, one-to-one. And then [he would say], "No! Come on, you know how to do this!" It ain't like, "Oh, now we've showed you this. If you can't get it, we'll have to have some extra work or something," you know? John will say, . . . "Come on, you can do this! Come on! Try it!" And then [he would] . . . help ya, just to *give you that little push*. . . . Yeah, he was good. I liked him.

Bill emphasized how important it was to him that John made learning fun and that he had an energy that he brought to the classroom. He told us that what made John a teacher who supported his learning was John's willingness to invest the extra time in helping him by giving him the explanation and "extra attention" he needed in order to learn. When asked about the kinds of supports John provided that facilitated his learning, Bill listed the behaviors John exhibited in the classroom (going around the room with "a lot of energy," "making learning fun," and "explaining"). Bill also said that John provided a source of external motivation for his learning; it seems that John's patient way of explaining and repeating explanations gave Bill the external "push" he needed to learn. The push seemed to be experienced by Bill as encouragement and a form of support.

Toward the end of this second interview, Bill told us more about how a good teacher (John) facilitated his learning:

> He made you think. And he used words, and he'd make us write them down, then he'd explain something. And he explained how to do it. And then, he'd make you write it in columns; you'd write down exactly how to do it. "Take the top number. Subtract it. Blah-blah-whatever-divide-add-and-then—then you'd get that problem *right*. And you [would learn] how [to] do it—when you do it on your little quiz. He made us take quizzes every day; you could use your notes, go back and look at your notes. . . . See how you did it. And then we'd do it. . . . And then he'd say, "Okay, let's try it without the book." And then we'd do it . . . without the book, and he'd show us one or two [problems]. . . . And he'd put a problem up try and explain exactly what you did right and wrong. He was an enthusiast.

Bill explained how John's behaviors supported his learning process; John explained things to Bill and Bill's classmates, he used words that made learning fun, and he *made* the learners write down "exactly" how to complete the math problems. This kind of step-by-step procedure, along with clear instructions and repeated explanation, was supportive to Bill's learning. John's teaching practices, which included scaffolding learners by allowing them to use their notes when first completing quizzes and later asking them to complete the quizzes without the notes, were experienced by Bill in a supportive way. Bill articulated a set of observable behaviors that good teachers exhibit.

Both Bill and Renada felt supported by the teachers' efforts to make themselves available for extra help after class and sometimes on weekends. During his third interview, Bill described a time, a few weeks earlier, when he had been seriously considering quitting the program. He told the research team that it was John who convinced him to stay.

He said to me, "Don't quit." He told me to come back, "You're doing good. We appreciate your being here. . . . " I enjoyed the hell out
of his math class. . . . I hate homework, but I enjoyed math class. I
like science. I hate science—it was just him. *He made me want to be
there.* And he offered to help me fix my computer. He said, "I'll take
a look at it. I'm not promising nothing." He's offered to be there Sat-
urdays for us—"I'll do whatever I can, come to my house." He gave
us his home phone number, "If you ever need anything at all, call
me." . . . [He] *made me come back.* I said, "Okay, I'll just give it another shot." [*Interviewer: Why do you think him saying that made
such a difference to you?*] I don't know. I don't know. He could
have said to me, "Well you know, it's too bad you have to, if you
have to, it's too bad." Reading from the script. He could have said
what everybody else probably would have said as far as I'm concerned. "Well that's too bad," but he come right out and said
"Don't, don't quit. Come on, stick it out. We can work something
out." *It was important to him that I stay. He gets paid whether I'm
there or not.*

When we asked Bill to tell us why John's encouragement meant so much
to him and why it helped him to continue in the program, Bill responded
by saying, "I don't know." He then focused on the concrete reality that
John, as a teacher, "gets paid whether I'm there or not." While Bill described this experience in concrete terms, he did say that he believed it
was important to John that he stay in the program. Bill was beginning to
acknowledge the relationship itself as being important—which marked an
important change in how Bill understood the teacher-learner relationship
(a newly emerging socializing way of knowing was evident).

During the last round of interviews with Bill and Renada, just before
graduation, we noticed subtle but important shifts in their understandings
of what makes a good teacher. Bill's understanding of his relationship with
his teacher Judith was also shifting. Bill was beginning to view Judith, the
life employment workshop teacher, as an external authority on whom he
relied to judge himself and his ability as a student. Bill's changed construction of "What makes a good teacher?" demonstrates that he no longer
viewed teachers *only* as transmitters of knowledge, creators of rules, and
instructors who gave him "the right way" to complete academic tasks. At
this point, the teacher's opinion of him mattered in a way that it had not
previously, showing his growth toward a socializing way of knowing.

For example, in the last interview when we asked him about the best
way for him to learn, Bill responded by telling us that Judith had told him
that he "never learned how to learn" when he was in school. He seemed

to look to Judith as a valued other—someone whose opinions were beginning to shape the way Bill viewed himself as a learner. Judith's feedback seemed to matter to him in a new way. Later in this interview, Bill talked more about what he thought made a good teacher and spoke about the ways in which the teachers supported him. This passage illustrates his new understanding.

A really good teacher? One who stays on you a little. I mean, they can't just, I know they're talking to sixteen of us, but these teachers, every one of them, make a valid effort to take care of us one at a time. . . . There was [no teacher] who said, "Well I, we can't do this." There was always somebody that would give you extra [help], they'd come early, they'd stay late. Every one of the teachers helped you no matter what you had to do, they'd help you. . . . Not just because you were in their program or nothing, just 'cause they wanted you to learn. And that's the way I felt about them.

Along with the list of teachers' behaviors that helped him to meet his learning needs, Bill made it clear that he *felt* that teachers were helping him and other learners not only because it was part of their jobs but because they *cared* about the learners. For the first time, we note glimmers of Bill's newly developing capacity to construct his relationship with his teachers not only in terms of what the teachers can do for him. Bill's thinking demonstrates evolution, a change from his earlier thinking, in that he was not only describing the teachers' behaviors—what they did for him—but their generosity, as demonstrated by what he experienced as their persistent efforts to support learners. He tells us that he knew the teachers' went beyond their formal roles by offering many different kinds of support to learners, and he also said he felt the concern teachers had for all learners in the program. This demonstrates the emergence of a socializing way of knowing.

The Instrumental/Socializing Way of Knowing

Like Bill and Renada, the seven learners poised between the instrumental and socializing ways of knowing (recall the X/Y position explained in Chapter 2) still wanted their teachers to explain things well and to speak at a rate that they could understand. It remained important to them that teachers provide concrete approaches to facilitating learning. But while Bill and Renada saw the teacher as someone who "makes you learn" by teaching step-by-step procedures, these learners, in transition to the socializing way of knowing, were already concerned with the quality of their relationship with the teacher. For them, it was important for teachers to be "patient" and "nice" and to make learners feel comfortable to ask questions when they didn't understand something. These learners spoke often about the importance of having a "respectful" relationship with teachers. Acceptance from the teacher was paramount, enabling learners to feel at ease asking questions, rather than "ashamed." These learners:

- See teachers as people who model good behaviors, and these learners seek their teachers' approval.
- Viewed teachers as experts who could tell them what they should know.
- Understand that both teachers and peers can give support.
- Want teachers to value their ideas and themselves, to really listen to them, and to care.
- Place importance on how teachers treat students; being respected by their teachers becomes increasingly important to them.
- Value teachers' caring manner and connection to learners.
- Are unlikely to criticize or challenge teachers and/or their practices because to do so would be experienced as threatening to their own selves; opinions of valued others, including the teacher, make up the way these learners feel about themselves.
- Begin to voice feelings of "being proud" of their teachers.

These learners internalize the perspectives of valued others. Importantly, they expected teachers to help them understand.

Several learners who demonstrated the instrumental/socializing way of knowing talked not only about the importance of having good teachers who speak slowly and explain concepts well; they were also oriented toward the interpersonal and abstract qualities that are characteristic of good teachers. They described good teachers as "patient," "kind," "caring," and "honest." These learners spoke repeatedly about how their relationships with their teachers made a difference in their learning. Their perspectives highlight the importance of the human connections between learner and teacher.[1]

Teresina: Learning from Care. Helena, Angelina, Hope, Veronica, and Teresina are learners who spoke emphatically about how good teachers treat learners with "respect," "listen" to learners, and "care" about them. Being valued and respected by teachers mattered greatly to them. During the first interview, for example, Teresina told us that it was important not only that she learn from her teachers but that they "learn something" from her.

In the second interview, Teresina told us why she thought John was a good teacher; he helped her to learn because he had "patience," explained things "clearly," and "repeated" what was said until she understood. In addition to naming the concrete behaviors that, in her view, make for a good teacher (e.g., good teachers "come to class on time" and "have everything organized"), Teresina valued the two-way nature of the teacher-learner relationship. Good teachers, for Teresina, were those who are "going to understand me and I understand the teacher. . . . She's going to repeat every question. . . . She has the patience to repeat [herself]."

In the last interview, when asked about what makes for a good teacher, Teresina said:

> I think that [teaching] is hard job, too, because sometimes you have students that don't care. They don't do the homework, they just go to play [in the] classroom. But the teachers, you have to respect them, just like your mother or father, because they spent their time to teach you something that's good for you later. Probably now you don't see the results [from] the teacher tell[ing] you to doing homework.

Teresina discussed the importance of respecting the teacher and had the capacity for some abstraction in her thinking. She compared the respect a person *should* give to teachers to the respect a person *should* give her mother and father. She also thought that the good teachers were teaching her something that would be helpful to her later, something she couldn't recognize now. In the above passage we see that she has appreciation for her teachers' experience; she saw their work as a "hard job" and understood that they invested their time into helping the students.

Helena: Finding Care in Little "Pushes." Helena, Veronica, Hope, and Angelina told the research team that good teachers are those who "make you understand." In addition to helping learners acquire skills, good teachers, in Helena's view, are "always there." In this first interview, Helena echoed several key themes that we heard from other learners who made sense of their experience in the instrumental/socializing of knowing. Helena explained,

> Because she give me homework, and she give me, you know, she make me writing. She's always there. I like the way she teaches. Some teachers, . . . if you don't understand something, they make you understand it. . . . Like if I don't understand something. I tell

you, "Can you repeat it again, I don't understand you." Then she explains again.

Like other learners with this way of knowing, Helena indicated that a good teacher helped her to feel comfortable, so that she could ask questions and gain an understanding of what she's studying. For Helena, learning was the result of a one-to-one exchange with someone who *cares* about her.

Like Bill, Helena said that a good teacher "pushes" the student. However, Helena experienced and named the push teachers gave her as a demonstration of their caring.

> He's the kind of teacher, he push, you know, I don't mean he push too much, but you have to let them . . . to teach you, push you little bit to make sure you learn. Because some teachers doesn't care.

While the source of some of her motivation was external, Helena understood the teacher's "push" as a caring expression of interest in her and her learning. At the same time, a good teacher was also someone who could help learners meet concrete, practical needs by *showing* the student what to do.

In the last interview, she spoke about a good teacher as being someone who requires a lot from the students. Helena responded to an interviewer's question about the best way for her to learn by talking about the teacher-learner relationship.

> I say the best way for me to learn if you have a good teacher to teach you. *To care about you, to care about you, then to teach you to make you understand.* Because, like Judith [the life employment workshop teacher], you have to learn from her, too. Because when she give you homework, you have to do it, you don't have no excuse. So that one make you learn more because like, okay, you go someplace on the weekend and say, "Oh, I have to do my homework when I go to school," Judith is going to say something, because she don't play. So you have to do it . . . and she never forget that, yes. She collect all the homework we do. She collect the homework, you don't have no choice, you have to do. . . . For me, I think is a good teacher, I don't complain about that. *Because a teacher like that make you learn—like if you have teacher don't care, so, you not gonna learn. I see they care, you learn.*

Helena's case highlights how these learners in our sample experienced care as an essential quality in the teacher-learner relationship. This caring was experienced as a support to their learning. Helena understood the teacher to be a valued authority, and she also saw a direct relationship between a teacher's caring actions and her learning.

The Socializing Way of Knowing

One of the strengths of the socializing way of knowing is that a person has the developmental capacity to internalize and identify with the perspectives of others. These learners in our sample were not only interested in fulfilling their teachers' expectations of them; they *identified* with their teachers' expectations of them. They did not have the capacity to separate their own expectations for their learning from their teachers' expectations. Their teachers' goals for learning became their goals. These learners viewed the teacher as a source of authority, but they also experienced the teacher as a supportive and encouraging guide who "helped" them understand. It was the teachers' genuine care and concern for them that mattered most.

Pierre: Looking to Experts. Many of these learners spoke about the importance of having a respectful relationship with their teachers and how that facilitated their learning processes. For example, in the second interview, Pierre elaborated on why John was a good teacher—"he knows his job" and "he's explaining like he's at school also." Like other learners with this meaning system, Pierre viewed the teacher as another learner in the classroom and talked about how John's ability to "explain" made learning accessible to all learners. He observed that John provided "everything, every angle to find the result, he knows about it and explains everywhere." At this time, Pierre also told us that he believed the teachers in the Polaroid program were of high quality: "I know a committee of this group know how the best ability to teach. So they're [Polaroid] not going to send us anybody. I know whoever came on board [as a teacher is going] to be good." Like other learners with this way of knowing, Pierre viewed the teachers as experts.

These learners voiced appreciation for their teachers' demonstrations of caring about them as people and "helping" them to learn. They looked to teachers, and their authority, to "know" when they had learned something and to tell them what they needed to learn. In addition to wanting teachers to be "patient" and give "clear and slow" explanations, these learners focused on the interpersonal relationships they had with their teachers, and their academic efforts were directed toward pleasing these important others. Pierre said he also wanted "the teacher [to have] enough experience to figure out what's good for me."

Pierre, like other learners with the socializing way of knowing, expected the teacher to anticipate his needs. His perceptions of himself as a learner are connected to how the teacher *feels* about him. A good teacher understands that he may need multiple opportunities to learn something and is willing to explain things several times.

In all of our interviews with Pierre, he told us that he expected teachers to "know what they are doing," so he felt that he did not need to think about their role that much. In the first interview, when asked how teachers think about their "job as teachers," he replied, "Oh, I don't have no idea about that." He added that over time, the teacher is "going to figure out the right way to make [you] learn." This illustrates Pierre's (and other socializing knowers') conception of the teacher-learner relationship; he viewed the roles of learner and teacher as givens. His role was to learn from the teacher, and he expected the teacher to know what he or she should do to help him learn.

When we asked these learners if there was anything about the program or their teachers' teaching that they would change, they rarely voiced any criticism of the teachers or their teaching practices. For example, the only criticism that Rita named about her experience in the program was that she "wished it were longer." Challenging or criticizing a valued other or authority figure is a threat to the self in this way of knowing. However, it presents an opportunity for the teacher to support these learners by encouraging them to voice their own thinking in classroom contexts. By supportively challenging these learners in this way, they may grow, over time, to have greater self-authorship in presenting their ideas and opinions. The socializing knowers in our sample talked less about their relationship with their teachers than did learners with other ways of knowing. One explanation for this may be that, as mentioned earlier, at this way of knowing a person is defined by and identified with the expectations and opinions of others and is not yet able to take a perspective on shared mutuality.

The Socializing/Self-Authoring and Self-Authoring Ways of Knowing

Four cohort learners Christopher, Paulo, Daniel, and Magda demonstrated a self-authoring way of knowing operating in combination with a socializing way of knowing at the program's beginning. Of these, the latter three learners demonstrated changes in their ways of knowing at program completion. Jeff, who demonstrated a fully and solely operating self-authoring way of knowing at both the beginning and end of the program, will also be discussed in this section.

One of the strengths of the self-authoring way of knowing is the learner's ability to take a perspective on interpersonal relationships and shared mutuality rather than being made up by (or completely identified with) relationships (Kegan, 1982). These learners saw not only their teachers as authorities who were sources of knowledge; importantly, they also viewed themselves and others as sources of knowledge.

Christopher: Appreciating Teachers' Techniques and Learners' Styles. In his first interview, Christopher, who was originally from the Caribbean, described good teachers as "humble" and "patient," and remarked that they have certain characteristics (they "consider you" and "don't ignore you"). After completing two trimesters, he was able to draw from his program experience to elaborate on what makes a good teacher. Christopher discussed John as an example.

> [John] always shows you things on the board. And he's a talker. He's a good explainer. . . . He kept explain[ing] all of the time, all of the time. Really try to put it inside your mind. . . . He shows you different ways. . . . Like I'm doing tax, which is very good . . . he shows you a different way, which is a good technique for him, too, I think. Because it's a good technique to teach.

Like other learners with this way of knowing, Christopher appreciated John's ability to use a variety of teaching "techniques" so that all learners could understand. As the above passage illustrates, he, like other learners with this way of knowing, reflects on how his teacher's techniques are working in the classroom. All of these learners were also able, to varying degrees, to offer their teachers constructive feedback. As discussed in Chapter 5, Jeff shared his perspective with John about how he could alter his teaching practices to better meet the needs of the class. Not only did he reflect on their teachers' teaching practices, but he was also able to take a perspective on and consider the needs of his fellow classmates.

Unlike socializing knowers, these learners were concerned with meeting their own goals and standards for learning on behalf of what they saw as their larger learning purposes. Several talked about how good teachers were those who supported them in meeting their own internally generated goals. They looked to themselves and their own expectations for learning and therefore took greater responsibility for their learning in and outside of the classroom. At the end of the study, Christopher talked about the student's responsibility for learning: "I need a good teacher. If I want to ask a question, I make sure there is something to talk about. There always something . . . to talk about a question, but some of them doesn't make sense. I always make sure mine is making sense. . . ."

Like other learners with this way of knowing, Christopher looked to himself, rather than the teacher, to determine whether or not his questions were "important" and "good." He had his own internally generated system for assessing this. At the same time, and like others with this way of knowing, he appreciated when teachers offered help when he was struggling, and he also mentioned that a teacher's human qualities were important to him because they helped him to decide whether or not he could approach the teacher. Christopher experienced this kind of support from teachers as helping him to achieve his own goals for learning, which helped him to "feel free." He demonstrates both a socializing and self-authoring way of knowing in the way he constructs his relationship with his teachers.

Several of these learners voiced their appreciation for the additional time teachers spent helping them to gain information or learn processes so that they could move toward their own larger goals (e.g., teaching them to navigate the Internet so that they could have access to information). Many of these learners understood how the teacher was helping them to achieve the self-generated goals they had set for themselves. They spoke about the ways in which they felt themselves "growing as people" and "feeling stronger" as a result of their experience in the program.

Daniel: Valuing Different Personalities and Perspectives. Daniel, like Christopher, had his own criteria for assessing whether or not a teacher is a good teacher; he described good teachers as "knowledgeable, patient, and polite." Also similar to Christopher, Daniel believed that a teacher's personality can make a difference in terms of supporting learning. For Daniel, it was also important that teachers have a wealth of information to share—he understood this as being important to helping him achieve his self-determined learning goals. In the second interview, he talked more about why it was important for him to see these human qualities in teachers:

> I think it's to be polite and to first of all, with the student, to be patient, a lot of patience. . . . There is a lot of people they don't understand a lot of things, and very simple things. I have people . . . that start work with me, and I'm nice, nice person and everything, good attitude. . . . I've got to focus on their personality. Because a lot of people they can learn quick, some people they have a difficult to learn.

This passage illuminates what Daniel means by "politeness" and "patience," two qualities he valued in his own work as a supervisor ("I'm . . . nice person, good attitude"). Daniel, like all other learners with this way of knowing,[2] stressed that it is important for teachers to listen to him. For Daniel, this need to be recognized seems to be embedded in a larger context than what other people think about him. In his view, listening to others requires skill ("you have to know how") and sensitivity to individual learning styles ("a lot of people they can learn quick, some people they have a difficult to learn"). Daniel valued patience and the ability to understand in his teachers and in his own supervisory work.

Daniel also appreciated teachers who could get students to work hard, as he says about a teacher named Margaret: "Try to make you work hard. Yes. It give you support, and she give you support and she tries you to, to make you work hard and learn more. . . . The way she tries to help us to express, everybody. I think she did good job." He also appreciated Margaret's ability to teach students how to say things in English. He added:

> A lot of times we were so comfortable, if you, sometime if you say something she will show you that, and so you can say [it] this way, or something like that. She'll not, she got a way to show us so not to be, for us not to be offended.

When an interviewer asked Daniel how Margaret was able to correct students without offending them, he replied, "I don't have no way to explain that." He did not yet have the capacity to fully take a perspective on why this happens. At the same time, he was able to understand the teacher's perspective as separate from his own, and seemed able to imagine what her intentions were in teaching. Daniel explained that he had to miss 6 classes and had to make up homework. Margaret gave him work to redo:

> I have to copy about all eight, eight of them. And she was a little strict also on one, in the end, because some of those stories I have to write short. I don't have to go too long. In the past I used to write a little longer. And because the time-wise, I'm very busy . . . where I work. . . . I don't have enough time for tons of homework. But she was doing her job and tried to make me, force me to do better, which I'm proud of that.

Daniel's understanding of this situation goes beyond his sense of how Margaret thinks of him. He locates the responsibility for her feelings in her and the feelings of pride in himself.

In the final interview, when asked to share his thinking about what makes a good teacher, Daniel responded by discussing the connection he sees between good teaching and good supervisory work. At this time, we noted an important change in Daniel's construction.

A good teacher you have to know how to explain. You have to
know how to deal with different people. I think the teacher is being
like . . . a good supervisor, you have to have a lot of patience, because especially if you, say you deal with the kids now, you have a
lot of kids, they use drugs, they go to school, you don't know what
kind of attitude they go to school with. . . . You get mad and things
like that. There's a lot of teaching that you have to know people.
You dealing with a lot of people, lot of different people and each one
got a different attitude. It's tough for a teacher. . . . But if you get
good students, they learn good, and you know how to express yourself also, to explain, that makes a good teacher. Like an English
teacher, he knows everything in the head, most things you ask him
for something, he—bang!—he tell you.

Daniel's explanation is not grounded solely in his experience at Polaroid,
but extends to teaching in general. At the end of the program he was able
to articulate a fuller and different appreciation for what he viewed as the
complexity of a teacher's work and the demands of teaching. His thinking
about the teacher-learner relationship demonstrates an important change.
For the first time, he talked about the idea that good teaching depends
on getting "good students." In his view, "No matter how good teacher
you have, if you don't really want to learn, you're not going to learn
nothing." At this time Daniel understood to a certain extent the motivation to learn as being independent of the teacher's influence. Daniel's new
conception of the teacher-learner relationships shows an important
change from his earlier way of knowing. He now assumed even greater
responsibility for his role in the learning process and seemed to have a
deeper understanding of the complexities of the teachers' role in that process.

Jeff: Considering Context and Acting on Beliefs. Jeff, like Daniel
and Christopher, also thought that good teachers employ different techniques to help learners with different learning styles and needs. Like Christopher, he talked about the subtle qualities in a teacher's personality that
make a difference. His ideas about what makes a good teacher remained
fairly consistent during the program, illustrating his fully and singly operating self-authoring way of knowing. During the first interview, in response
to a question about what makes a good teacher, Jeff replied:

The person who's teaching has to, let's say, make it interesting. You
can't just go in and say, "Well, today we're gonna do math, this is
how you do it, you do it this way, . . . you add this number to this

number," you know. [*Interviewer: So how does a teacher make it interesting?*] Teaching but not teaching. . . . Well, just like we're sitting here talking now . . . just casual talk. You put a number up on the board and, you know, you got to make it interesting. You got to keep the attention of the student. [*Interviewer: Are there other things you think make a good teacher?*] Well, personality and all that. [*Interviewer: What's the right personality to be a good teacher?*] . . . [They should be] stern, but casual, loose. But yet keep control of the situation.

Jeff has definite ideas about what makes a good teacher. In determining what makes a good teacher, Jeff looked inside himself to make the decision and considered a variety of factors—including the context. He appreciated both a teacher's work and learners' needs.

In his final interview, Jeff mentioned other factors that he believed made for a good teacher: namely, personality, the context in which the teacher teaches, and ability to meet the needs of learners who have different learning styles, preferences, and strengths. Jeff observed the situation and considered the larger context in which the teaching occurs. Also, in this last interview Jeff spoke about a good teacher as someone who "can, say, carry out directions and explain things . . . in an easy, simple format," so that learners can understand. Jeff's assessment of teachers and their practices suggests that he has the capacity to step back from the teacher-learner relationship to observe what they do. He had his own way of determining what constitutes good teaching, and he used internally generated values to make this assessment.

As discussed in Chapter 5, Jeff also had the developmental capacity to critique his teachers' teaching practices and offer constructive feedback. He named several occasions when he did this because he thought that his feedback might help teachers to better support learning. For example, in his third interview, Jeff talked about how he had criticized Kirk, a teacher who had arrived late for class several times. Not only did Jeff share this directly with Kirk, but he also told the interviewer that he made CEI program administrators aware of Kirk's tardiness. He believed that this kind of information could help CEI improve the diploma program. In this same interview, Jeff told us about another decision he made to approach John and tell him that he was teaching sophisticated mathematical concepts in a way that was not working for the class. These two examples demonstrate Jeff's capacity to act on his own beliefs and values for the good of the class, himself, and the CEI teaching enterprise as a whole. This shows the extent of his understanding of the complexity and interconnectedness of the *system*, which in this case involved the program and all of its participants.

SUMMARY AND CONCLUSIONS

Support, in its broadest sense, is confirmation of the learner and his or her current efforts. . . . Challenge, in its broadest sense, is encouragement to stretch beyond what is currently familiar and comfortable in order to achieve some new level of competence. It focuses on what remains to be done, rather than what is already accomplished. (Taylor, Marienau, & Fiddler, 2000, p. 326)

The cases I presented in this chapter show how learners with qualitatively different ways of knowing perceive their learner-teacher relationships. These examples also demonstrate how, in some cases, learners' conceptions of these relationships were not fixed, but rather changed during the program.

I examined how Bill and Renada, both instrumental knowers, wanted teachers to provide clear explanations and step-by-step procedures in order to *make* them learn. They assessed their own learning by means of their ability to demonstrate expected behaviors and by the grades they received from teachers. When learning, they focused on their own concrete needs and felt supported when teachers gave them information. They also felt supported by teachers' efforts to provide extra assistance when they needed it. At the end of the program, they had both changed their conception of the teacher-learner relationship. Bill and Renada began to recognize an internal and abstract experience. In both cases, I highlighted the emergence of a socializing way of knowing.

Like Bill and Renada, learners who made sense of their experience with the instrumental/socializing way of knowing felt supported in their learning when teachers explained concepts well and talked slowly so that they could understand. Unlike Bill and Renada, these learners expected their teachers to be good role models, and they wanted teachers who valued them and their ideas. They felt most supported by teachers who really cared about them. For example, like Bill, Teresina initially told us that good teachers *made* her do her homework. However, unlike Bill, Teresina felt that good teachers also helped her to feel comfortable. By the program's end, Teresina's understanding of the teacher-learner relationship had changed. She had become able to talk more abstractly about this relationship, saying that a person should show teachers the same respect that is shown to parents.

Socializing knowers were not only interested in fulfilling teachers' expectations of them, but also identified with these expectations. In other words, they took the teachers' goals for learning as their own goals for learning. Pierre, like other socializing knowers, expected the teacher to *know* what he needed to learn. Although Pierre could feel (internally) when he had learned something, he needed the teacher's acknowledgment to solidify, or complete, that feeling. In this way of knowing, having good relationships with teachers facilitates the learning process. Interpersonal connections were important supports. Because the idea of challenging or criticizing a teacher is experienced as a threat to the self for these learners, a productive challenge could take the form of encouraging them to voice their thinking in the classroom. By supportively challenging socializing knowers, they may grow, over time, to have greater self-authorship in presenting their own ideas and opinions.

Learners with the self-authoring way of knowing not only saw their teachers as valued authorities and sources of knowledge, but also saw themselves and their fellow learners as generators of knowledge. Unlike socializing knowers, they were able, to varying degrees, to reflect on their teachers' practices and offer constructive feedback. Like socializing knowers, they voiced appreciation for teachers who employed a variety of teaching techniques to meet learners' needs. Unlike learners with other meaning systems, they were concerned with meeting their own goals and internal standards on behalf of what they saw as their larger learning purposes. Good teachers, in their view, supported them in meeting their own goals. These learners did not look to meet teachers' expectations for their learning but rather looked to themselves and their own expectations. In addition, they took greater responsibility for their learning. For instance, Daniel grew to understand his teachers' perspectives as separate from his own. He developed a capacity to appreciate the complexity of a teacher's work and understood that the motivation to learn, to a certain extent, was independent of the teacher's influence. Providing opportunities for self-guided learning and decision making while connecting classroom learning with self-identified goals would support and challenge self-authoring learners.

The CEI program teachers seemed to enact their role in a way that provided learners with multiple forms of support, so that the challenges of being "an adult" in school and managing the demands of this role in addition to other roles were not overwhelming. Not only were CEI teachers able to do this effectively, but learners emphasized their appreciation for their teachers' efforts to do so. Some learners valued the teachers' ability to make learning fun or interesting. Most talked about the importance of having teachers who cared about them as people or who were "there for them."

Wendy Luttrell (1997), in *School-Smart and Mother-Wise: Working-Class Women's Identity and Schooling*, describes how the women in her study conceptualized and negotiated gender, race, and class relations. She writes, "There is an ongoing dialogue about how gender shapes what and how women know" (p. 134); she calls for new research "to shed light on how the teacher-student bond gets negotiated differently by different groups of students" (p. 139). While this research did not incorporate analysis of how the women and men at any of the three study sites may have experienced their relationships with their teachers in similar or different ways, such an analysis would certainly be useful. A study informed by both gender and developmental analyses could yield important lessons.

In concluding this chapter, I will respond to the question of how developing a better understanding of learners' expectations of their teachers—and the criteria they use to assess good teachers—might inform teacher practice.

As teachers, we have the privilege and responsibility of supporting and challenging learners to facilitate and gently guide their learning and development. Attending to learners' diverse needs, preferences, and ways of knowing can all serve to inform practice. Oftentimes, we serve in many roles: as guides, advocates, counselors, and mentors (Belenky et al., 1986; Brookfield, 1987; Cranton, 1994; Daloz, 1986). Through our relationships with learners, we aim to support them in both academic and nonacademic ways. Throughout this process, we strive to shape classroom contexts in which it is safe for learners to take risks, to share their thinking, and to ask questions. We also realize that what constitutes safety for one learner may be experienced as overly challenging for another. Helping learners increase their sense of self-efficacy, self-confidence, and competency is at the heart of a teacher's mission. Taylor, Marienau, and Fiddler (2000) highlight the importance of teacher-as-mentor:

> Though some people succeed in growing and changing without [a mentor or] guide, it is a much lonelier and more difficult process, and like any challenging journey undertaken alone, more prone to missteps, injury, and losing one's way. (p. 330)

The cases presented in this chapter illuminate how learners, depending on their way of knowing, have different views of their teachers and different psychological relationships with the "teacher as authority figure." Understanding the role that culture plays in learners' constructions of their relationships with teachers and in their perception of teachers' authority can also inform teaching practices.

One of the research team's initial questions concerned how a learner's native culture, especially with respect to the way it regards teachers, might influence what a learner was willing and able to share. I have presented examples of how learners from the same home country and with similar educational experiences made sense of their relationships with teachers and of how they understood what it means to be a good teacher. The cases illustrate how two people can come from the same home country, live with similar expectations, and have a similar educational background yet demonstrate different ways of knowing. These examples show that while culture strongly influences experience, it is not the single ruling variable that can predict the way in which a person understands that experience. It is *through the lens of a person's underlying meaning system* that he or she understands his or her experiences of teachers. Following are a few examples.

Bill and Jeff are two learners who were born and raised in the United States and who dropped out of school before completing high school. Neither of them had histories of positive learning experiences. In fact, both had trouble telling team members about any positive experiences from past formal learning. However, each of them, while sharing the same home-country culture and similar prior educational experiences, had different expectations for their program teachers and experienced the teacher-learner relationship differently. Culture and personal educational histories are not the only variables that shaped their understandings of what makes for a good teacher. As demonstrated, their conception of what makes for a good teacher is significantly shaped by their way of knowing. Consequently, each needs different forms of support and challenge from their teachers.

Recall that as an instrumental knower, Bill thought that good teachers were those who told him "exactly" what he needed to do to get the right answer. Bill felt that he needed to follow the teachers' rules to get a good grade (a cause-and-effect relationship). Jeff, a self-authoring knower, viewed good teachers as those who helped him to access the information he needed to make his own decisions and to achieve his self-determined goals. Jeff saw the teacher as one source of knowledge, and saw himself and his classmates as other sources.

Similarly, Christopher and Pierre shared the same home country in the Caribbean and had lived in the United States for close to the same amount of time. Yet they had different ideas about what it takes to be a good teacher, and they thought about the responsibilities of the teacher and learner in qualitatively different ways. As a socializing knower, Pierre looked to his teachers for validation and acceptance. While he could feel (internally) when he had learned something, he needed his teacher to acknowledge his learning. Pierre oriented to the relational qualities of the teacher-learner relationship (good teachers "show they care"). Christopher, a socializing/self-authoring knower, respected and appreciated teachers who were there for him (in terms of supporting his learning). However, unlike Pierre, Christopher had internally generated criteria for assessing his teachers' instructional practice and for deciding whether or not his own questions were "good." Christopher felt best supported in learning when teachers helped him to meet his own learning goals. As I have shown, learners' ways of knowing importantly shape their understanding of the teacher-learner relationship.

All of the other learners who completed this program, except Tough (who was from an Asian country) and Hope (who was from a different home country in the Caribbean than Pierre and Christopher), shared the same home country in West Africa. This exploration shows that while learners shared some common cultural ideas about their own country and its educational system, their experiences of the same showed subtle differences.

Another important lesson to which all of the cases presented in this chapter point is that learners can change and grow in terms of their expectations of teachers and of their own learning when given the appropriate challenges and supports.

"We're Trying to Get Ahead": Changes in Learners' Conceptions of Themselves, Their Skills, and Their Relationship to Work

> The workforce issues that plague employers—including high turnover, poor performance and low morale—may be symptoms of a serious, underlying problem of workforce literacy. Moreover, without employer intervention, the problem is likely to get worse. . . . The skills deficit among U. S. workers will continue to be a critical issue for business, regardless of the ups and downs in the U. S. economy.
> —Center for Workforce Preparation, Spring 2002

THE NATURE OF WORK and the skills and competencies we need to function as competent workers are becoming increasingly complex. The need for more sophisticated skills and competencies is, according to the Center for Workforce Preparation, "an urgent business issue that demands employers' attention" (2002, p. 2). How can educational programs, such as the Adult Diploma Program provided by the Continuing Education Institute (CEI), help adults to enhance their skills, improve their competencies, and increase positive feelings about themselves as workers? How might a developmental framework inform our understanding of how to best support adults as they grow to demonstrate new skills and competencies and better manage the complexities of work—and possibly their other roles as parent, partner, and citizen?

In this chapter I show some of the ways in which participation in the diploma program at Polaroid changed the participants, in particular their lives as workers (i.e., their skills, competencies, feelings of self-efficacy), as they were "trying to get ahead," a phrase used by Jeff to describe how the program was helping him at work and in life.[1]

Our research team found that learners experienced three kinds of change: (1) informative, (2) transformative, and (3) acculturative (Drago-Severson, 2001; Drago-Severson & Berger, 2001; Helsing, Broderick, & Hammerman, 2001; Popp & Boes, 2001; Portnow, Diamond, & Rimer,

2001). The program supported informative change—increases in skills and knowledge—in all of the learners at the Polaroid site and at the other two study sites. The program also served as a dynamic transitional space that supported and challenged some learners as they underwent transformative changes—changes in their capacities of mind or ways of knowing. This kind of change is less about a change in the amount or type of skills or knowledge a person possesses than about a change in the very way a learner understands himself or herself, the world, and the relationship between the two. Transformational changes thus effect a broadening of perspective on oneself (seeing and understanding different aspects of the self) and others (Cranton, 1994; Kegan, 1982, 1994; Kegan & Lahey, 2001; Mezirow, 1991). Learners who experienced transformational change grew to demonstrate new and more complex ways of knowing. This type of change occurred at all three sites, although it was most evident at the Polaroid site, where one-half of the learners showed transformational change. That these qualitative shifts in learners' ways of knowing would occur for this many learners over the short period of one year is quite noteworthy (Drago-Severson, 2001; Drago-Severson et al., 2001b; Kegan et al., 2001a, 2001b).

The third type of change documented in the study, acculturative change, indicated by learners' improved fluency in both the English language and American culture, was especially prevalent in learners at the community college (see, e.g., Helsing, Broderick, & Hammerman, 2001) and family literacy sites (see, e.g., Portnow, Diamond, & Rimer, 2001), most of whom had recently immigrated to the United States. The adult learners at the Polaroid site were older than the learners at the other two sites and had lived in the United States for an average of 20 years. While acculturative change was certainly a part of their experience, informative and transformational changes were predominant. (It is important to note that learners at all three sites with the same way of knowing gave descriptions of change that were strikingly similar [Kegan et al., 2001b].)

In this chapter I focus primarily on informative and transformational change. I show how learners made sense of their learning as contributing either to ongoing or hoped-for improvements in many aspects of their lives, including their sense of identity, their careers, their social and economic status, their home lives, and their confidence in themselves.

While I am not suggesting that *all* of the changes to be discussed here can be entirely attributed to being part of a consistent and enduring cohort, I do believe that the cohort—as a program design feature—was one robust contributor to remarkable changes in the learners. Similarly, I suggest that just as peer support was a powerful contributor to change, teacher-learner relationships stand out as importantly propitious (Drago-Severson, 2001).

HOW PROGRAM LEARNING INFLUENCED LEARNERS' WORK LIVES

By carefully attending to and documenting both the content and the contours of these adults' thoughts about their learning and the ways in which it transferred to their lives outside the classroom, our research team was able to identify both commonalties and differences in how these learners made sense of their experiences. Not only did we discover these patterns and differences, but we also witnessed how learners' understandings of their work, their skills and competencies,[2] their relationships at work, and themselves as workers changed during the 14 months of the program.

The Instrumental Way of Knowing

Many of the learners, no matter what their way of knowing, reported their belief that their concrete English skills had improved during the program and that this was helpful to them at work.

Bill and Renada: Developing Abstraction. Recall that when Bill and Renada began the program, each demonstrated a fully operating instrumental way of knowing. Upon program completion, each grew to demonstrate the emergence of a socializing way of knowing. These instrumental knowers talked about work and their role as workers in concrete terms (i.e., in terms of their behaviors at work and job requirements).

Renada and Bill talked about how their skills had changed as a result of program participation. They both said that the skills they learned in diploma program classes were helping them to change the way they did their work. Both remarked that they had become better able to communicate their ideas. Bill said he had become "more aware" of his writing, showing his emergent abstract thinking, and Renada talked about being better able to communicate her ideas verbally. She said that people at work had told her that she could now "explain herself better," acknowledging the importance of others' needs and perspectives.

Both Renada and Bill also reported feeling better able to help their children with their homework because of the math and English skills they had learned in the program. Their new math skills, they explained, also changed the way they performed their job (both reported that they had to do mathematical computations on the job).

In the second interview, Bill said that he was able to do math on his own and that he didn't use the calculator as often.

> I'll have a, like an invoice coming in, and I'll just turn it over and it's two hundred pieces, and I got forty boxes with thirty-five pieces in

each. I just, "Yup. Yup. Okay, that's right." Click. Before I'd run
over to the calculator and add it up. Now I'm not.

Doing the math in his head helped him to do his work more efficiently. In
the last interview, Bill elaborated on this: "So I think it made me a little
better employee, less time running around, hanging around the office there.
I stay out at my machines more, I do my inventories. I don't depend on the
calculator no more." Bill's new math skills also saved him time. Demonstrating his instrumental way of knowing while his abstract thinking developed, he understood the situation in terms of a cause-and-effect relationship: If I work more efficiently and do better at my job, the consequence
will be a reward—an increase in my salary.

His capacity for abstraction was more evident in his writing. Bill also
reported that skills he learned in the program had helped him with writing
at work by changing the way he was able to communicate with others. For
example, he said that "now" (during the second trimester) he thought
about putting commas in sentences where he would not have before. Bill
mentioned this in the context of sharing his views about how learning in
the program helped him to be more "aware of what [he's] writing."

Significantly, Bill's socializing way of knowing was most apparent in
his new orientation to his coworkers (marking the emergence of a socializing way of knowing, 2(3)). During his last interview he spoke more about
his relationship to his colleagues (this was one of a very few times when
Bill talked about other workers). He talked about how people who worked
for him gave up their breaks and filled in for him because he was in class
and said that he wanted to write them thank-you notes. In Bill's words,
"Guys who lost their breaks because I wasn't there, guys who went too
late, lost their coffee and stuff because I wasn't there, so I'm gonna send
them all thank-you letters." These examples illustrate a subtle but important shift in Bill's way of understanding his role as a worker; he was beginning to orient toward his inner psychological experience (though the context is concrete). Not only did Bill demonstrate this growing orientation
toward abstract psychological experience with fellow workers, but he also
showed this emerging capacity with family members. For example, Bill told
us that he now thanks his children for waiting for him when he picks them
up after dropping his wife off for work.

The Instrumental/Socializing Way of Knowing

Seven participants in the diploma program demonstrated fully operating
instrumental and socializing ways of knowing. At program completion, Sal
and Hope demonstrated an evolution in their way of knowing, and Rita's
thinking evolved to a fully and solely operating socializing way of knowing.

Like Bill and Renada, many of the instrumental/socializing knowers had a concrete orientation to their work goals. For example, these learners explained that they wanted to have a diploma or a better position at Polaroid because they wanted to "make more money." Nonetheless, when asked if there were other reasons why an education was important, they talked more about what earning a diploma or being promoted at work meant in abstract terms. Many oriented to their own inner experience and discussed the influence of work on their emotional states.

Helena: Finding New Perspective. While Veronica, who had been laid off, still felt appreciation for Polaroid, Helena, who was still employed at Polaroid, felt that the company did not "care" about its employees. At the start of the program Helena was worried about being able to find another job if she were to be laid off from Polaroid. But by the end of the program, Helena's understanding of her work situation had changed. She voiced new confidence in being able to find a new job, should she need to:

> I think if I lose my job, I find another one. I think God help me. . . . Because if you worry, you can't think, you can't help it. So why you worry, I calm down. So this is the way I feel. It come. I say, "Why I worry, maybe never come to be." So I don't worry anymore. Because if it happen, gonna happen anyways. So if he didn't want to give me [a severance] package, if I worry or I don't worry, they give me anyways. They don't care about me anyway . . . So why I worry?

At this time, Helena was able to talk about her internal experience of worrying or not worrying about the possibility of being laid off and about knowing that God would help her; she was thinking more abstractly about her experience, demonstrating a socializing way of knowing. In the above passage, she shares her internal conversation about the pros and cons of how she understood her situation at work, thus, taking a perspective on the fact that she is worried. For Helena, being laid off has an emotional component to it—it is about more than losing a job. While Helena also talked about Polaroid not caring about people, which demonstrates a socializing way of knowing, her explanation is discussed in concrete terms, which demonstrates an instrumental way of knowing.

All learners with this way of knowing told us that they enrolled in the program because they thought that their expressive English skills would improve and that this would help them to express themselves in their relationships with supervisors and coworkers. With improved expressive English skills, they could be "better team members"; this was important to them and to their work, they said. Almost all spoke about the need to improve their expressive English skills because of the changes they saw in the workplace (they were aware of how the recent layoffs were influencing their working lives). Improved skills would help them keep their jobs, they explained, and create possibilities for promotion.

Outcomes for the Instrumental/Socializing Learners

At the end of the program, all of these learners reported feeling better able to communicate with supervisors and coworkers, and they attributed these changes to skills they had learned in the program. Several said that they were "proud" of themselves and that they felt better about not having to ask coworkers and supervisors for help as much anymore. Program learning, they explained, helped them to do a better job of reading the logs left from the previous shift and writing notes to convey information to the next shift of workers. Improved expressive English skills (e.g., proper pronunciation and increased vocabulary), they said, helped them to no longer feel "scared" to ask questions, which, in turn, seemed to empower them both in their workplace and in the classroom.

Learners with this way of knowing talked about how they "pushed" themselves at work. People's opinions of them and their performance mattered greatly. Earning approval from a supervisor was especially important; these learners looked to their supervisor both for approval and to make sure that they were doing a good job (an external rather than internal evaluation of their work). Many of these learners told us how much they valued support and approval from supervisors and spoke about it over and over again throughout the program. Angelina and Helena also talked often about how their supervisors encouraged them. This kind of encouragement became increasingly important to learners as they began more fully to demonstrate a socializing way of knowing. As discussed earlier in the book, people making meaning with a socializing way of knowing take on other people's opinions of themselves and turn to others in order to determine when they've done a good job and what things they should be most proud of.

All of these learners reported that their skills had increased as a result of their learning and that this helped them at work. Specifically, they mostly referred to improved communication skills. Initially, many said that they had been "afraid" to ask questions, both at work and in the classroom; however, all explained that this had changed for them. Many said that other people at work told them that they had become better communicators.

Teresina and Angelina: Learning to Improve Communication. Teresina, a nonnative speaker of English who was originally from West Africa, felt that not only was she better able to express herself verbally, but was also doing a better job completing paperwork (i.e., writing). In response to the question about ways in which the program has made things better for her at work, Teresina said the following:

> Before I have a problem to talk in meetings. My job they have meeting groups. You have to say something about the job. I have a problem. Very difficult. I have some ideas, but I don't know how [to say them in English]. Now I have a little problem, because I talk better English. I think this class I have this semester help me a lot. I have a lot of friends who speak English. Now I talk to them better. If I have some problem now for making the papers at the end of the night, you have to make your paperwork, now I make better [papers] than before . . . about how the machine works, what problems you have. You have to put on the paper. That's called the paperwork.

In the last interview, Teresina said that these improved skills helped her to feel "more confident" when talking with other people at work and in using the skills she learned as a result of her participation in the program (most of these are "concrete" skills).

Teresina said her relationship with her boss had also changed. Before the program, she did not ask questions during team meetings, since she felt that her boss would not listen to her because she did not speak English well. When she spoke about her relationship with her supervisor at the program's end, she emphasized how her improved communication skills were helping her at work, describing a change that she saw in herself as a worker:

> Before I don't talk. If . . . he [the boss] ask me something [I would say], "No. I don't have nothing to say," because I scared. . . . Sometimes [before] I have something to say about the job, but I keep my mouth shut because I think they gonna laugh at me if I say. But now I don't have this problem. After I came for this course, I understand better English. . . . Now he [her supervisor] talks so lovely, talks play. I say, now, he know I know better English, now. If he's tell me something, I [understand] to answer. I don't keep my mouth shut no more. I gonna say something.

Teresina's newly refined expressive English skills seemed to enable her to feel more empowered in her relationship with her supervisor and to present her views in work meetings.

Many learners with this way of knowing also spoke about how the program helped them in their relationships with coworkers. For some, this meant an improved ability to explain their ideas more clearly and to do more at work on their own. Teresina talked about having been afraid of people laughing at her at work (fear of what other people would think of her) before learning to express herself better in English. Angelina, during the second through fourth interviews, also talked about feeling increasingly confident when talking with coworkers and her supervisor because she felt that her expressive English skills had improved. In the final interview, Angelina made the following comments about how these relationships had changed:

> Sometime [at work], I get stuck. I don't know what I'm doing. I don't want to ask her [a coworker], because they already tell me [how to do the procedure] . . . so many times. But, I don't want to go forward, because I don't want to make a mistake. So it's kind of, [I get], sometimes, well, I get upset. . . . But then I came back again to do [my work] every day. Then I say to myself, "I'm going to do this now." Every day until I learn myself. Then, now, I'm doing it every day.

Angelina, like many learners, talked about how she learned to do more on her own at work and also how she was better able to understand coworkers when they "explained" procedures to her. Her comment about not wanting to ask coworkers for help after they had explained something to her already suggests that she felt some embarrassment or fear that they would be angry. Angelina voiced an implicit concern for what her coworkers thought of her and what their reaction would be. At the same time, she was unable to articulate a fuller internal experience of what this was like for her. Angelina's case shows how a person with a socializing way of knowing is identified with opinions that others hold of her. The responses of Angelina's coworkers have a tremendous influence on the way she sees herself as a worker.

Some participants talked about how program learning helped them in other social roles. For instance, Teresina explained how program learning changed the way she was able to enact her role as a parent. In the last interview, she reported that she was better able to help her son with his homework and that she attributed this change to skills learned in the program.

> My kid in the school, he ask me for [help with] something, "Mama, show me how to read this, how to write." Now, I have to teach him to do, to write. [*Interviewer: Before you couldn't help him so much?*] No. Because I don't [know] how to write something. I don't [have] every words, but the important words I have, I know how to write.

And he's, some, when he bring me something from preschool, I know I understand better.

Teresina spoke about how she was better able to help her child in concrete terms. After the program, she reported feeling that she now had the needed skills to help him with his writing and to understand the communications he brought home from school.

Hope: Developing New Skills. While many learners explained how the skills they were learning in the program helped them at work, home, and in relationships, Hope spoke specifically about how skills she'd learned in the program had helped her to better manage the demands of her increasingly complex work on the shop floor. Hope's case illuminates how she understood her new work responsibilities and how she felt better able to manage the multiple requirements in her three different jobs.

In the first interview, Hope, who emigrated from her home country in the Caribbean 30 years ago, spoke with great confidence as she described her competency as a worker. In fact, at that time, she told me that she wished her teachers in the program could visit her on the job so that they could see how complex her job was—and how good she was at performing her tasks. However, in January 1999, after working at Polaroid for more than a decade, Hope was told that rather than doing the one job she had always done, she would need to do two additional jobs. The changing nature of the workplace demanded greater competencies from Hope. In the third interview, after managing her new and multifaceted job responsibilities for several months, Hope shared her understanding of her relatively new situation and reflected on what it was like when she was first told about the change.

> The first day when I was told to go downstairs and do the training I was a little bit upset, but I didn't let my supervisor know I was upset. I kept it to myself. And then the person who was training us, I said to him, "Do you have any paper or pamphlet for me to read?" They said no. They said, "I'm showing you and that's it." So I guess what it boils down to now is they want you to learn the job and it's not, you're shown and, then you can go ahead and do it while you are learning [and] ask questions.

Although Hope had thought of herself as a "hands-on" learner earlier in the program, she now asked for pamphlets to help her learn what she needed to know to carry out her new responsibilities. She needed the reading materials, she explained, because she wanted to learn "the right way" to operate the machines in her new jobs. Hope said she didn't let her supervisor know that she was upset that there was no reading material, but she did approach the person who was doing the training to ask him for help. What mattered, in Hope's view, was having the skills necessary to do the job or jobs. In addition to the required skills to perform her new tasks competently, Hope also needed to tolerate the ambiguity of not knowing which of the three jobs she would work when she arrived for her 11 p.m. to 7 a.m. shift after an hour-long commute from home.

In the third interview, Hope discussed the changes in her workplace, the changes in what was required of her, and the reasons why she was disappointed with the way she had been trained to do these jobs. She also highlighted how learning in the program was helping her to succeed.

> I've come a long way with everything that was going on, and there's a lot of changes on my job. . . . And since January, I have to learn two more jobs. . . . And the way they are teaching us those jobs is hands-on training. You don't have any paperwork, nothing to go back on. So whatever they show you, you got to do. And I think with this program, it gives me, my mind to more thinking. [The program helped me with my job] because I can go in tonight and they say "Okay go back to your regular job." I can go tomorrow night and they say go to [another job]. I can do the new job, but not as perfect as the one that I have been on. Well, I think my mind to think more because before I don't think, if I wasn't in this program if I could, I didn't say I couldn't handle it but I don't think I could go into it and get involved and get to know it as fast as I did.

In Hope's view, the program "helped [her] mind to think more," and this, in turn, helped her to perform more competently in her work. She also talked about how she thought that, as a result of program learning, she was better able to adjust to not knowing which of her three jobs she would be doing when she began work each day. Before participating in the program, she would have had more trouble handling this. At the end of the program, Hope explained that she had changed, and noted the specific aspects of her life that supported her in making these changes—namely, the program, her teachers, and work:

> I appreciate the program, and what Polaroid did. And . . . I appreciate the time the teachers took with us, when we didn't understand, and show us, to let us understand. And [the teachers] didn't think because we are grown-up, we should have known. I'm proud of myself.

And I'm proud that Polaroid gave us the opportunity [so] that we could . . . do it.

Hope demonstrated a change in how she understood her role and her work. She grew more able to talk in more abstract ways about the appreciation she felt for Polaroid and to orient to her inner psychological experience (feeling proud of herself and of Polaroid), indicating that a socializing way of knowing was now prominently organizing her meaning system.

The program seemed to provide a holding environment that supported Hope as she grew to better manage the complexities of her work and her life.

The program helped her to look ahead to the future. In her words,

I'm proud that, what I started, I finished. Because when you start something, and you finish it, it really make you look ahead, to see that you could do more than you thought you could do. . . . It's never too late to get an education. And you're never too old. And there are a lot of opportunities out there. You just gotta reach for it.

The Socializing Way of Knowing

Every one of these learners, all nonnative speakers of English, said that one of the reasons they enrolled in the program was to improve their expressive English skills. They told our research team that they wanted to improve their speech so that they would be able to understand others and be understood by others. Most said that they did not want their coworkers or supervisors to think that they were "stupid" just because their English skills were not well developed.

These learners discussed how their relationships with supervisors mattered to them. When faced with a situation or dilemma at work, rather than turning inward to decide what they needed to do, they would turn to a supervisor, a valued authority, to see what they *should* do. Being understood and listened to by others, especially supervisors, was of critical importance to these learners. In fact, when we asked them about aspects of their own work and work competencies, they (except Pierre) often replied by talking about what other people had told them about how they performed their jobs.

Pierre: Building Confidence from Others' Respect. Two learners, Pierre and Tough, demonstrated an exclusively socializing way of knowing at both program start and completion. Rita grew to demonstrate an exclusively socializing way of knowing at program completion. Being understood and feeling respected by other people in the workplace (supervisors and coworkers) were of key importance to these learners. They identified with other people's opinions of them or, in Pierre's case, with what he imagined to be other people's perceptions.

Pierre, a learner who rarely talked about his supervisor (perhaps because his boss left before the end of the program), also rarely mentioned his coworkers (except to say that one of the other learners in the program, Christopher, worked in his department). However, Pierre appreciated the vote of confidence his boss demonstrated by signing the papers to approve Pierre's request to enroll in the program. Interestingly, Pierre could envision how he, as a worker, would be better able to support his boss with more highly developed skills.

> My boss so happy for me to come and get that [diploma] because he knows that I'm capable, but just for a little thing to hold me back. So with that chance, with that opportunity, I could help him more. And he's so happy to . . . take money from his budget to pay for me and then I can get here.

Pierre valued his boss's approval but, unlike other learners with this way of knowing, he did not talk about him as a major source of support or encouragement.

Pierre, Rita, and other socializing knowers reported feeling better able to communicate with people at work, and in the world, at the program's end. For example, most of Pierre's self-confidence was directly tied to both his expressive English ability and the way he thought other people perceived him. This is especially important, because learners with a socializing way of knowing derive their view of their own competence from others' perceptions of their ability. For nonnative English speakers who are socializing knowers, this characteristic seems especially profound because they believe others find them incompetent when they have difficulty expressing themselves. While all of the learners in the Polaroid cohort who were nonnative speakers spoke of wanting to improve their English, Pierre's case illuminates, as discussed earlier, how this experience is understood from a socializing way of knowing.

In his final interview, Pierre showed himself as someone who wants the respect of others and who believes that limitations in his expressive English skills are getting in the way, particularly in the context of his department at Polaroid. As a quality control person, he had to be able to "explain the negative and positive impact of every single thing" he did at work.

I want to feel comfortable here because without good English speaking here, you don't get *good respect*. Most people at the class, they were all machinery people, [they] do one job—start the machine. . . . Myself, I don't do that. I am on the quality team and I have to explain the negative and positive impact on every single thing I am doing. I have to explain, if I don't do it, why? And if I have to [monitor machine performance], I have to know plus or minus. I have to say, okay, I am going to increase the temperatures, what that does for that. So that means speaking. . . . I call my department "talk radio" because you have to say something all the time. I call it "talk radio" because they are mostly talking.

Communicating with coworkers and supervisors was important, Pierre explained, "[Because] what's come to your [mouth] is how your mind sound . . . the way you sound, that's the way people judge." He reported that he, like other learners, felt better able to express himself and to understand others as a result of program learning.

Rita: Building Confidence from New Skills. Rita's case also illuminates how she understood the program learning to be helpful to her at work. During the second interview, she spoke with confidence about her newly developed competency in math. "I never knew those things," she said. "But now I feel the confidence doing any kind of job with any kind of math. It changed my life." Rita described this "confidence" (locating it in herself) when she talked about how program learning was helping her to do things at work that she "never knew" how to do before.

Although many learners talked about how important it was for them both personally and professionally to develop their skills, Rita's experience demonstrates the meaning and importance of developing skills within the organizational culture of Polaroid. These new skills, she reported, not only made her job easier, but also gave her confidence to feel that she could handle demands to do math in other jobs.

Rita, like many learners, named the importance of the Applied Knowledge Program at Polaroid. In fact, her supervisor reminded her that even if she were to leave Polaroid, she would "still have her education" (highlighting one of the company's intentions in offering the program). During her second interview, Rita discussed other ways that the program made things easier for her at work:

Before sometimes when I'd say something at work and they'd say "Wait a minute, speak English." I'd tell them "English is my fourth language." And it's very hard for me to speak like you do because I never study like you. But, if I study twenty years ago, if I went to school believe it or not, now I would speak different. Now sometimes when I tell them something they say, "Now you go to school." I say "Yes. And I will learn step by step." But I will learn different things every day . . . Before, if they told me write something, sometimes I say, "My goodness, I have a friend I say how you spell this, how you spell that?" Now I don't have too many problems no more.

Rita observed concrete changes in her skills at work. For instance, when asked to write, she had fewer spelling problems. This was important to her because being able to spell well had great impact on her job performance.

During her final interview, Rita spoke in greater depth about other changes that she noticed in herself that she attributed to program learning. She talked about feeling confident in her capacity to learn. Like others, Rita noticed that she was no longer "ashamed" to ask questions:

I learn a lot that . . . before, that I never know. . . . I had a lot of problems before I learn, and I felt so confident now to open up any book and read and understand what I read. Because before sometime I used to read and then I don't know what I read and I was confused. And then I was ashamed to ask, people, "What is this?" Because they said, "You've been in America so long, you don't know what to do?" . . . [*Interviewer: So what's the most important thing about the learning that you've done?*] The history of America. . . . Because I live here and I *should* know. If anybody asks me for anything, and I will be glad to answer them back. [*Interviewer: And why would it feel so good to be able to answer them back?*] To be myself. If anybody ask me right now, Rita, "What you been [doing] in these [fourteen] months?" I don't feel ashamed to tell them I been in school. Or if they ask me, "What did you learn in [fourteen] months?" I will tell them, which before if they asked I would say, "well, I never go to school," [and] that [felt] bad.

Learning in the program helped Rita to feel more confident when asking other people questions. Importantly, for Rita and other participants, her learning in the program inspired self-confidence. As Rita said, it helped her to be herself.

The Socializing/Self-Authoring and Self-Authoring Ways of Knowing

Four learners—Christopher, Paulo, Daniel, and Magda—demonstrated a socializing/self-authoring way of knowing at the program's start. Of these,

Paulo, Daniel, and Magda demonstrated new meaning systems at program completion. In addition, Jeff demonstrated a solely operating self-authoring way of knowing at both the beginning and end of the program.

All of these learners, except Magda, talked about how learning in the program helped them to "feel stronger" about enacting their roles as workers. All of them seemed to take greater responsibility and ownership of their work. They had a clear sense of (and a capacity to reflect on) how program learning helped them to be able to access information that they would then use to help them make their own decisions in their worklife. They were excited about and wanted to understand how to make better decisions for themselves.

Throughout data collection, our team asked all learners who or what they thought contributed to the changes they noticed in themselves. Many learners, no matter what their way of knowing, named their program teachers as having helped them to learn. Others also named specific pedagogical practices that were employed by teachers (as discussed in previous chapters). Several talked about program experiences (such as walking the Freedom Trail in Boston) as being supportive to their learning. However, unlike the great majority of learners, who exhibit other ways of knowing, these learners named *themselves* as supports to their learning in addition to other people or program features.

When they spoke about increasing self-confidence, unlike most other learners, they talked about how their learning made them less reliant on other people. These learners described how education and program learning provided them with more opportunities at work and in life. They shared a common goal—wanting to be "better educated"—and they reported that this would help them in their work. These learners reflected on both the cognitive and abstract psychological experience of their work. Learning in the program helped them to feel stronger at work.

Christopher and Paulo: Learning for Strength. Christopher's goal as a worker was to become better educated. As he explained during the first interview, "Without a diploma for me, in [his Caribbean home country] or here, you're nothing." In addition, he had the goal of learning more in order to "feel strong." His desire to feel strong at work and to be able to work independently changed from being a goal to an accomplishment, which Christopher attributed to his program learning. During his third interview, in response to a question about how, if at all, program learning helped to make things better at work, Christopher replied:

> At work, I'm using different equipment. . . . So now, [to use] the [latest] technology . . . you have to be educated. . . . When you are very

educated . . . then you would be [able] to do all kind of things . . .
where you can do things yourself. You don't have to ask for people
all of the time. If there is something in front of you, you can do it—
what the paper says, and then I don't need to go to [anyone] for help
. . . which is very good.

This ability to work more independently contributes both to Christopher's
positive sense of himself as a worker and to his feelings about his job. The
better he understood the work—the process that the machine goes through
or the process that is involved in making film—the more responsibility he
said he was able to take for his work and the better equipped he felt he was
to work independently. This sense of responsibility for his work seemed to
be very gratifying to him. Christopher said that if he was able to do more
at work, it would lead to a "high class," meaning that he would be eligible
to have a higher position, one in which he would be able to work even
more independently, exhibiting the internal authority of a self-authoring
knower.

Like Christopher, Paulo said that education would help him to feel
"strong" and to be better able to fulfill the requirements of his work in
dome lamination at Polaroid. Like all of the nonnative speakers with this
way of knowing, Paulo voiced a desire to improve his communication skills
and thought that with improved communication skills he could do his
work more effectively. In the first interview, Paulo described the kind of
writing skills required by his job and explained what it would mean to
write better reports.

Paulo needed to be able to convey information to other workers, engineers, and supervisors in his written reports. This was an important theme
that was common to learners with this way of knowing: They all spoke
about trying to "push" themselves to do a better job. Doing their jobs well,
and pushing themselves (internally), was important to them. At the same
time, Paulo was concerned about writing reports that would *please* important others (his supervisors and the engineers with whom he works).

Paulo felt that his writing skills had improved, and he discussed how
this was helpful to him at work. Before the program, he could see defects
in products but was not always able to describe what he saw in writing,
and he did not know whether what he wrote accurately conveyed what he
wanted to say. But in the third interview, Paulo reflected on the change he
noticed in himself and his ability to do his work:

Before I work on a very interesting machine to inspect some sheet for
some glass. . . . But I don't know how I write my paperwork when I
find a defect in a material, or I don't know how I [could] explained

on a paper. So now I can explain anything on a paper, write myself.
. . . Before I have a lot of things to say on a meeting, but I can't say
nothing because I feel shy to say something if I say it wrong.

The distinction between what Paulo knew and saw and what he was able
to explain in English is implicit. Paulo reflected on his own job qualifica-
tions, his demonstrated abilities, his actual abilities, and the changes he
noticed in how he was doing his work.

Feeling "very, very, very strong" represents an important change in
Paulo's self-confidence and in his perceptions of improved competence as
a worker. In the third interview, he spoke for the first time about feeling
"strong." He reflected on his internal psychological experience and feelings
of greater self-efficacy, explaining the changes he noticed in his life and
what it meant to him to feel "strong":

The kind of strong I feel, is because now I can . . . [with] this program,
I understand everything. I feel free. . . . I feel free to explain anything
to say anything, to understand. . . . When you help your kids look for
better school than before. So you feel strong. When you go to the doctor you, so now you're confident with you and your doctor. You can
speak to your doctor. So your doctor tells you anything, you understand exactly; you go to dentist or you go anyplace else. . . . You feel
strong when you help yourself or your family.

Like other learners with this way of knowing, Paulo had an appreciation
for how program learning helped him change his behaviors and thinking.
Having a greater sense of being able to communicate with others—both at
work and in other domains of his life—made Paulo feel strong.

Like others with a socializing/self-authoring way of knowing, Paulo
felt that his new knowledge and more highly developed skills changed his
worklife. At the end of the program, he felt that he was a more confident
and competent worker and a more empowered person who could navigate
effectively within the American system. His experience in the program
highlights a critical theme prevalent among learners with this way of knowing: Education provides access to greater opportunities.

Paulo, like others with this way of knowing, had an understanding of
what was going on at work and in meetings and had self-determined solutions that were, initially, hard to offer because of his lacking English skills.
In the beginning of the program, Paulo talked about how he wanted to
share his knowledge and ideas with fellow workers. However, at that time,
he reported that he did not always have the language skills necessary to
communicate his ideas. In the second interview, Paulo noticed an important

change in his communication skills. His improved communication skills, he said, enabled him to work more independently; he reported being able to communicate his ideas effectively without needing assistance.

It was also important to him to demonstrate to his supervisor that he was not "wasting time" while he was away from work (rather, he was learning). It seems that he had an internally generated value for using class time, which was time away from work, productively. Paulo now had a larger perspective on his supervisor's perspective (though it is unclear how much the supervisor's perspective influenced his thinking). He noted, "I think my supervisor feels happy to support me."

During his final interview, Paulo described a change he observed in himself: He was now able to contribute his ideas in work meetings. At this time, the team noted an important change in Paulo's way of knowing: He now demonstrated a full self-authoring way of knowing alongside his socializing way of knowing. Paulo explained his new way of contributing at work as follows:

> So one day I'll have a meeting with my supervisor to plan, to manage. So it was before, when I go to that meeting, I have lot to say, but I can't say nothing, I say just one thing, so I be quiet until finish. But now, I have good ideas, I try to change a lot of things, like to change how we do the work in my area. So I'm better at meeting.

Paulo's enhanced communication skills changed the way he was able to express his thinking in meetings at work. This helped him take greater initiative in making improvements at work, which was satisfying to him. Not only did Paulo feel a greater sense of confidence and competence in his work, but he also reported that the way he felt about himself was positively influencing other areas of his life. He felt that he needed to understand various sources of information so that he could weigh them and make his own decisions. During his final interview, he recalled what it was like before the program, when his English language and communication skills were not well developed.

> When you have to go someplace, you look all day for somebody go with you. So nobody can have a chance to go with you because [they] work. So you feel . . . kind [of] mad, "Why I don't understand for myself?" Say when go to the meeting on the school, they say something's maybe good for your children, but you don't know if it's good or not.

Education, in Paulo's view, made it possible for him to make more informed decisions for himself and his family. Paulo's experience points to the ways in which knowledge and education can be empowering—enabling him to make better decisions and giving him more control over his life. At this time, he spoke specifically about how his knowledge helped him in his role as a parent.

Paulo was able to make the decision to transfer his daughters to better colleges because he had greater access to important information and a deeper understanding of it, which then enabled him to weigh that information when making a decision. In addition, he explained that his recent promotions at work provided him with greater financial resources to support his choices.

At the end of the program, Paulo reflected on the process of learning. It was important to him that he made his own decisions. Paulo mentioned that he understood the value of education and how it helped him with his decision making:

> Just those kinds of decisions I make. But whatever, if I work two jobs, I'd have money in the bank, but I don't know how I'd spend my money. But when you have education, you start [to] understand so you can decide what you're supposed to do. . . . I have the information.

Having knowledge and information enabled him to make his own decisions about how to manage his money and his life. Being better able to understand different sources of information and then use them to inform his decision-making processes changed the way he enacted his roles as worker and parent. This, in Paulo's view, helped him to "feel strong," and it also helped him work toward meeting his larger, more abstract goal of helping his children "be free" by supporting them in their educational journeys and providing them with a home.

In elaborating on what "strong" meant to him, Paulo revealed that his understanding of strength is multilayered. Feeling strong means being able to communicate both verbally and in writing with people at work. It also means being able to help his family, being able to speak to a doctor, and being able to help himself—being able to be more independent. Feeling "strong" helps Paulo to "feel free." Paulo frees his mind and his self through learning. Knowledge and education empower him to "feel free." Importantly, Paulo feels free *knowing* he can do these things at this point in the program—and not because he is simply *carrying out* these important responsibilities to meet other people's expectations. His understanding of "strong" goes beyond concrete tasks; it also represents abstract things for him, including self-reliance, greater independence, and freedom.

Outcomes of Learning from a Socializing/Self-authoring Way of Knowing

Learners with a socializing/self-authoring way of knowing told the research team how learning in the program was changing the way they enacted their roles as workers. They said that they were now able to work more efficiently and with greater confidence. There were three main ways in which they transferred learning—ways that changed the way they worked. These learners reported that the program helped them to improve their writing skills, allowing them to make better and more informative reports; employ new mathematical and computer competencies in their work; and access information, which helped them in their work and private lives.

Magda and Jeff: Working with New Confidence. Magda, for instance, needed to write reports to do her work at Polaroid. Magda worked mainly on a computer; taking measurements and looking for data in the computer were part of her everyday tasks. In the second interview Magda talked about having greater confidence in her writing and about how this maturing competency helped her at work. Before the program, when she had to write something down on paper, she needed to look it over several times before typing it into the computer. In response to a question about how program learning was helping her at work, Magda said,

> . . . [N]ow I can like just type it in. I still do some of the things like a hard word, I put it next to the paper and I look at it, but things that I think are normal things like everyday things I just type it in. That makes my life easy . . . and then I feel more confident.

In the third interview, Magda described her increased self-confidence in reading and writing; she felt "more comfortable to do certain things, or write things, or read." Program learning, Magda said, helped her to feel better about being able to understand "certain words." Magda made the following comments on changes she perceived in how she did her work:

> I've been doing it for so long that I, even then, I know what I was doing and, but again, [I] certainly see it more clearly. I knew what I was doing. I was trained to do them. But now, especially when I'm on the computer, . . . I can be more confident to change things. Before like I was a little bit intimidated.

Magda makes an important distinction between doing a job she was trained to do and doing a job that she feels more confident doing. The former seems to focus on doing what is needed to get a job done, while the latter involves deeper understanding. This development enabled her to recognize areas that needed attention and also gave her greater confidence that she could change things. It is important to keep these statements in the context of her work, because Magda does technical work in which "doing something wrong" could affect product quality.

All learners making meaning with this way of knowing reported how program learning helped them to feel increasingly confident in their roles as workers. For example, Jeff spoke about an important change he noticed in himself—namely, an increase in his self-confidence in the intellectual realm. This was an area in which he had never felt confident before, he said. At the end of the program, he saw himself as smarter than he had thought he was:

> I guess, getting the satisfaction out of knowing that, some of the thing I thought I had forgot in math . . . and the English part, and the science part. It was gratifying to know that, once we started and got into the course, that a lot of the stuff was easier to pick up. I picked up really fast . . . especially on the math. I surprised myself. . . . There's more up there than I thought there was . . . as far as knowledge. . . . But I guess it's like once you open something, it just pours out. . . . It's there. It's just getting you out, I guess, which is what happened through this course.

Summary: Changes in Learners' Conceptions

I have shown some of the powerful ways in which program learning helped these learners to generate new goals, new skills and competencies and, in some cases, new understandings of themselves and their work. I highlighted changes: changes in their skills, changes their in knowledge, changes in their self-confidence, changes in how they understood their relationships, and changes in their ways of knowing.

All learners reported greater self-confidence, improved efficiency in their work, and improved communication skills. I have illustrated how learners across a wide range of ways of knowing made sense of these changes and how, in many cases, learners changed the very ways they understood their roles as workers.

For example, the learners who were instrumental knowers focused on how developing new skills or improving existing skills helped them demonstrate new behaviors at work. Learning in the program and earning a diploma would make them more eligible for better jobs or promotions (this demonstrates a cause-and-effect relationship between the two). Socializing knowers, in particular, oriented to the ways in which their enhanced skills and competencies helped them not only in their improved capacity to work more effectively, but also in their improved communication skills, their greater understanding of other people (such as supervisors and coworkers), and their ability to express themselves better. Because socializing knowers are identified with other people's perceptions of themselves, being better able to express themselves was of critical importance to them in the workplace and in their lives.

While self-authoring knowers valued their improved skills and competencies, they appreciated these on behalf of their own larger learning purposes. Program learning helped them to have greater access to information that they needed to make their own decisions that would, in turn, help them to achieve their larger, self-determined goals. Overall, learning in the program made them feel strong.

CONCLUSION

Adult educators with an interest in supporting transformational learning can look to constructive-developmental theory as a source of ideas about (1) the dynamic architecture of "the form which transforms," that is, a form of knowing; and (2) the dynamic architecture of "reforming our forms of knowing," that is, the psychological process of transformations in our knowing. (Kegan, 2000, p. 53)

In this chapter I demonstrated how learners in the diploma program at Polaroid experienced the process of education as one that affected their *selves*—in Kegan's words, "the dynamic architecture of 'the form which transforms' " (2000, p. 53). My hope was to show how a constructive-developmental perspective can be used as a tool for better understanding how adult learners make sense of important aspects of their program experiences and how their learning influenced their lives as learners, workers, and, in some cases, as parents. In so doing, my intention has been to illustrate the *motion of change* (Kegan, 1982) in these adults' lives and to broaden conceptions about how better to support them in their educational processes.

The CEI Adult Diploma Program design and curricula explicitly and deliberately made connections between program learning and workplace needs (see Chapter 4 for a discussion of CEI's program design and curricula). The curricula themselves, and their emphasis on what CEI refers to as "pervasive standards" (i.e., communication, critical thinking, problem solving, presentation skills, and computer competencies); the program design (e.g., the cohort model and program classes taking place during work-days); and teacher practices (e.g., employing collaborative learning) helped learners develop skills and competencies needed in the workplace.

In Chapter 4 I discussed Polaroid's competency development Star Model, which consists of five components and core skill sets. One component of this model is team participation, and another is a high-performance workstyle. Many CEI program features seemed to support the development of these workplace competencies. For example, in all program classes learners worked in collaborative groups—comparable with working in teams on the shop floor—in which group members taught one another while developing problem-solving skills and exchanging feedback on their work. These skills and competencies correspond with skill sets articulated by the Polaroid competency model (which is part of "team participation"). As I have shown, many learners reported being better able to actively engage with their teams, a competency they attributed to learning in the program. All learners reported feeling a greater self-confidence in their ability to do their jobs. And learners across ways of knowing reported that program learning helped them do their work more efficiently and faster. (These are skills listed under the high-performance workstyle part of Polaroid's competency model.)

Bridging ABE/ESOL program curricula with the multifaceted curricula of the 21st-century workplace will help workers to develop the skills and competencies they need to manage the multiple demands of modern-day work. In other words, contextualizing curricula and attending to how adults with different ways of knowing demonstrate skills and competencies and make sense of their learning and work experiences will help to meet the call for building what Comings and colleagues (2001) refer to as a "level playing field" for workers, in which all have the chance to develop the skills necessary to meet the demands of work in the 21st century.

In concluding this chapter, I revisit one more notable finding, linked to what Kegan (2000) refers to as "the form which transforms . . . [and] the dynamic architecture of 'reforming our forms of knowing' " (p. 53). In addition to a gain of important and life-enhancing skills, increased competency, and increased self-confidence reported by learners, one-half of these cohort learners demonstrated a qualitative change in their meaning system from program start to finish, a fact that the research team found remarkable, given the relatively short duration of the program. The illustration below furthers the discussion in Chapter 2 in depicting the continuum and progression of change in Kegan's ways of knowing, specifically from instrumental (the second way of knowing) to socializing (the third way of knowing).

$$2 \longrightarrow 2(3) \longrightarrow 2/3 \longrightarrow 3/2 \longrightarrow 3(2) \longrightarrow 3$$

instrumental   socializing

Movement among the other ways of knowing parallels this notation. Table 7.1 summarizes the changes observed in the cohort's ways of knowing and shows the number of participants who demonstrated each type of structural change at this site.

In previous chapters, I illuminated some of the ways in which this program created a dynamic and robust holding environment, one that was

Table 7.1. Changes in Learners' Meaning System from Program Start to Finish

Way of Knowing [1]	Number of Learners with This Way of Knowing at Program Start	Change in Way of Knowing from Program Start to Finish [1]	Number of Learners Who Demonstrated This Type of Change at Program's End
Instrumental knowers (2)	2	2→2(3)	2
Instrumental/ socializing knowers (2/3 or 3/2)	7	2/3→3/2 or 3/2→3	3
Socializing knowers (3)	2	3→3(4)	0
Socializing/ self-authoring knowers (3/4 or 4/3)	4	3/4→4/3	3
Self-Authoring knowers (4)	1	4→4(5)	0

Adapted from Drago-Severson, 2001, p. 609.

[1] The symbols in the first and third column denote the knower's position in the continuum from the first to the fifth way of knowing in Kegan's theory. Please refer to Chapter 2 of this volume for an explanation of the notation used to characterize movement along the continuum.

roomy enough to support and challenge learners with different ways of knowing. In this chapter I reported on the many and varied ways in which learners said that their program learning transferred to their work lives. Development and change, as demonstrated in this group of learners, occurred by meeting learners where they were and by carefully scaffolding them by offering a variety of forms of support and challenge (e.g., concrete and relational supports as well as access to information and opportunities for self-reflection). Cohort relationships, collaborative learning, teacher-learner relationships, curricula, pedagogical practices, and program structure seemed to work synergistically to support and challenge these adult learners across a wide range of ways of knowing. This dynamic and multi-faceted holding environment held learners as they developed greater capacities to manage the challenges and complexities of their lives.

CHAPTER 8

Implications of a New Pluralism for Program Design, Curriculum Development, Practice, Policy, and Research

> Although most education is not consciously and explicitly directed toward psychological development, the process of education itself implies growth and development.... Even in highly technical or skills-based courses, the learner is concerned with questions that impact the self.
>
> —Tennant & Pogson, 1995

THE RESEARCH ON WHICH this book is based was intended to stretch conceptions about how best to support adult learners in the educational process. Many forms of diversity are present in an adult basic education (ABE) or English for speakers of other languages (ESOL) classroom, including gender, age, race, class, religion, and ethnicity. The research presented in the preceding chapters suggests the importance of another form of diversity, a new kind of pluralism—namely, the developmental levels, meaning-making systems, or ways of knowing that adults bring with them to the classroom. Like those more familiar forms of diversity, developmental diversity must be acknowledged. This new pluralism, diversity in learners' ways of knowing calls for a correspondingly diverse collection of pedagogical approaches and an awareness that these ways of knowing can evolve given the appropriate challenges and supports.[1]

The interesting regularities and patterns in ways of knowing that I have discussed with regard to learners at the Polaroid site in this book also emerged at the family literacy and community college sites in the study (see, e.g., Drago-Severson, 2001; Drago-Severson & Berger, 2001; Helsing, Broderick, & Hammerman, 2001; Popp & Boes, 2001; Portnow, Diamond, & Rimer, 2001). As discussed, these findings shed light on how learners constructing their experiences with a specific meaning system commonly understood (1) their experiences of program learning, (2) themselves as students, (3) their expectations of teachers, and (4) their social roles. Adults of noticeably different ages, cultures, and regions of the world demonstrated these commonalities.

154

At each of the three research sites, the team discovered that an instrumental way of knowing was dominant for at least one learner, that a self-authoring way of knowing was dominant for several learners, and that a socializing way of knowing was dominant for most learners.[2] The team also found that the differences in the complexity levels of adult learners' meaning-making systems were *not* highly associated with level of formal education (see, e.g., Drago-Severson et al., 2001c; Kegan et al., 2001b). In other words, some learners with limited formal schooling nevertheless demonstrated developmentally complex ways of knowing.

All three of this study's core findings revolve around the concept of a new pluralism (Drago-Severson et al., 2001c; Kegan et al., 2001a, 2001b). These findings, which have been explored here and in the team's larger study across all three sites (Kegan et al., 2001b), concern (1) the variety of importantly different ways of knowing that adults bring to the ABE/ESOL classroom; (2) the importance of the cohort, or what I call a *community of connection*, for adult learning; and (3) the possibility for and variety of significant change for adults in ABE/ESOL settings, even during a period of only about 1 year.

In this chapter I will highlight the practical implications of these findings for program design, curriculum development, teacher practice, policy-making, and research in ABE/ESOL practice specifically, and in other adult learning enterprises more generally.

DESIGNING PROGRAMS THAT CENTER ON THE COHORT AND COLLABORATIVE LEARNING

One of the central findings of this study was the power of the cohort in supporting adult learners with varying ways of knowing. In this section I will discuss this finding as it relates to previous research on the value of cohorts, provide suggestions for multiple ways to infuse the cohort into program design, and share an example of how including the cohort can have implications for retention.

Informing the Research on Cohorts

The research team's finding on the power of adult learning in the cohort parallels findings reported by Beder and Medina (2001). In their qualitative study of 20 ABE classrooms with highly diverse populations learning in a range of contexts, the authors describe the disappointing effects that "[Enrollment] turbulence, unstable classroom environments where learners are going and coming on a continuous basis" have on adult learning, classroom culture, and the possibility of developing "shared meanings" (p. 123). In this study of basic literacy, family literacy, and workplace literacy programs where classes were conducted in public schools, community colleges, libraries, community centers, churches, and workplaces in eight different states, Beder and Medina discovered that "mixed levels and continuous enrollment are very serious problems, problems over which teachers have very little control, problems that most teachers simply cannot cope with effectively" (p. 20). These critical problems, they argue, contribute importantly to teacher burnout and lack of learner success in ABE programs.

Beder and Medina maintain that mixed levels in ABE classrooms and enrollment turbulence have important "implications for the open entry/ open exit norms of adult literacy education as well as the time limits placed on student participation due to welfare reform and other adult literacy education policies" (p. 20). Additionally, they suggest that the continuous enrollment policy, while often necessary to ensure funding, has important consequences.

They contend, for example, that continuous enrollment influences learners who have a propensity for "tuning out" in classrooms because presented material is too easy or too difficult and, as a result, they become bored or cannot follow instructions (Beder & Medina, 2001). Furthermore, Beder and Medina suggest that "tuning out" may be characteristic of a learner who is nearing dropout. Although they suggest that continuous enrollment and mixed levels—i.e., various levels of language and skill abilities—are likely to remain aspects of ABE programs, Beder and Medina argue for new approaches: (1) systematic evaluation of best practices for addressing enrollment and diverse skill levels; and (2) dissemination of these practices.

In Chapter 5, I illustrated how cohort learners with different learning needs and different ways of knowing experienced *academic, emotional,* and *cognitive* benefits from working in collaborative groups, a classroom practice that may help address aspects of the "mixed-level" problem raised by Beder and Medina.

After reviewing the research team's monograph (Kegan et al., 2001b), Dr. Sondra Stein, senior research associate and national director of Equipped for the Future (EFF), commented on the value of the practice of building cohorts, noting that she felt such cohorts are essential best practices because they create consistent environments for emotional and academic transformational learning. Furthermore, the success of peer cohorts remind us of the limitations of "limits of one-to-one instruction" and "open-entry/open-exit" classroom structures (S. Stein, personal communication, May 16, 2001). Thus, the findings of this study reinforce previous notions of how the cohort in ABE programs can provide a potential avenue for alleviating the issues of mixed levels and continuous enrollment and for supporting adult learners' academic learning, emotional well-being, and cognitive development.

Incorporating the Cohort and Variations of Cohorts into the Classroom and Program Design

While working and learning together in cohorts has great benefit for adult learners, it may not be feasible to build the same kind of consistent and enduring cohort structure into all programs, given the complexities of adult learners' lives, program restrictions, and funding requirements under which many ABE programs operate.

Importantly, I do not claim that any one particular cohort design is favorable. Instead, I suggest that good matches to a variety of ways of being supported or challenged might be more crucial to success than a particular structure regarding entry and exit (Drago-Severson, 2001; Drago-Severson et al., 2001b; Kegan et al., 2001a).

Lessons from the Polaroid site in particular, but also from this research in general (Kegan et al., 2001b) suggest that ABE/ESOL programs would benefit from incorporating features of the cohort design into existing program structures in order to enhance learning, to better support the development of classroom communities in particular and learning communities in general, and to increase learner retention (Drago-Severson, 2001; Drago-Severson & Berger, 2001; Drago-Severson et al., 2001b). Such *communities of connection* could take the form of having learners meet in small groups of about eight to ten people for regular discussion of particular topics that relate to their life experiences. These alternatives could include a focus or theme of:

1. Discussions of current events.
2. Peer support and even tutoring from fellow classmates.
3. Peers serving as mentors to fellow classmates and thereby sharing their expertise.
4. Groups meeting regularly to discuss other issues of importance to them in their social roles as adults (parents, workers, learners).
5. Discussion groups focusing on particular workplace issues.
6. E-mail listserves for class members so that they can communicate with each other and possibly discuss how issues and questions raised in class relate to their lives.

These groups could meet, for example, twice a month during a program's duration, and the program could secure physical spaces for such meetings.

Additionally, a teacher could facilitate such discussion, or different members of the group could assume this kind of leadership role during the course of meetings.

As a teacher, I employ many such practices (collaborative learning activities, small and large group discussion, free writing, peer commenting, e-mail listserves, and pair-triad exercises) in teaching graduate-level courses on leadership for supporting adult learning, and also in teaching research methods classes. These methods have proven very successful for supporting adult learning and for building peer relationships and classroom communities that extend beyond the walls of the classroom (see, e.g., Drago-Severson, 2004; Drago-Severson, Asghar, & Stuebner Gaylor, 2003).

An Exemplary Program: Bridge to Learning and Literacy

While the majority of adult learners in the Continuing Education Institute (CEI) Adult Diploma Program at Polaroid were given paid release time while they attended classes, there are other ways in which these communities of connection can and do develop in ABE/ESOL learning contexts. To illustrate the power of cohorts in a different context, I will discuss how this strategy has been used in another program and how it has influenced the learning environment and outcomes.

Carol Kolenik is the dynamic and vivacious leader directing the Harvard Bridge to Learning and Literacy, which is part of a series of initiatives that the president of Harvard, Lawrence Summers, implemented in January 2002. These initiatives are aimed at "improving the compensation and quality of work life for service workers on the Harvard campus" (At Work @ Harvard, 2002).

Harvard's Bridge to Learning and Literacy is a worker education program open to all hourly wage employees. Harvard employees who are interested in enhancing their work skills in their current positions or in acquiring new skills for different positions can attend 2-hour classes twice a week. There are currently 450 adult learners in the program, and 8 full-time and 8 part-time teachers, in addition to Kolenik (personal communication, October 25, 2002). Classes are offered on campus during work hours, and Kolenik has arranged for classes to meet in various classrooms throughout the university (each professional school at Harvard University has allocated space at no charge). Harvard employees can select from classes in ESOL, speaking and listening, literacy, GED/academic preparation, and computers. One hundred employees have completed courses, and many of them are now enrolled in Harvard University's Extension School. Bridge also makes one-on-one tutoring sessions available to students on request. Tutors, who are mostly volunteers from all parts of the university (including undergraduates, graduates, staff, administrators, and faculty), are available to work with students on campus before and after work hours.

Building Relationships. Maricel Santos, while a doctoral candidate at the Harvard University Graduate School of Education, helped design the contextualized curricula this program implements. She commented on the ways in which the adults in the program have formed important relationships, similar to those demonstrated by cohort learners at the Polaroid site. According to Santos, they are "diehard committed to one another; they meet outside, at the dining hall, on their work breaks, and they study together" (personal communication, October 16, 2002).

Gaining Respect. Similar to the Polaroid learners, adult learners in Bridge are given paid release time while they are taking classes, which is unheard of in many workplaces and ABE centers, says Kolenik. Being paid for time away from work, Kolenik explained, helps the adult learners in Bridge feel that they are doing something important—and they are. Like their supervisors and other learners at this university, these hourly wage employees are able to focus on learning and development. Kolenik's words make clear the importance of how being in the program and having paid release time from work helps these adults to feel respected:

> I've heard from hundreds of students that the respect they get here is the greatest thing about coming. It's [that] they are respected here, as if they are a Harvard student. They see how Harvard students are treated and now they feel like when they come here, they're also Harvard students. (C. Kolenik, personal communication, October 25, 2002)

This description of what it means for these adults to be allocated time away from work for learning reminded me of what many of the Polaroid learners had emphasized: Learning in the program helped them to gain the respect of their peers and supervisors.

Developing Communities of Connection. Santos explained that the learners in this program identify as part of a community through the Bridge program, despite only attending 2 hours of class a week. Clearly, there are ways to build what I call communities of connection that include elements of a cohort design without having formal, structured cohorts. However, the design features of a cohort (sharing a common purpose, meeting for a longer period of time) need to be woven into existing program structures, and these features can take any of the forms listed above, wherein adults are given scheduled and regular opportunities to talk with each other, learn from each other, and reflect on their own and other people's experiences over a period of time. These contexts, in which adults can build relationships that may support them in academic, emotional, and cognitive ways, can also be established in the workplace and education settings in addition to their ABE programs, provided that resources (human, time, and financial) are allocated to them.

Ancillary Supports

Learners in the Polaroid program, like the learners at the other two research sites, benefited from various additional supports. These included teachers, tutors, contextualized curricula (such as the Life Skills Workshop), programmatic structures (cohorts), technology (computer access and software programs), career and academic counseling, and psychological counseling (see, e.g., Coleman, 2002). These program design features helped to provide learners with important support no matter what their way of knowing.

Additional features that also support learners include mentoring by community members and/or peers, and community outreach. Many ABE/ESOL programs benefit from the services of volunteers from neighboring communities who help adult learners in important ways, including academic, emotional, career planning, networking, computer applications, tutoring, and so on. Building these additional supports into program design holds great promise for supporting adult learners who have different ways of knowing.

CREATING A DEVELOPMENTAL CURRICULUM

Differences in how adults make meaning essentially make all adult learning classes mixed-level classes. Learning activities need to be structured that can effectively address the multiple needs/expectations of adults at multiple developmental as well as skill levels to most effectively reach and teach all students. (S. Stein, personal communication, May 16, 2002)

Adults' different ways of knowing can help explain how it is that the same curriculum, classroom structures, activities, assignments, and/or teaching behaviors can leave some learners feeling stimulated and well supported while others feel abandoned or lost (Drago-Severson et al., 2001c). In such instances, teachers may unknowingly be using materials, classroom designs, or teaching strategies that are more appropriate for learners who have one way of knowing while inadvertently neglecting others. The teaching of any subject matter only as an aggregation of concrete facts and rules to be learned may feel frustrating to adult learners who have socializing and self-authoring ways of knowing (Drago-Severson et al., 2001c; Helsing, Drago-Severson, & Kegan, 2003). At the same time, this kind of teaching and learning would likely feel satisfying and supportive to adult learners who make sense of their experience with an instrumental way of knowing, who orient to a concrete, step-by-step approach when learning. Teachers who have a developmental understanding of how adults engage in the learning process will have an enhanced capacity to support all learners in their classrooms, across a range of ways of knowing. This kind of developmental mindfulness can increase the likelihood that greater numbers of adults will feel recognized and valued in their learning.

Making Connections to Learners' Lives

Infusing ABE/ESOL and workplace education curricula with links to learners' workplaces and to real-life experience (both personal and professional) can support and challenge learners with different ways of knowing and help them to transfer learning. What shape might such curricula take?

Rossiter (1999), along with Kerka (2002) and Brooks and Clark (2001), recommends that instructors invite learners to write their autobiographies as a way to support and promote development. Development requires consideration of personal history and imagining multiple future pathways, and drafting an autobiography "externalizes it so that one can reflect on it [and] become aware of its trajectory and the themes within it" (pp. 68–69).

While educators may not necessarily assign the writing of autobiographies to students, it is developmentally helpful when instructors can relate assignments to learners' life experiences. In addition to building curricula that help learners to develop skills, it is useful to create curricula aimed at supporting learners as they set goals and begin to reflect on their goals. Additionally, linking ABE curricula to learners' work and personal lives can support learners. These curricula need to be accompanied by appropriate scaffolding and support to meet a range of learner needs (see, e.g., Drago-Severson, 2004). Instrumental knowers, for example, would likely find a skill-oriented curriculum better suited to their needs and would need different forms of support to engage with this process. Socializing and self-authoring knowers, who think abstractly about their experiences, would need other forms of support and challenge.

Such reflective exercises (discussed in more detail later on in this chapter, sections on "Contextualizing the Curriculum" and "Creating Opportunities for Development in the Classroom") could be similar in nature to the exercises that CEI teachers assigned, which helped scaffold and support learners in their thinking (e.g., the life stories exercise and research conducted independently and in collaborative groups with support from the teachers, as discussed in Chapter 5). Creating opportunities for adults to work together and engage in dialogue and reflection in smaller groups that meet regularly to discuss workplace issues and/or solve problems (see, e.g., Cofer, 2000; Imel, 2001; Marsick, Bitterman, & van der Veen, 2000) is an option that could support both informational and transformational learning (similar to the ways in which a cohort does).

Applying Skills to Real Life

Other exercises (written and oral) that encourage learners to reflect on applying the skills learned in class to real-life situations can also support learners' development (e.g., creating opportunities to apply math principles to assist learners in figuring out financing for purchasing a home, mortgages, etc.; see, e.g., Dirkx, Amey, & Haston, 1999; Imel, 2000). These exercises would support and challenge learners as they unearth their assumptions, achieve a new relationship to their thinking, see new possibilities, and develop new aspirations. Creating opportunities for learners to share these exercises with teachers and classmates will not only support the development of classroom community but will also help learners consider alternative ways of thinking, as they benefit from peer and teacher feedback and questions.

Educators in ABE/ESOL, workplace learning programs, and other educational contexts (both formal and informal) need multiple ways to attend to learners' needs and a variety of curricula that help learners reflect on their learning by connecting it with their work and their lives outside the workplace. Employing practices that support this kind of self-reflection can be developmentally helpful in two ways. First, a space is made for learners to reflect on their lives and develop a new relationship to their own thinking and assumptions. Second, educators learn how better to support and challenge learners in their striving to become more empowered workers who can meet the demands of the modern workplace. Creating these opportunities could very well enhance possibilities for them as learners and workers, and for us as educators.

Attending to the Developing Cognition of Different Individuals

Workplaces and ABE/ESOL programs can also benefit from awareness of the ways in which adults' meaning-making systems can become more complex over time. As I have noted, careful attention to the ongoing nature of development can assist teachers in recognizing learners' emerging capacities so that they can better support learners' growth by scaffolding them in this process. It is important for educators to be vigilant about both the costs and benefits of development. In effect, beneficial learning asks that teachers meet students "where they are" cognitively by considering and attending to their existing ways of knowing (Drago-Severson, 2001; Kegan et al., 2001a, p. 24).

I agree with Rossiter (1999) about the importance of balancing challenges with enough support to keep learners from dropping out of programs; however, I suggest that the forms of support and challenge that facilitate learning need to be developmentally appropriate for learners (Drago-Severson, 2001, 2004). This does not mean, as Tinberg and Weisberger (1997) contend, that it is necessary to create multiple lesson plans to attend to learners' and workers' needs. Instead, it is crucial to incorporate multiple and developmentally appropriate forms of support and challenge in teacher and workplace practice, curricular and program design, and ABE/ESOL and workplace classrooms.

Useful tools for educators to embed in classroom practice include:

- journal writing,
- small discussion groups in which learners have the opportunity to reflect in writing and then by sharing their thinking with others, and
- assignments that help learners to explore new topics and their perspective on them (in pairs or triads).

Such exercises can sufficiently and appropriately support and challenge learners with different ways of knowing—and will likely help them to learn more.

Stein and her Equipped for the Future (EFF) team have created a ten-step cycle tool for developing learning activities that are integrated with assessment. This tool is based on EFF's conceptual framework, which is centered on constructivism (see, e.g., Bingman & Stein, 2001; Gillespie, 2002a, 2002b; Stein, 2002). The teaching-learning cycle tool was built on the experiences of practitioners and adult learners using the EFF framework and content standards. It includes guiding questions and sample tools for each step of the process to assist teachers in developing curricula and assessing learners' progress along a developmental continuum.[3] Like the research team's work, EFF's work emphasizes and provides tools for teachers that help us better understand and appreciate perplexing differences in adult learners' responses to teacher practices through a developmental perspective so that we can better assess, support, and monitor learning.

Importantly, a developmental perspective neither favors nor criticizes one particular educational philosophy or pedagogical style or one approach to program design or curriculum development. In fact, the research team suggests that educators move from an "either/or" stance to a "both/and" position when considering how to best help adults learn.

What sorts of curriculum and program design issues would lend themselves to a developmental analysis? Consideration of students' own naturally different needs and preferences will enhance the design of practices for instruction. These evaluations must be developmentally oriented in order to facilitate more complex thinking in a reasonable amount of time (Drago-Severson, 2001; Kegan et al., 2001a).

As teachers we would be wise to attend to the different ways in which curricular demands may be perceived by learners with different ways of knowing (Drago-Severson, 2001; Drago-Severson et al., 2001c; Kegan et al., 2001c). This developmental mindfulness is a first step toward improving the fit between learner challenge and learner capacity. Actively interpreting specific educational demands through a developmental lens is an important second step toward supporting adult learning. For example, teachers and program designers would benefit from considering what the program or teacher is demanding of learners from the perspective of their current way of knowing. The team also suggests that as a third step, we as teachers need to ask ourselves: "What way (or ways) of knowing does a particular pedagogical design favor?" and, now that we are aware of unintentionally neglecting and/or favoring some way(s) of knowing, "What can we do to insure we are *also* engaging the other way(s) of knowing?" (Kegan et al., 2001a).

CONTEXTUALIZING THE CURRICULUM: GOAL SETTING

> Research shows that learning transfers from one context to another more effectively when the learner understands not only the facts but also the "big picture"—the underlying principles, patterns, and relationships—that is acquired through the application of knowledge (Glaser, 1992; Bransford, Brown, & Cocking, 1999; Greeno, Resnick, & Collins, 1997). (Gillespie, 2002b, p. 1)

Contextualizing curricula can help learners transfer their learning from one context to another. It emphasizes the social nature of knowledge construction, and supports the idea that knowledge and skills are acquired in culturally diverse social contexts (Baumgartner & Merriam, 2000; Comings & Cuban, 2002; Gillespie, 2002b). Importantly, it also allows learners to apply classroom learning in real-world activities.

Contextualizing curricula and creating classroom conditions in which adults are periodically invited to reflect on their learning goals, personal goals, and role-specific goals (e.g., work goals and life goals) can support learners with different needs and different ways of knowing. These practices create opportunities for adults to envision and reflect on the concrete steps needed to achieve their goals. Learners might also be encouraged by their teachers and peers to formulate new (more abstract) goals after participating in this process. Along with this curriculum, teachers could create forums for their classes in which learners could work (both independently and in discussion groups) with teacher and peer support to outline steps for achieving goals.

This kind of curriculum for goal exploration (Drago-Severson, 2001), like the life stories exercise discussed in Chapter 5, would be robust enough to support and challenge learners with a wide range of needs and a diversity of ways of knowing. It could include both oral and written exercises (e.g., structured with guiding questions related to goals) that could be integrated into existing program classes.

For example, learners could become more aware of their goals by responding to questions such as, What do you consider to be your goals for this year? How do you feel about your goals? What do you think a goal is? EFF (see Gillespie, 2002b) is currently developing curricula and tools to assist teachers in designing curriculum activities that will help teachers to better understand how adult learners in ABE/ESOL, and adult education in general, make sense of their roles and role requirements to better support their learning and development. This is especially important given that learners with different ways of knowing need appropriate forms of support and challenge from both teachers and peers to benefit fully from engaging in this process.

Taylor, Marienau, and Fiddler (2000) highlight the important ways in which creating opportunities for learners to reflect on their own experiences in the classroom can help them to generate trust in their "own voice" (p. 313). By using their own voices, students are empowered as their lives become central to their learning, though not to the exclusion of other texts.

Contextualizing for Different Ways of Knowing

Developmentally minded educators would benefit from consideration of how learners with different ways of knowing might be supported *and* challenged as they engaged in what I refer to as "curriculum for goal exploration" (Drago-Severson, 2001). For example, instrumental knowers would benefit from supportive challenges that encourage consideration of more abstract goals. Adults with a socializing way of knowing who look to their teachers and/or valued colleagues for validation when setting goals, would benefit from explicit encouragement from teachers and peers to view themselves as able to author their own learning and life goals. Learning how to access the information they need to pursue self-generated goals might best support self-authoring knowers. I will share one possibility for how this curriculum for goal exploration could be woven into the fabric of ABE/ESOL classrooms and other adult learning contexts.

Writing about Learning Goals. At the start of such a program, teachers invite learners to work independently by writing about goals in response to structured questions. Structured questions might include the suggestions I mentioned above, as well as questions that relate to important issues in adults' lives. For example, What kinds of goals do you have for yourself at work? How would you like your learning in this program to help you achieve any goals you have set for yourself at work? What kinds of goals do you have for your family life? What kind of learning might help you in achieving these goals? Next, learners have an opportunity to share whatever goals they feel comfortable sharing with teachers and members of their own small, collaborative group of classmates.

Collaborating in Peer Groups. As discussed in Chapter 5, collaborative group work offers both support and challenge to learners with a variety of ways of knowing. In this case, collaborative group work creates a context within which learners share goals, reflect on fellow group members' goals and questions (an opportunity to clarify goals and possibly to broaden perspectives), and perhaps help each other develop concrete steps to be taken toward accomplishing goals. Teachers could also create forums (toward the end of the semester) in which learners are invited not only to revisit and assess their goals but also to check in with teachers and peers and to reflect independently by writing about their goals. Building curricula like this into program design and classroom practice holds the potential to better support and challenge the range of learners who are likely to populate all ABE/ESOL and other adult learning classrooms and to meet learners—wherever they are—as they strive to meet their goals. Such practices may enhance classroom community, which might help learners persist in achieving their goals and in learning programs in general.

Referencing Books and Other Print Materials. Another curriculum idea is to give learners books or newspaper articles in which other people are discussing their goals and even the ways in which they achieved them.

These readings could become part of the curriculum for goal setting discussed above, and learners could be given opportunities to

- write about learning from the readings and the ways in which they connect to other people's stories (i.e., by drawing from one's own experiences),
- discuss the readings in small groups (with questions to guide the discussion), and
- share the ideas discussed in small groups with the larger class so that all could benefit from shared experience.

Teachers could also create assignments in which learners use the Internet (if computers are available) to explore goal setting in other literature. All of these activities can support learning and development.

Comings, in discussing some of the differences between the K–12 and the adult education system, echoed the importance of contextualizing the curriculum in adult education settings. Adults, unlike child learners, are not immersed in their learning environments; rather, they face a myriad of other responsibilities, and their schooling is but one small aspect of their lives. Their learning should reflect this dynamic by contextualizing their curriculum to the other facets of adult life (J. Comings, personal communication, September 13, 2002).

Relating curricula to adult learners' real-life needs supports meaningful learning. As Knowles's (1980) path-finding theory of androgogy put forth long ago, adults learn best when the content matter they are learning is of clear and current importance to them.

CONCEPTUALIZING COMPETENCY
AS A DEVELOPMENTAL CONTINUUM

The research team conceptualizes competency development along a continuum and believes that the ways in which we demonstrate competencies are influenced by our way of knowing. Our study shares the philosophical view of EFF in "conceptualizing adult literacy as something bigger than the acquisition of basic skills" (Portnow, Popp, Broderick, Drago-Severson, & Kegan, 1998, p. 25) and in defining competence within the context of the individual adult learner's life demands. Similar to EFF, our view is that the "something bigger" is the person who is making meaning of his or her own skills and developing competencies, the person who through his or her own way of knowing is actively constructing an understanding of what behaviors need to be exercised (Drago-Severson, 2001; Portnow et al., 1998; Popp & Boes, 2001).

Understanding the "Hidden Curriculum"

An adult learner's life demands, more specifically, can be looked at in the context of his or her many social roles. In fact, like EFF (Stein, 2000, 2002), the research team has been interested in what Kegan (1994) refers to as the "hidden curriculum" of adult life. In other words, Kegan contends that inherent in each of the social roles common to most adult lives, there is a hidden curriculum that adults must manage to function well in their various roles. Role demands surface in our personal lives (in our roles as parents and partners) and in our public lives (in our roles as workers and citizens). As adults, we assume a variety of social roles, and each of them is infused with a set of mostly unrecognized psychological tasks and demands that must be resolved satisfactorily if we are to succeed in each role (Drago-Severson, 2004; Kegan, 1994; Popp & Boes, 2001). EFF has identified a number of these role-related tasks and also discusses their implications for adult learning (see, e.g., Gillespie, 2002a, 2002b; Stein, 2000, 2002).

Popp and Boes (2001), members of the research team, describe how the adults in our study—from across all three research sites—demonstrated competency in their social roles (as parent, learner, and worker) differently, depending on their way of knowing. The team examined the specific question of whether the ways people will understand and carry out the tasks of a given social role are importantly influenced by their more general way of knowing (Kegan et al., 2001b). Specifically, Popp and Boes (2001) examine the tasks that EFF identifies in various social roles and focus on how learners across all three research sites demonstrated competency differently. From a developmental perspective, competence is defined in the following way: "[T]here is an increased sense of confidence when one experiences a new sense of mastery and capacity in a particular area" (Popp & Boes, 2001, p. 641). The confidence and mastery act reciprocally, each motivating the development of the other. In other words, this work shows *how* learners demonstrate the same tasks differently depending on their way of knowing.

CREATING OPPORTUNITIES FOR DEVELOPMENT IN THE CLASSROOM: TEACHING PRACTICE

It has never been any secret that we change as we age. The only question is how? (Daloz, 1986, p. 43)

Realizing that learners' goals change over time—and that the way in which learners understand their goals may change over time—has implications for teacher practice (Drago-Severson, 2001). As teachers, we can design classroom structures and classroom assignments that will support learners as they develop the skills needed to create, articulate, and reflect on their own goals. It is also essential to understand that learners with different ways of knowing need developmentally appropriate forms of support and challenge as they engage in this process.

To do this, we must meet learners *where they are* and provide appropriate scaffolding as they engage in goal setting. This, in the view of our research team, constitutes a new kind of *learner-centeredness*—one that calls for attention to how learners with different ways of knowing experience and need different forms of support and challenge. I will now discuss specific ideas for creating such opportunities in the classroom.

Reflective Practices for Learners

To support learning, whether it be an adult's or a child's, we need to start with the learner's experience. Examining one's own experiences and ways in which curricula connect to one's own life and work can facilitate the development of reflective judgment (Kitchener & King, 1994). Incorporating the use of reflective journals (either on the computer or in paper journal books), papers in which students respond to questions about readings and other types of assignments in which they are invited to share their perspectives and receive feedback, can spur new thinking and situate the learner and the teacher in the individual's experience. Kerka (2002) emphasizes the importance of journal writing as a method for helping adults to process new information, make sense of it, incorporate it with current knowledge, and bring into being new meaning. She identifies the following purposes of journal writing:

- invigorating stagnant thinking
- fostering metacognition
- promoting mindfulness of tacit knowledge
- exploring the self
- problem-solving

Using journals helps adults come to new understandings of their learning and also provides them with a method for demonstrating what they know and understand and what their questions are. Brooks and Clark (2001) concur with Kerka (2002) in suggesting that constructing narratives "pushes us to integrate and reformulate new information, ideas, and ultimately our own identity" (p. 1). Employing journal writing as a tool for learning not only provides learners with a chance to articulate their thinking in words (writing is thinking); it also helps teachers to "informally assess students' assumptions about knowledge and how beliefs should be justified" (Kitchener & King, 1994, p. 240) and to consider how adults' assumptions and thinking—for example, about their own goals—may change over time.

Similarly, Brookfield (1987) encourages teachers to engage in "critical teaching," in which emphasis is placed on the importance of teachers assuming multiple roles in our efforts to act as "catalysts of discussion and inquiry" (p. 80). Inviting learners to reflect through writing in journals and other reflective processes can create opportunities to enact the important and various roles emphasized by Brookfield.

Reflective Practice Groups for Teachers

Creating opportunities for teachers to engage in reflective practice groups is an important step toward supporting teacher learning. In fact, it is the leading developmental tool for practitioners as described by scholars in the field of adult learning (Brookfield, 1995; Cranton, 1994, 1996; Helsing, Drago-Severson & Kegan, 2003; Kegan & Lahey, 2001; Osterman & Kottkamp, 1993; Schön, 1983). Inviting teachers to reflect on their own professional practice—both privately, and together with colleagues—has proven successful when implemented with K–12 teachers (Drago-Severson, 2002b, 2004; Killion, 2000; Rogers & Babinski, 1999). Teachers in adult education contexts could also benefit from this kind of practice, if time and structures are in place to support it.

The guiding idea behind exploring assumptions in a reflective context is that when encouraged to become more aware of his or her own assumptions, which guide thinking and behaviors, a person will be freer to understand how assumptions inform problem solving and be better able to engage in learning—and conflict. Examining assumptions is essential for the development of lasting change and new practices (Brookfield, 1987). Stephen Brookfield (1995), in discussing how to help teachers become critically reflective practitioners, describes assumptions as our "taken-for-granted beliefs . . . that seem so obvious to us as not to need stating explicitly" (p. 2). It is essential that we as educators examine our assumptions because, as Brookfield explains, taking practices for granted may lead to profound frustration when things do not seem to manifest as we intended.

To make lasting changes in our teaching practices, it is crucial that teachers—and all adults, for that matter—have opportunities to examine assumptions. Incorporating these kinds of opportunities into ABE/ESOL programs and workplaces can assist practitioners in developing a heightened awareness of their assumptions, so that they can examine their influence on performance (Osterman & Kottkamp, 1993). Doing so creates opportunities for transformational learning.

Reflective practice groups can support teachers as they develop the capacities to better manage the complexities and challenges of their work. Through systematic reflection with colleagues, practitioners can learn to understand the assumptions that underlie their beliefs and actions. In so doing, they may become better able to view their thinking multiple times through the reflected lenses of others around them, which can lead to alternative frameworks for thinking and action.

One goal of reflected practice groups is to stop events so they can be reviewed—the power is in the reviewing and consideration of alternative and more effective ways of thinking and responding. Once issues/questions are raised to a conscious level, practitioners can then take steps to address or rethink them. The problem for practitioners is that they often have difficulty doing more than responding from assumption and instinct, because the demands on them are great and the time and tools for reflection are limited.

Suggestions for Implementing Reflective Practice. Many topics for reflection and dialogue (such as developing assessment and accountability systems, integrating new innovations, developing strategies to measure achievement, developing a shared mission) can be contextualized so that they arise out of teacher practice and/or a program's unique needs. In addition, monthly faculty meetings can serve as mechanisms for developing an agenda of topics for discussion, reflection, and learning to be explored during reflective practice group meetings.

Incorporating reflective practice groups into ABE/ESOL and other educational programs can provide a supportive, safe learning environment for practitioners to develop greater awareness of their beliefs and assumptions, which guide behaviors and deeper thinking. Reflecting with colleagues in this way can support envisioning alternative ways of thinking, acting, and/or behaving. Securing, prioritizing, and guarding these spaces in which adults can engage in reflection and discussion of thinking and assumptions holds the potential for transformational learning.

POLICYMAKING IN SUPPORT OF DEVELOPMENTAL LEARNING

In the October 2002 *Report on Literacy Programs*, which highlights news of basics skills training and workplace literacy, Russ Whitehurst, the assistant secretary who heads the former Office of Educational Research and Improvement, reports that "the Education Department will only fund programs that are based on scientific evidence, and that evidence must meet rigorous scientific standards" (p. 154). He also explains that education officials from 16 states gathered in early October to learn more about the ramifications of the "No Child Left Behind Act" and discuss how this reading program "imposes tough standards on that and many other programs, including ESL instruction and teacher training" (p. 154).

Strong policies are those that provide enough guidance and also allow enough autonomy for each unique context, so that they can be responsive to different program needs. A developmental perspective can provide policymakers with knowledge about how learners make sense of learning opportunities, and these insights can be useful to improvement efforts and to developing stronger accountability systems. This perspective has important implications for ABE/ESOL teachers and policymakers. A constructive-developmental framework enables us to understand that many of the skills and competencies inherent in our roles as workers, parents, and learners can be successfully performed from a broad range of ways of knowing. And this framework also helps us see that the purposes and nature of the performance will differ as a function of a person's way of knowing (Kegan et al., 2001a).

Therefore, teachers, educational programs, and workplaces would benefit from considering the various ways in which adults with different ways of knowing will demonstrate skills and competencies, and from considering the match between their program's overall goals and expectations and adults' ways of knowing. In other words, we would be wise to consider how our programs, curricula, and classroom practices might inadvertently require adults to perform tasks and demonstrate competency at a certain way of knowing. Popp and Boes (2001) summarize important implications for employing a developmental view of competency, and stress how this approach recognizes and builds from one success to the next. Among these implications, they argue that the empowerment that succeeds the demonstration of competence provides "a way to mark, value, and celebrate the learner's growth" (p. 641).

Because adult learners understand and *demonstrate* skill and competency development in developmentally different ways, it is critical that ABE/ESOL and workplace education curricula be shaped to

- recognize this developmental diversity,
- acknowledge competency development as a process, and
- link to learners' lives as workers.

Realizing that learners construct their roles as workers, their relationships with supervisors and coworkers, and their skill development in qualitatively different ways—and that these conceptions can change over time—has important implications for program curricula and for how we understand competency and skill mastery in the workplace (see, e.g., Bingman & Stein, 2001; Gillespie, 2002a). Considering skill and competency development as processes can help us to acknowledge and meet a worker where he or she is and offer supports and scaffolds to support him or her to where he or she wants to go in terms of skill and competency development. Creating policies based on what we know about how adults learn and develop and how they demonstrate competency holds great promise for strengthening adult learning within the United States. Moreover, this knowledge offers an effective way to monitor, assess, and improve the quality of ABE/ESOL and other educational programs.

The research team's findings on the power of the cohort and collaborative learning also have implications for policymaking. The formation of learner cohorts, whether they be as structured as the one at the Polaroid site or unstructured but frequent occasions where learners work together in groups, could, as this research suggests, help to increase persistence and retention rates, especially if such structures could be in place when learners enter ABE/ESOL programs. The mechanism of working together in a group that is sustained over time is crucial.

Quigley (1997) highlights that ABE programs risk losing up to a third of students in the first 3 weeks of a course. If programs had learner cohorts or derivatives of them in place when learners first entered their programs, it could reduce the risk of their dropping out and enhance learner persistence.

Policymakers could also go far by supporting professional development for teachers. A constructive-developmental approach can help us to understand adult learners' skills, knowledge, and constructions of knowledge in a new light. The findings reported in this book point to the importance of creating opportunities for teachers and workplace educators to develop a knowledge base—or to strengthen their already existing knowledge—about how constructive-developmental theory can inform teaching practices, curricula development, classroom structure, and their understanding of the diversity of ways in which learners make sense of their experiences (see, e.g., Bingman & Stein, 2001; Gillespie, 2002a). This means creating opportunities for teachers to learn about both the principles of constructive-developmental theory and their implications for practice, and possibly providing incentives for such coursework through professional development credits. The EFF approach to assessment, accountability, and improvement (Stites, 2002) and their *EFF Teaching and Learning Toolkit* (Nash & Gillespie, 2002) is one model that could also provide meaningful guidance to educators both in terms of assessment and structuring curricula.

However, in order for this—and other possible initiatives for supporting teacher learning—to occur, ABE/ESOL and workplace programs and policymakers must make available the resources (human, financial, and time) needed to support this kind of teacher development (Drago-Severson, 2002b, 2004; Helsing, Drago-Severson, & Kegan, 2003; Kegan et al., 2001a).

Finally, providing workers with paid release time to attend classes will also yield great benefits (as evidenced by the Polaroid learners and the learners in Harvard's Bridge to Learning and Literacy). Adult education policies need to be enhanced to include enough financial support to enable learners to take advantage of learning opportunities to improve their skills and to grow.

Equipped for the Future: An Exemplary Model to Consider

While policymakers and employers might certainly consider several promising ABE/ESOL models, the scope of this book allows me to explore and recommend EFF, as it is grounded in the developmental principles that informed the research team's study. EFF is developing a model and approach to testing and assessment, the EFF Assessment Framework, which is informed by principles of developmental theory (Stites, 2002). This system reform initiative and approach is directed toward improving practices and assessing results in the ABE field. This model identifies and applies criteria for the development of tests and assessments for high-stakes accountability and improvement.

By employing EFF's model, or others organized by a developmental and pluralistic framework, policymakers could better support adults' development by focusing on the more long-term, overarching purposes of literacy rather than measuring successful growth in terms of instantaneous, measurable change (Bingman & Stein, 2001; Fingeret & Drennon, 1997; Helsing, Drago-Severson & Kegan, 2003; Nash & Gillespie, 2002; Stites, 2002). This perspective can help us to improve and expand policies and can also inform program designers in their decision making about how to create programs that will attend to teachers' and students' actual preferences and needs (Helsing, Drago-Severson, & Kegan, 2003). Educational improvement depends on educational policymakers' attention to the ways in which a constructive-developmental perspective can inform adult learning and assessment procedures. EFF's groundbreaking work and the team's research provide rich results for informing adult education policy.

Moreover, the work done by the research team and EFF can also be used to inform the Adult Education and Family Literacy Act, Title II of the 1998 Workforce Investment Act (WIA), which compiled employment, training, and literacy programs into three grants to states to support family literacy, adult education, adult employment, training services, and disadvantaged youth services (National Institute for Literacy Policy Update, 1998). WIA's mission is to better serve adults, within each state, in their efforts to gain access to job training, education, and employment. WIA has set 12 criteria that states must consider when determining a program's potential for funding (including accountability, reporting, program content and quality, staffing, and attention to community needs).

WIA established quality criteria for assessing program quality. The research team's findings about the need to reenvision competency development, the benefits of incorporating a constructive-developmental perspective when considering how best to support adult learning and development, and the power of creating cohorts (or derivatives of them) hold immense potential for helping to rethink WIA's program quality assessment measures and funding allocation.

Put simply, more effective policies can be created if they are informed by constructive-developmental theory and lessons from the team's research, which contribute to the knowledge base by illuminating how adult learners' meaning making influences their expectations and experiences in adult literacy programs. EFF's leading work also provides meaningful guidelines and curricula for shaping and improving ABE programs. Using these pieces of the bigger picture to inform policy will likely benefit practice and help us to better meet the demands of 21st-century work and life.

PROMISING AVENUES FOR DEVELOPMENTAL RESEARCH

After reading the team's research monograph (Kegan et al., 2001b), Wendy Luttrell of Harvard's Graduate School of Education commented that it would also be important to extend the team's research by examining "the relationship between developmental position, perceptions of control, and a person's analysis of power" (personal communication, June 11, 2002). Moreover, in light of the team's findings, Luttrell suggested that future research needs to examine the critical pedagogy literature that focuses on literacy as a social practice that is embedded in institutional contexts and power relations. This literature illuminates how people make sense of their reading, writing, and math activities (see, e.g., Barton & Hamilton, 1998; Beder, Medina, & Eberly, 2000) and could benefit from being brought into conversation with adults' meaning-making processes.

Another promising avenue for research is to examine ABE/ESOL and other teachers' ways of knowing. Studying effective teachers and employing a constructive-developmental lens to better understand teachers' meaning-making systems, may help us to better understand aspects of professionalism associated with success despite the contextual constraints (Kegan et al., 2001b).

In the K–12 school systems, teachers are benefiting from strong research connections with universities, businesses, and community organizations (Drago-Severson, 2002b, 2003, 2004; Drago-Severson & Pinto, in press). Many K–12 teachers are also reaping benefits from conducting research in their own classrooms. Training ABE/ESOL teachers to become researchers not only enhances leadership, but also helps to improve practice. Developing partnerships with universities and community programs (such as those offered by museums) also holds promise for enhancing teaching and learning practices in the field of ABE/ESOL. Such relationships and partnerships will likely help us as we strive to "level the playing field" (Comings, Reder, & Sum, 2001), enhance adult learning, and support adults in becoming more able to meet the demands of 21st-century work and life. Policies that support programs as they work to develop strong partnership with universities, businesses, and community organizations may indeed help the field to conduct the research urged by the above-mentioned authors. Such policies may also help the field to be strengthened.

The cohort and collaborative learning are features of the programs from this research that served as important and powerful mechanisms for supporting adult learning. While the research team did not conduct a gender analysis of data from the larger study, this is a fruitful area for future research. Bringing a gender analysis in conversation with a constructive-developmental analysis could yield important findings. Also, conducting further research in workplace literacy programs with an eye toward careful examination of gender as well as race, class, and development is another rich area for exploration. Inviting workers themselves to conduct action research toward examining workplace issues is yet another fruitful arena for exploration (see, e.g., D'Amico, Lentz, Smith, & Taylor, 2002).

Viewing this lifelong learning system as an "economic development program," as Comings et al. (2001, p. 23) suggest, should render a positive return on this essential investment, create a positive social impact, build a citizenry that is better equipped for and able to change their lives, strengthen our workforce with the skills and capacities we need to meet the demands of life in this century, and help all adults help their children to succeed in school (see, e.g., Comings, Sum, & Uvin, 2000).

AN APPETITE FOR LEARNING

To improve the economic and humanistic health of our nation and to support adults as we strive to meet the complex demands of the modern workplace, we must attend to workers' learning needs.

Stein and her colleagues at EFF conducted research aimed at devising a content framework and setting benchmarks for measurement (2000, 2002) to answer the following questions, among others: "What do we mean when we say adults need to 'compete in a global economy, to exercise rights and responsibilities of citizenship'? What do they need *to do* in order to carry out these responsibilities?" (2002, p. 3). They asked these crucial questions before addressing the following questions: "What do adults *need to know* to carry out these roles [as citizens, family members, workers] effectively? How many Americans have the knowledge and skills necessary to carry out these roles effectively?" (2002, p. 3).

To answer these questions and develop a meaningful content framework, Stein and her research team invited 1,500 adults from across the United States to assess their roles in the global economy, including descriptions of the "rights and responsibilities of citizenship" (p. 3) and the skills they believed were required to perform such responsibilities. Their research identified a set of common fundamental purposes, across roles, that motivated the adults in the study to look for knowledge and skills that related to successful performance in these roles (Stein, 2000, 2002). Equipped for the Future (EFF) describes these purposes as:

> *Access* so that individuals can gain information and access to perform in their roles.
> *Voice so that ideas can be shared with confidence and heard.*
> *Independent action* in order to make decisions without having to depend on others' assistance.
> *Bridge to the future* to keep pace with an evolving world.
>
> (Stein, 2002, italics in original)

Building on the team's partnership with EFF, the research team investigated how program learning helped adults to meet their larger purposes. The team examined how learners understood the transfer of skills and competencies that they developed in this program as helping them to better meet and manage the complex demands of 21st-century worklife, which calls for new skill sets (Comings et al., 2000; Murnane & Levy, 1996; Stein, 2000). Not only did program learning support the development of learners' skills and competencies, but in many cases learners grew to have a new relationship to their work.

After reviewing the team's work (Kegan et al., 2001b), Stein commented that it is important to consider learners' different ways of knowing because educators may be able to understand students' capacity for cognition in ways that even the student cannot fully grasp (S. Stein, personal communication, May 16, 2001).

In Chapter 7, I presented the various ways in which learning in the CEI Adult Diploma Program helped the adults in this study to develop their capacities for more effectively performing their roles as workers. In EFF's terms, these stories illuminate how program learning helped these learners gain access to information, knowledge, and skills so that they felt they were better able to orient themselves in the world. They reported that program learning also helped them to voice their ideas and opinions with greater confidence. They emphasized how this helped them in their relationships with supervisors and colleagues at work, as well as in other domains of their lives. Learners also explained how they felt they were able to act more independently, to solve problems more effectively, and to make more informed decisions without having to rely on others' help. I illuminated how these learners made sense of their improved skills and competencies—and often their new sense of personal and professional empowerment—through their individual meaning systems. Put simply, I have shown how learning in this program made a difference in learners' lives. Learning opened up the world for these learners.

What specific kinds of changes did workers notice in themselves as they participated in this program? How did the skills workers learned in the program translate to their work lives? Learners across ways of knowing reported feeling better able to manage the complexities of their work. The skills and competencies they named as improved align with what workplaces in this technological age demand (see, e.g., Comings et al., 2000; Murnane & Levy, 1996; Purcell-Gates, 1995). Specifically, learners said that they had:

- improved communication skills
- improved writing skills
- greater productivity
- increased self-confidence (at work generally, and in delivering oral presentations)
- greater appreciation for and ability to work with people from diverse backgrounds
- enhanced facility with personal computers and the Internet
- greater reading comprehension
- sharpened/expanded mathematical skills.

Learners reported that these skills and competencies helped them to become better team members, more effective communicators, and more efficient workers. Significantly, all learners expressed a desire for additional formal learning after completing their Adult Diploma Program. It appears that learning in this program not only supported learners as they developed and enhanced skills and competencies needed for work, but it also stimulated a craving to continue learning. May they continue to joyfully sing their songs.

Graduation: A Red-Letter Day

Life is full of opportunities; you just have to reach out and grab one. Never give up your dreams.

—Hope, program graduate, June 1999

JUNE 27, 1999, was a sunny, warm, and clear Sunday afternoon in Boston, Massachusetts. Shortly after noon a few members of our research team left Cambridge, traveling to the University of Massachusetts Boston campus. UMASS Boston's Harbor Campus is located just steps away from the John F. Kennedy Presidential Library on a piece of land offering an inspiring view of Boston's waterfront and harbor islands.[1] We were on our way to join Polaroid Corporation's adult learners for their graduation from high school. The Continuing Education Institute holds graduation ceremonies each year at this campus. The adults who participated in CEI's diploma program classes would receive their high school diplomas. This was a day to celebrate and a time to remember.

Adult learners from five CEI-sponsored Adult Diploma Programs in the greater Boston area gathered together on this special day with their families, friends, coworkers, CEI teachers, and program administrators, as well as the CEI president, Dr. Lloyd David. Distinguished guest speakers came to celebrate and recognize the graduates' impressive achievement: completing the CEI Adult Diploma Program and earning a high school diploma. On that sparkling Sunday afternoon, each adult learner who had successfully completed all graduation requirements during the 14-month program at Polaroid and other CEI sites would be awarded a high school diploma from Boston's Cathedral High School.

While traveling from Harvard's Graduate School of Education to the University of Massachusetts/Boston campus, we talked about our deep admiration for all that the learners in the Polaroid cohort had accomplished during their program. We reminisced about our first meeting with these special people—just 15 months earlier—when we introduced ourselves as researchers while inviting their participation in this research study. On that opening day, the adult learners in the Polaroid program attended an orientation and welcoming event, "The Kickoff," at Polaroid's Norwood, Massachusetts, facility in the meeting room where their program classes would take place.

As some of us traveled to the graduation ceremonies, we remembered these learners telling us about their initial feelings of trepidation about enrolling in the program. During that trip we also talked about how rewarding it was to have witnessed changes in how the Polaroid participants thought about their own learning and themselves. In the months between kickoff and graduation, learners had told us about certain changes in their sense of confidence. They had shared with us the important difference that learning in this program had made for them—both at work and at home. I was moved by how much these learners had talked about themselves, both individually and as a group, as changed as a result of their program participation. I was inspired by the relationships they had developed with one another and with their teachers and by how these relationships supported their learning. Learning and earning the diploma meant so very much to them.

Conducting research with these adult learners opened our minds and our hearts to their sense making. While I conducted research, and especially on that Sunday I celebrated the privilege of accompanying these exceptional people along their important learning journey. I was then, and I remain, grateful for all they have taught me about their worlds.

Upon entering the auditorium a few minutes before ceremonies were to begin, we searched the several hundred faces and scores of seating sections to find "our group" of learners. Our eyes darted about the large, tiered assembly room as we made contact, one by one, with the Polaroid cohort graduates. Seventy-four adults would receive their diplomas that day, 16 of which represented the Polaroid cohort we had come to know so well. Graduating men were dressed in robes of green, and women wore gold gowns. The room brightened with faces beaming with the kind of joy wished for us all at times of commencement. We located our seats in a center-section row toward the rear of the now-buzzing auditorium. Throughout the room, small children gripped helium-filled balloons emblazoned with "Congratulations." Adults moved quickly here and there, offering one another congratulatory handshakes and hugs, mixing green with gold and gold with green as they reached out to each other with extended arms.

"Pomp and Circumstance" played as the graduates marched down the auditorium aisles. CEI teachers and CEI's program president and program director, followed the graduates. The commencement speaker, Dr. Ismael Ramirez-Soto, dean of UMASS/Boston's College of Public and Community Service, followed the CEI group to the front of the auditorium. Graduates seated themselves in the first dozen rows while CEI people and guest speakers passed by to take their places on the elevated stage. Speakers representing students at each of CEI's five program sites sat with their cohort groups, as each site group had elected its own class speaker to express a few thoughts about their learning journeys on this important day.

Kathy Hassey, CEI's program director and a dedicated educator who once taught high school math and science, opened the ceremony. She talked about this graduating class as a "diverse, kind, and spirited" group of learners who spoke 14 different native languages in addition to English. After these opening remarks, Dr. David presented the Class of 1999. He shared his initial vision for CEI, which was founded in 1977 to help adults in the workforce earn high school diplomas. He spoke of his hope to help "every adult to become more literate and possess the knowledge and skills necessary to compete in an international economy." CEI was founded to create innovative educational and training programs for adults in the workplace who needed English and academic skills, and more than 7,000 adults have participated in these programs so far. Dr. David proudly reported that this was CEI's 18th graduation. He said that receiving a high school education is important for many reasons—among the more practical, access to job opportunities with better salaries.

Dr. David congratulated graduates before passing the baton back to Kathy Hassey, who introduced graduation speakers. Hope, the class-elected speaker from the Polaroid Corporation cohort, was the fourth person to speak. Dressed in her flowing gold robe, Hope approached the podium with grace and self-assuredness. During a focus group meeting we'd held just 1 week earlier, Hope had excitedly told us how happy she was to have been elected speaker for her cohort. She said that she had worked very closely with her classmates to be sure that the ideas she presented at graduation represented the cohort's thoughts. During that focus group session, Hope also told us and her cohort colleagues that she had created a second speech, on her own, and that she was hoping that the group would help her decide which of the two speeches she should deliver on graduation day. After much discussion, Hope was convinced that it would be better to deliver the collaborative speech rather than her own.

Many of the Polaroid learners told me they had dreamed of graduation day both before and during the program. During the research I often heard learners say that it was harder for them to learn, because they were adults or "grown-ups" with multiple responsibilities. Often I heard learners say how proud they were of themselves for being able to stick with it even when they doubted their abilities. Support from family, classmates, teachers, coworkers, and supervisors gave them the encouragement they needed to continue. Hope spoke:

> We, the graduating class, would also like to thank our friends, family, classmates, and coworkers. It was hard work because we had

families and other obligations, but we accomplished our goals. After
all of this hard work, we are proud of ourselves and excited to be receiving our diplomas. We serve as an example to others to open
doors of opportunity. You are never too old and it is never too late
to get an education. Life is full of opportunities; you just have to
reach out and grab one. Never give up your dreams.

After the final class speaker delivered his speech, Dean Ramirez-Soto delivered the commencement address. He told the graduates and all of us in the
auditorium that the ceremony was a "celebration of your culture." And
then he applauded graduates for their hard work and energy. As an inspiring surprise, he also invited all of the graduates to continue their education
by earning a bachelor's degree at UMASS-Boston. "There is a place for
every program graduate" he said; "This school was created for people like
you." He reminded graduates that they had earned an important degree
and encouraged them to use it as a "stepping stone."

Sr. Patrice, the assistant principal of Cathedral High School, the di-
ploma-granting Boston school, then offered the graduates congratulatory
remarks. After her greeting, she and Dr. David awarded the diplomas. We
watched as each graduate proudly walked to center stage to receive the
"piece of paper" encased in a hunter-green folder. Applause and cheers
filled the air as each graduate's name was announced. The ceremonies con-
cluded with Kathy Hassey dedicating a heartwarming poem to CEI program teachers. We were all invited to attend a reception for graduates in
the school cafeteria.

We walked the short distance to the cafeteria by way of an overpass
that overlooked the John F. Kennedy Library and which provided a stunning view of Boston Harbor. In the cafeteria, all waited to greet and again
congratulate the graduates—in our case, especially the Polaroid Corporation graduates. One by one they entered the room, faces beaming. We congratulated. We took photographs. Diplomas were circulated and admired.
We were honored to meet many families, children, and friends of graduates. Polaroid graduates talked with us about plans for future schooling.
After celebrating with these wonderful learners, we wished them continued
great success, and we bid them farewell.

Each and every adult who participated in our study, and all they had
to say, became important to us as researchers and as learning colleagues.
The CEI diploma program and its teachers shepherded participants
through courses of study that helped them achieve dreams for personal
development and enhanced opportunities for their work and life. In many
ways, it was also the pathfinding Polaroid Corporation of Massachusetts
that made so much of this learning and opportunity possible for so many.

Over the years, Polaroid had hired many people who did not have a high school education, and as shifts in the economy initiated a push for more skills at the company, management had decided that education was a better path than layoffs or downsizing (although the latter would also eventually occur at the Polaroid Corporation). No words could adequately acknowledge the generous contributions made by Polaroid and its many employees toward helping their adult workers to learn, earn high school diplomas through the CEI program, and change their lives and themselves.

On the way home to Cambridge, we shared our thoughts and impressions about the wonderful experience and the success of the Polaroid learners and all program graduates. We wondered where they would be and what they would be doing years from now. We expressed our sense of awe at how much they had accomplished and how meaningful the learning experiences had been for them as they worked their way through the program. We talked about the ways in which these special people had told us about learning that had made a genuine difference in their lives. I shall always remember these remarkable people, the pride they showed on graduation day, my relationships with them, and all that they have helped us learn.

Notes

Chapter 1

1. Some of the ideas presented in this discussion appear in the research team's monograph (Kegan et al., 2001b) and are cited herein.

2. Such theories include age-phasic (e.g., Arnett, 2000; Erikson, 1964, 1968; Knowles, 1970, 1984; Knox, 1981; Levinson, 1978, 1996; Mezirow, 1991, 1994, 1996; Mezirow & Associates, 1990, 2000; Scarf, 1980; Vaillant, 1977; Wigfield et al., 1996; Wortley & Amatea, 1982); relational theories focusing on girls' and women's development (e.g., Baxter Magolda, 1992; Belenky, Clinchy, Goldberger, & Tarule, 1986; Brown & Gilligan, 1992; Caffarella & Olson, 1993; Gilligan, 1977, 1982; Goldberger, Tarule, Clinchy, & Belenky, 1996; Jordan, Kaplan, Miller, Stiver, & Surrey, 1991; Miller, 1976, 1991; Ross-Gordon, 1999; Taylor, 2000; Taylor, Marienau, & Fiddler, 2000); theories focusing on boys and men's development (Gurian, 1996, 1999; Gurian & Henly, 2001; Kindlon & Thompson, 1999; Newberger, 1999; Pollack, 1998, 2000); and theories prevalent in educational psychology (Ackerman, 1998; Carney & Levin, 1998; Fischer, 1980; Fischer & Granott, 1995; Froman, 1994; Granott, 1994, 1998; Pascual-Leone & Irwin, 1998; Smith & Pourchot, 1998; Torff & Sternberg, 1998). (I acknowledge Maria Broderick for creating the first three of these categories. For a more detailed discussion of the theories and their specific application to adult learning, see Helsing, Broderick, & Hammerman [2001] and Helsing, Drago-Severson, & Kegan, 2003).

3. Some of the ideas presented in this discussion also appear in Drago-Severson et al., 2001a, 2001b, 2001c; Drago-Severson & Berger, 2001; Helsing, Drago-Severson, Kegan, Popp, Broderick, & Portnow, 2001; Kegan et al., 2001a; Kegan et al., 2001b); these are cited herein.

Chapter 2

1. This research includes that by the research team (Drago-Severson et al., 2001a; Kegan et al., 2001a, 2001b) as well as earlier research (Basseches, 1984, Belenky et al., 1986; Daloz, 1983, 1986, 1999; Drago-Severson, 1996; Goodman, 1983; Kegan, 1982, 1994; Kohlberg, 1984; Piaget, 1952, 1963, 1965; Weathersby, 1976).

2. Some of the ideas discussed in this section also appear in Drago-Severson, 2004; Drago-Severson et al., 2001a; Drago-Severson & Berger, 2001; and Kegan et al., 2001a and are cited herein.

3. For a more detailed discussion of Piaget's theory, see Duckworth, 1987; and Kegan, 1982, 1994, 2000.

4. Other descriptions of Kegan's ways of knowing are presented in Drago-Severson, 2004; Kegan (1982, 1994); and Lahey et al. (1988).

5. The Golden Rule as commonly stated is "Do unto others as you would have them do unto you," from the Gospel of Matthew 7:12 and Luke 6:31. It is a common ethic of reciprocity in many of the world's religions.

6. For additional discussions of the time required for movement from one way of knowing to another, see Kegan (1982, 1994), and Helsing, Drago-Severson, and Kegan (2003).

Chapter 3

1. Several sections of this chapter describing the team's research methodology appear in a similar form in Chapter 2 of Kegan et al. (2001b) and are cited herein. Also, some descriptions of the CEI Adult Diploma Program appear in similar form in Drago-Severson (2001) and are cited herein.

2. Interrater reliability in studies using the original SOI measure has ranged from .75 to .90. Several studies report expectedly high correlations with like measures (cognitive and social-cognitive measures) (Kegan, 1994; Lahey et al., 1988).

3. After analyzing participants' initial responses to this measure, we decided not to administer it during our final data collection. This and other survey-type measures were the only protocols that we did not tape-record and transcribe.

Chapter 4

1. All Polaroid employees and program participants in this study are referred to by pseudonyms that I assigned, in accordance with confidentiality agreements.

2. My team, the Polaroid subteam, was able to interview only one of the three adults who did not complete the program. This employee, from the nearby company from which three adults initially enrolled, said that he needed to leave the program because he no longer had transportation from his workplace to the Polaroid site where the classes took place.

Chapter 5

1. Sections of this chapter appear in similar form in Drago-Severson and Berger, 2001.

2. A bit of explanation about how learner quotations are handled throughout the book. Words or phrases that are italicized in learner quotations highlight the structure of the learner's meaning-making. Ellipses in quotations note places where learners either repeated what was already said or stopped midway through and did not complete the thought. To provide a context, I have sometimes included the interviewer's questions; these are in italics and noted as "Interviewer." The interviewer's words/questions, however, are omitted from most quotations to place em-

phasis on the participants' words. All learners' names have been changed to aliases that I have assigned, in accordance with confidentiality agreements.

3. I acknowledge Jennifer Garvey Berger for her thoughtful contributions to parts of this section in the research monograph (Drago-Severson & Berger, 2001).

Chapter 6

1. Hope and Teresina spoke about the relational qualities of their teachers. Initially each demonstrated a 2/3 way of knowing. (In the X/Y position of the continuum from the instrumental to the socializing way of knowing, 2 represents an instrumental way of knowing, and 3 acts as the socializing perspective. See Chapter 2 for further explanation.) Toward the end of the program the team assessed Hope's meaning making to be 3/2. Although I will not discuss her case here, she also talked about the mutual trust and respect that is essential between teachers and learners. Helena, Angelina, and Veronica demonstrated a 3/2 way of knowing and also spoke about the relational qualities of their teachers.

2. Wanting to be recognized could be a demonstration of either a socializing or self-authoring way of knowing, depending on how a learner makes sense of what it means to be recognized.

Chapter 7

1. Some sections of this chapter illuminating the adult learners' program experiences appear in altered form in Drago-Severson, 2001.

2. Evers, Rush, and Berdrow (1998) point to the lack of clarity in defining what skills and competencies mean. They cite Attewell's (1990) definition of a skill—"the ability to do something"—and suggest that skill implies increasing ability—"while skill is synonymous with competence, it evokes images of expertise, mastery, and excellence" (p. 433, cited in Evers, Rush, & Berdrow, 1998, p. 24). Arguing that skills are "not possessed in isolation," Evers and colleagues suggest that "base competencies represent functionally related skill sets. All skills can be viewed on continua from low to high levels of competency" (p. 25). The research team agrees and maintains that it is essential to consider how workers with different ways of knowing demonstrate skills and competencies so that we might better support and challenge them (Popp & Boes, 2001). A developmental conception of competency is discussed in Chapter 8.

Chapter 8

1. A version of how the team understands this new pluralism appears in different form in Drago-Severson, 2001; Drago-Severson et al., 2001b, 2001c; and Kegan et al., 2001a, 2001b, as cited herein.

2. As shown in this book and discussed in Chapter 2, a person can be making sense of his or her experience with two ways of knowing operating concurrently. For example, in the constructive-developmental scoring system (Lahey et al., 1988),

a person can be making meaning at any of four transitional phases between two full ways of knowing. Across sites we found that when a person was making meaning with a socializing way of knowing operating along with the instrumental or self-authoring way of knowing, the socializing way of knowing was dominant.

3. Information about this ten-step cycle tool is available at the EFF Web site: http://www.nifl.gov/linc/collections/eff

Epilogue

1. A version of this text appears in Drago-Severson, 2001.

References

Ackerman, P. L. (1998). Adult intelligence: Sketch of a theory and applications. In M. C. Smith & T. Pourchot (Eds.), *Adult learning and development: Perspectives from educational psychology* (pp. 145–158). Mahwah, NJ: Lawrence Erlbaum Associates.

Arnett, J. J. (2000). Emerging adulthood: A theory of development from the late teens through the twenties. *American Psychologist, 55*(5), 469–480.

Aslanian, C. B., & Brickell, H. M. (1980). *Americans in transition: Life changes as reasons for adult learning.* New York: College Entrance Examination Board.

At Work @ Harvard (2002). Available from Harvard University, Office of Human Resources Web site: http://www.atwork. harvard.edu

Attewell, P. (1990). What is skill? *Work and occupations, 17,* 422–448.

Atwell, N. (1987). *In the middle: Writing, reading, and learning with adolescents.* Portsmouth, NH: Heinemann.

Barnett, B. G., & Muse, I. D. (1993). Cohort groups in educational administration: Promises and challenges. *Journal of School Leadership, 3*(4), 400–415.

Barton, D., & Hamilton, M. (1998). *Local literacies: A study of reading and writing in one community.* London: Routledge.

Basom, M., Yerkes, D., Norris, C., & Barnett, B. (1996). Using cohorts as a means for developing transformational leaders. *Journal of School Leadership, 6,* 99–112.

Basseches, M. (1984). *Dialectical thinking and adult development.* Norwood, NJ: Ablex.

Baumgartner, L., & Merriam, S. B. (Eds.). (2000). *Adult learning and development: Multicultural stories.* Malabar, FL: Krieger.

Baxter Magolda, M. B. (1992). *Knowing and reasoning in college: Gender-related patterns in students' intellectual development.* San Francisco: Jossey-Bass.

Beder, H. (1994). The current status of adult literacy education in the United States. *PAACE Journal of Lifelong Learning, 3,* 14–25.

Beder, H., & Medina, P. (2001). *Classroom dynamics in adult literacy education.* NCSALL Report #18. Boston: World Education.

Beder, H., Medina, P., & Eberly, M. (2000, June, Vancouver, British Columbia). *The adult literacy classroom as a social system.* Paper presented at the Adult Education Research Conference (AERC).

Belenky, M., Clinchy, B., Goldberger, N., & Tarule, J. (1986). *Women's ways of knowing.* New York: Basic Books.

Bingman, B., & Stein, S. (2001). *Results that matter: An EFF approach to quality using Equipped for the Future.* Washington, DC: National Institute for Literacy. Available from http://www.nifl.gov/linc/collections/eff/results_that_matter.pdf

Bosworth, K., & Hamilton, S. J. (Eds.). (1994). *Collaborative learning: Underlying processes and effective techniques.* San Francisco: Jossey-Bass.

Bransford, J. D., Brown, A. L., & Cocking, R. R. (Eds.). (1999). *How people learn: Brain, mind, experience, and school.* Washington, DC: National Academy Press.

Brod, S. (1995). Outreach and retention in adult ESL literacy programs. *ERIC Digest.* Washington, DC. (Eric Document Reproduction Service No. EDO-LE-95-01)

Broderick, M. A. (1996). *A certain doubleness: Reflexive thought and mindful experience as tools for transformative learning in the stress reduction clinic.* Unpublished doctoral dissertation, Harvard University Graduate School of Education, Cambridge, MA.

Brookfield, S. (1987). *Developing critical thinkers.* San Francisco: Jossey-Bass.

Brookfield, S. (1995). *Becoming a critically reflective teacher.* San Francisco: Jossey-Bass.

Brooks, A., & Clark, C. (2001, June, East Lansing, MI). *Narrative dimensions of transformative learning.* Paper presented at the Adult Education Research Conference (AERC) annual meeting. Available from: http://www.edst.educ.ubc.ca/aerc/2001/2001brooks.htm

Brown, L. M., & Gilligan, C. (1992). *Meeting and the crossroads: Women's psychology and girls' development.* New York: Ballantine Books.

Caffarella, R., & Olson, S. (1993). Psychosocial development of women: A critical review of the literature. *Adult Education Quarterly, 43*(3), 125–151.

Calkins, L. M. (1986). *The art of teaching writing.* Portsmouth, NH: Heinemann.

Carney, R. N., & Levin, J. R. (1998). Mnemonic strategies for adult learners. In M. C. Smith & T. Pourchot (Eds.), *Adult learning and development: Perspectives from educational psychology* (pp. 159–175). Mahwah, NJ: Lawrence Erlbaum Associates.

Center for Workforce Preparation (2002, Spring). *A chamber guide to improving workplace literacy: Higher skills Bottom-line results.* Washington, DC: Center for Workforce Preparation, U.S. Chamber of Commerce.

Chappell, C. (1996). Quality & competency based education and training. In *The Literacy Equation* (pp. 71–79). Red Hill, Australia: Queensland Council for Adult Literacy.

Chevalier, M. (1994). Developing a trusting community: Dilemmas in ESL adult instruction. *Adult Basic Education, 4*(1), 3–8.

Ciulla, J. B. (2000). *The working life: The promise and betrayal of modern work.* New York: Random House.

Cofer, D. A. (2000). *Informal workplace learning.* Practice Application Brief no. 10, 1–5. Available from http://www.cete.org/acve/docgen.asp?tbl=pab&ID=100

Coffey, A., & Atkinson, P. (1996). *Making sense of qualitative data: Complementary research strategies.* Thousand Oaks, CA: Sage.

Coleman, C. (2002). Who helps the helpers? Supporting counselors in adult basic education. *Focus on Basics, 6*(A), 1–8. Available from http://ncsall.gse.harvard .edu/fob/2002/ coleman.html

Comings, J., & Cuban, S. (2002). Sponsors and sponsorship: Initial findings from the second phase of the NCSALL persistence study. *Focus on Basics, 6*(A), 1–5. Available from http://ncsall. gse.harvard.edu/fob/2002/comings.html

Comings, J., Parrella, A., & Cuban, S. (2001, April). *So I made up my mind: A study of adult learner persistence in library literacy programs.* Paper presented at the American educational research association conference (AERA), Seattle, WA.

Comings, J., Reder, S., & Sum, A. (2001). *Building a level playing field: The need to expand and improve the national and state adult education systems.* NCSALL [Occasional Paper]. Boston: World Education.

Comings, J., Sum, A., & Uvin, J., with Fogg, W. N., Palma, S., Santos, M., Soricone, L., & Trub'skyy, M. (2000, December). *New skills for a new economy: Adult education's key role in sustaining economic growth and expanding opportunity.* Boston: The Massachusetts Institute for a New Commonwealth.

Continuing Education Institute (1992). *Program materials.* Watertown, MA: Author.

Continuing Education Institute (1997). *Program materials.* Watertown, MA: Author.

Cranton, P. (1994). *Understanding and promoting transformative learning: A guide for educators of adults.* San Francisco: Jossey-Bass.

Cranton, P. (1996). *Professional development as transformational learning: New perspectives for teachers of adults.* San Francisco: Jossey-Bass.

Cross, K. P. (1971). *Beyond the open door: New students to higher education.* San Francisco: Jossey-Bass.

Cross, K. P. (1981). *Adults as learners: Increasing participation and facilitating learning.* San Francisco: Jossey-Bass.

Daloz, L. A. (1983). Mentors: Teachers who make a difference. *Change, 15*(6), 24–27.

Daloz, L. (1986). *Effective teaching and mentoring.* San Francisco: Jossey-Bass.

Daloz, L. (1999). *Mentor.* San Francisco: Jossey-Bass.

D'Amico, D., Lentz, D., Smith, R. L., & Taylor, M. L. (2002). Building participation in workplace learning programs. *Focus on Basics, 6*(A), 1–9. Available from http://ncsall.gse. harvard.edu/fob/2002/damico.html

Diener, E., Emmons, R. A., Larsen, R. J., & Griffen, S. (1985). The satisfaction with life scale. *Journal of Personality Assessment, 49,* 71–75.

Dirkx, J. M., Amey, M., & Haston, L. (1999). Context in the contextualized curriculum: Adult life worlds as unity or multiplistic? In A. Austin, G. E. Nynes, & R. T. Miller (Eds.), *Proceedings of the 18th Annual Midwest Research to Practice Conference in Adult, Continuing, and Community Education* (pp. 79–84). St. Louis: University of Missouri at St. Louis. (ERIC Document Service Reproduction No. 447 269)

Drago-Severson, E. (1996). *Head of school as principal adult developer: An ac-*

count of one leader's efforts to support transformational learning among the adults in the school. Unpublished doctoral dissertation, Harvard University Graduate School of Education, Cambridge, MA.

Drago-Severson, E. (2001, August). "We're trying to get ahead": A developmental view of changes in Polaroid learners' conceptions of their motivations for learning, expectations of teachers, and relationship to work. In R. Kegan, M. Broderick, E. Drago-Severson, D. Helsing, N. Popp, K. Portnow, & Associates (Eds.), *Toward a "new pluralism" in the ABE/ESL classroom: Teaching to multiple "cultures of mind"* (pp. 477–614). NCSALL Monograph #19. Boston: World Education.

Drago-Severson, E. (2002a, April). *Adult development researchers' reflections on using multiple research methods with ABE/ESOL populations.* Paper presented at the annual meeting of the American Educational Research Association, New Orleans, LA.

Drago-Severson, E. (2002b, April). *School leadership in support of teachers' transformational learning: The dramatic differences resources make.* Paper presented at the annual meeting of the American Educational Research Association, New Orleans, LA.

Drago-Severson, E. (2003, March). *Building leadership capacity and supporting adult development: Innovative practices for transformational learning.* Paper presented at the Association for Supervision and Curriculum Development (ASCD) conference, San Francisco, CA.

Drago-Severson, E. (2004). *Helping teachers learn: Principal leadership for adult growth and development.* Thousand Oaks, CA: Corwin Press.

Drago-Severson, E., Asghar, A., & Stuebner Gaylor, S. (2003, April). *Reflections on teaching a qualitative data analysis course: Creating a space for researcher development.* Paper presented at the annual meeting of the American Educational Research Association, Chicago, IL.

Drago-Severson, E., & Berger, J. G. (2001, August). "Not I alone": The power of adult learning in the Polaroid cohort. In R. Kegan, M. Broderick, E. Drago-Severson, D. Helsing, N. Popp, K. Portnow, & Associates (Eds.), *Toward a "new pluralism" in the ABE/ESL classroom: Teaching to multiple "cultures of mind"* (pp. 379–476). NCSALL Monograph #19. Boston: World Education.

Drago-Severson, E., Helsing, D., Kegan, R., Portnow, K., Popp, N., & Broderick, M. (2001a, October). Describing the NCSALL adult development research. *Focus on Basics, 5*(B), 3–6.

Drago-Severson, E., Helsing, D., Kegan, R., Popp, N., Broderick, M., & Portnow, K. (2001b, October). The power of a cohort and of collaborative groups. *Focus on Basics, 5*(B), 15–22.

Drago-Severson, E., Kegan, R., Helsing, D., Broderick, M., Popp, N., & Portnow, K. (2001c, October). Three developmentally different types of learners. *Focus on Basics, 5*(B), 7–9.

Drago-Severson, E., & Pinto, K. (in press). From barriers to breakthroughs: Principals' strategies for overcoming challenges to teachers' transformational learning. *The Journal of School Leadership.*

Duckworth, E. (1987). *"The having of wonderful ideas" and other essays on teaching and learning.* New York: Teachers College Press.

Eble, K. E., & Noonan, J. F. (1983). *Learning in Groups.* San Francisco: Jossey-Bass.

Ecclestone, K. (1997). Energizing or Enervating? *Journal of Vocational Education and Training, 49*(1), 65–79.

Erikson, E. (1964). *Childhood and society.* New York: W. W. Norton.

Erikson, E. (1968). *Identity: Youth and crisis.* New York: W. W. Norton.

Evers, F. T., Rush, J. C., & Berdrow, I. (1998). *The bases of competence: Skills for lifelong learning and employability.* San Francisco: Jossey-Bass.

Fingeret, H. A., & Drennon, C. (1997). *Literacy for life: Adult learners, new practices.* New York: Teachers College Press.

Fischer, K. (1980). A theory of cognitive development: The control and construction of hierarchies of skills. *Psychological Review, 87,* 477–531.

Fischer, K., & Granott, N. (1995). Beyond one-dimensional change: Multiple, concurrent, socially distributed processes in learning and development. *Human Development, 38,* 302–314.

Flannery, J. (1994). Teacher as co-conspirator: Knowledge and authority in collaborative learning. In K. Bosworth & S. J. Hamilton (Eds.), *Collaborative learning: Underlying processes and effective techniques* (pp. 15–23). San Francisco: Jossey-Bass.

Froman, L. (1994). Adult learning in the workplace. In J. D. Sinnot (Ed.), *Interdisciplinary handbook of adult lifespan learning* (pp. 159–170). Westport, CT: Greenwood.

Gerlach, J. M. (1994). Is this collaboration? In K. Bosworth & S. J. Hamilton (Eds.), *Collaborative learning: Underlying processes and effective techniques* (pp. 5–14). San Francisco: Jossey-Bass.

Geertz, C. (1974). "From the native's point of view": On the nature of anthropological understanding. *Bulletin of the American Academy of Arts and Sciences, 28,* 221–237.

Gillespie, M. K. (2002a). EFF research principle: An approach to teaching and learning that builds expertise. *EFF Research to Practice Note, 2,* 1–8. Washington, DC: National Institute for Literacy.

Gillespie, M. K. (2002b). EFF research principle: A contextualized approach to curriculum and instruction. *EFF Research to Practice Note, 3,* 1–8. Washington, DC: National Institute for Literacy.

Gilligan, C. (1977). In a different voice: Women's conceptions of self and of morality. *Harvard Educational Review, 47,* 481–517.

Gilligan, C. (1982). *In a different voice: Psychological theory and women's development.* Cambridge, MA: Harvard University Press.

Glaser, R. (1992). Expert knowledge and processes of thinking. In D. F. Halpern (Ed.), *Enhancing thinking skills in the sciences and mathematics.* Hillside, NJ: Lawrence Erlbaum Associates.

Glaser, B. G., & Strauss, A. L. (1967). *The discovery of grounded theory: Strategies for qualitative research.* Hawthorne, NY: Aldine de Gruyter.

Goldberger, N. R., Tarule, J. M., Clinchy, B. M., & Belenky, M. F. (1996). *Knowledge, difference, and power: Essays inspired by women's ways of knowing.* New York: Basic Books.

Goodman, R. (1983). *A developmental and systems analysis of marital and family communication in clinic and non-clinic families.* Unpublished doctoral dissertation, Harvard University Graduate School of Education, Cambridge, MA.

Gowen, S. G. (1992). *The politics of workplace literacy: A case study.* New York: Teachers College Press.

Granott, N. (1994). Microdevelopment of coconstruction of knowledge during problem solving: Puzzled minds, weird creatures, and wuggles. *Dissertation Abstracts International, 54*(10–B), 5409.

Granott, N. (1998). We learn, therefore we develop: Learning versus development—or developing learning? In M. C. Smith & T. Pourchot (Eds.), *Adult learning and development: Perspectives from educational psychology* (pp. 15–34). Mahwah, NJ: Lawrence Erlbaum Associates.

Graves, D. H. (1991). *Build a literate classroom.* Portsmouth, NH: Heinemann.

Green, B. (1995). *Setting performance standards: Content, goals and individual differences.* Paper presented at the annual William Angoff Memorial Lecture. Princeton, NJ: Education Testing Service.

Greeno, J. G., Resnick, L. B., & Collins, A. M. (1997). Cognition and learning. In D. Berliner & R. Calfee (Eds.), *Handbook of educational psychology* (pp. 15–46). New York: Simon & Schuster Macmillan.

Grow, G. (1991). Teaching learners to be self-directed. *Adult Education Quarterly, 41*(3), 125–149.

Gurian, M. (1996). *The wonder of boys: What parents, mentors, and educators can do to shape boys into exceptional men.* New York: Putnam.

Gurian, M. (1999). *The good son: Shaping the moral development of our boys and young men.* New York: Jeremy P. Tarcher.

Gurian, M., & Henley, P. (2001). *How boys and girls learn differently!: A guide for teachers and parents.* San Francisco: Jossey-Bass.

Hamilton, S. J. (1994). Freedom transformed: Toward a developmental model for the construction of collaborative learning environments. In K. Bosworth & S. J. Hamilton (Eds.), *Collaborative learning: Underlying processes and effective techniques* (pp. 93–101). San Francisco: Jossey-Bass.

Hammer, M., & Champy, J. (1993). *Reengineering the corporation: A manifesto for business revolution.* New York: HarperCollins.

Harbison, A., with Kegan, R. (1999). *Best practice programs in professional education: A working paper prepared for programs in professional education, Harvard Graduate School of Education.* Unpublished manuscript.

Heard, G. (1989). *For the good of the earth and sun: Teaching poetry.* Portsmouth, NH: Heinemann.

Helsing, D., Drago-Severson, E., & Kegan, R. (2003). Applying Constructive-Developmental Theories of Adult Development to ABE/ESOL Practice. *The Annual Review of Adult Learning and Literacy, 4.* Mahwah, NJ: Lawrence Erlbaum Associates.

Helsing, D., Drago-Severson, E., Kegan, R., Popp, N., Broderick, M., & Portnow, K. (2001, October). ABE/ESL learners' experiences of change. *Focus on Basics, 5B,* 10–14.

Helsing, D., Broderick, M., & Hammerman, J. (2001, August). A developmental view of ESL students' identity transitions in an urban community college. In R. Kegan, M. Broderick, E. Drago-Severson, D. Helsing, N. Popp, K. Portnow, & Associates (Eds.), *Toward a "new pluralism" in the ABE/ESL classroom: Teaching to multiple "cultures of mind"* (pp. 77–228). NCSALL Monograph #19. Boston: World Education.

Hill, M. S. (1995). Educational leadership cohort models: Changing the talk to change the walk. *Planning and changing, 26,* 179–189.

Horsman, J. (1991). From the learner's voice: Women's experiences of il/literacy. In M. Taylor & J. Draper (Eds.), *Adult literacy perspectives.* Ontario, Canada: Cultural Concepts.

Hunter, C., & Harman, D. (1979). *Adult illiteracy in the United States.* New York: McGraw-Hill.

Hyland, T. (1994). *Competence, education and NVQs: Dissenting perspectives.* London: Cassell.

Imel, S. (2000). *Contextual learning in adult education.* Practice Application Brief no. 12, 1–5. Available from http://www.cete.org/acve/docgen.asp?tbl=pab &ID=102

Imel, S. (2001). *Learning communities/communities practice.* Trends and Issues Alert no. 26, 1–5. Available from http://www.cete.org/acve/docgen.asp?tbl= tia&ID=148

Jordan, J. V., Kaplan, A. G., Miller, J. B., Stiver, I. P., & Surrey, J. L. (Eds.). (1991). *Women's growth in connection: Writings from the stone center.* New York: The Guilford Press.

Josselson, R. E. (1992). *The space between us: Exploring the dimensions of human relationships.* San Francisco: Jossey-Bass.

Kegan, R. (1982). *The evolving self: Problems and process in human development.* Cambridge, MA: Harvard University Press.

Kegan, R. (1994). *In over our heads: The mental demands of modern life.* Cambridge, MA: Harvard University Press.

Kegan, R. (2000). What "form" transforms?: A constructive-developmental approach to transformative learning. In J. Mezirow and Associates (Eds.), *Learning As Transformation* (pp. 35–70). San Francisco: Jossey-Bass.

Kegan, R., Broderick, M., Drago-Severson, E., Helsing, D., Popp, N., & Portnow, K. (2001a). *Executive summary: Toward a "new pluralism" in the ABE/ESOL classroom: Teaching to multiple "cultures of mind."* NCSALL Monograph #19a. Boston: World Education.

Kegan, R., Broderick, M., Drago-Severson, E., Helsing, D., Popp, N., & Portnow, K. (2001b). *Toward a "new pluralism" in the ABE/ESOL classroom: Teaching to multiple "cultures of mind."* NCSALL Monograph #19. Boston: World Education.

Kegan, R., & Lahey, L. L. (1984). Adult leadership and adult development. In B.

Kellerman (Ed.), *Leadership: Multidisciplinary perspectives* (pp. 199–230). New York: Prentice-Hall.

Kegan, R., & Lahey, L. L. (2001). *How the way we talk can change the way we work: Seven languages for transformation.* San Francisco: Jossey-Bass/Wiley.

Kerka, S. (1998). *Competency-based education and training: Myths and realities.* Washington, DC: Office of Educational Research and Improvement. (ERIC Document Reproduction Service No. ED 415 430).

Kerka, S. (2002). *Journal writing as an adult learning tool: Practice application brief.* Available from http://ericacve.org/docgen.asp?tbl=pab&ID=112

Killion, J. (2000, December/January). Exemplary schools model quality staff development. *Results, 3.*

Kindlon, D., & Thompson, M. (1999). *Raising Cain: Protecting the emotional life of boys.* New York: Ballantine Books.

King, K. M., & Kitchener, K. S. (1994). *Developing reflective judgment: Understanding and promoting intellectual growth and critical thinking in adolescents and adults.* San Francisco: Jossey-Bass.

Kirsch, I., Jungeblut, A., Jenkins, L., & Kolstad, A. (1993). *Adult literacy in America: A first look at the results of the national adult literacy survey.* Washington, DC: U.S. Department of Education.

Kitchener, K. S., & King, P. (1994). *Developing reflective judgment.* San Francisco: Jossey-Bass.

Knowles, M. S. (1970). *The modern practice of adult education: Androgogy versus pedagogy.* New York: Association Press.

Knowles, M. S. (1975). *Self-directed learning: A guide for learners and teachers.* New York: Association Press.

Knowles, M. S. (1980). *The modern practice of adult education: From pedagogy to androgogy.* New York: Association Press.

Knowles, M. S. (1984). *The adult learner: A neglected species* (3rd ed.). Houston, TX: Gulf.

Knox, A. B. (1981). *Adult development and learning.* San Francisco: Jossey-Bass.

Kohlberg, L. (1969). Stage and sequence: The cognitive-developmental approach to socialization. In R. A. Goslin (Ed.), *Handbook of socialization theory and research.* New York: Rand-McNally.

Kohlberg, L. (1984). *Stage and sequence: The cognitive developmental approach to socialization: The psychology of moral development.* San Francisco: Harper & Row.

Lahey, L., Souvaine, E., Kegan, R., Goodman, R., & Felix, S. (1988). *A guide to the subject-object interview: Its administration and interpretation.* Unpublished manuscript.

Levinson, D. J. (1978). *The seasons of a man's life.* New York: Ballantine Books.

Levinson, D. J. (1996). *The seasons of a woman's life.* New York: Ballantine Books.

Loevinger, J., & Wessler, R. (1970). *Measuring ego development: Volume one.* San Francisco: Jossey-Bass.

Luttrell, W. (1997). *School-smart and mother-wise: Working-class women's identity and schooling.* New York: Routledge.

Lytle, S. L. (1991). Living literacy: Rethinking development in adulthood. *Linguistics and Education, 3,* 109–138.

Lytle, S. L., & Cochran-Smith, M. (1990). Learning from teacher-research: A working typology. *Teachers College Record, 92*(1), 83–103.

Lytle, S., Marmor, T., & Penner, F. (1986). *Literacy theory in practice: Assessing reading and writing of low-literate adults.* Unpublished manuscript, University of Pennsylvania, Graduate School of Education, Philadelphia.

Lytle, S. L., & Schultz, K. (1990). Assessing literacy learning with adults: An ideological approach. In R. Beach & S. Hynds (Eds.), *Developing discourse processes in adolescence and adulthood.* Norwood, NJ: Ablex.

Malicky, G., & Norman, C. (1997). Participation patterns in adult literacy programs. *Adult Basic Education, 4*(3), 144–156.

Marsick, V. J., Bitterman, J., & van der Veen, R. (2000). *From the learning organization to learning communities toward a learning society.* Information Series no. 382, Columbus: ERIC Clearinghouse on Adult, Career, and Vocational Education, Office of Education and Training for Employment, College of Education, The Ohio State University. (ERIC Document Service Reproduction No. ED 440 294). Available from http://ericacve.org/majorpubs.asp

Maxwell, J. A. (1996). *Qualitative research design: An interactive approach.* Thousand Oaks, CA: Sage.

Maxwell, J., & Miller, B. (1991). *Categorization and contextualization as components of qualitative data analysis.* Unpublished manuscript.

McEwan, H., & Egan, K. (1995). *Narrative in teaching, learning, and research.* New York: Teachers College Press.

Merriam, S. B. (1998). *Qualitative research and case study applications in education.* San Francisco: Jossey-Bass.

Merriam-Webster's dictionary (8th ed). (1974). New York: Pocket Books.

Meyers, C., & Erdmann, D. (1985). Using a sensitive topic in teaching lecture comprehension. *MinneTESOL Journal, 5,* 75–83.

Mezirow, J. (1991). *Transformative dimensions of adult learning.* San Francisco: Jossey-Bass.

Mezirow, J. (1994). Understanding transformation theory. *Adult education quarterly, 44*(4), 222–244.

Mezirow, J. (1996). Contemporary paradigms of learning. *Adult education quarterly, 46*(3), 158–172.

Mezirow, J. (2000). Learning to think like an adult: Core concepts of transformation theory. In J. Mezirow (Ed.), *Learning as transformation: Critical perspectives on a theory in progress* (pp. 3–33). San Francisco: Jossey-Bass.

Mezirow, J., & Associates. (1990). *Fostering critical reflection in adulthood: A guide to transformative and emancipatory learning.* San Francisco: Jossey-Bass.

Mezirow, J., & Associates. (2000). *Learning as transformation: Critical perspectives on a theory in progress.* San Francisco: Jossey-Bass.

Miles, M. B., & Huberman, A. M. (1994). *An expanded sourcebook: Qualitative data analysis.* Thousand Oaks, CA: Sage.

Miller, J. B. (1976). *Toward a new psychology of women*. Boston: Beacon Press.

Miller, J. B. (1991). The development of women's sense of self. In J. Jordan, A. Kaplan, J. B. Miller, I. Stiver, & J. Surrey (Eds.), *Women's growth in connection*. New York: Guilford Press.

Mishler, E. G. (1986). *Research interviewing: Context and narrative*. Cambridge, MA: Harvard University Press.

Murnane, R., & Levy, F. (1996). *Teaching the new basic skills*. New York: The Free Press.

Nash, A., & Gillespie, M. (2002). *EFF teaching and learning toolkit*. Knoxville, TN: EFF National Center and Assessment Consortium. Available from http://www.nifl.gov/linc/collections/eff

National Institute for Literacy Policy Update (1998). Workforce Investment Act offers opportunities for adult and family literacy. Available from http://www.nifl.gov/policy/98-9-23.htm.

Newberger, E. (1999). *The men they will become: The nature and nurture of male character*. Reading, MA: Perseus Books.

Osterman, K. F., & Kottkamp, R. B. (1993). *Reflective practice for educators: Improving schooling through professional development*. Thousand Oaks, CA: Corwin Press.

Pascual-Leone, J., & Irwin, R. (1998). Abstraction, the will, the self, and modes of learning in adulthood? In M. C. Smith & T. Pourchot (Eds.), *Adult learning and development: Perspectives from educational psychology* (pp. 35–66). Mahwah, NJ: Lawrence Erlbaum Associates.

Pearlin, L., & Schooler, C. (1978). The structure of coping. *The Journal of Health and Social Research, 19*, 2–21.

Pedersen, J. E., & Digby, J. E. (1995). *Secondary schools and cooperative learning: Theories, models, and strategies*. New York: Garland Publishing.

Peirce, B. N. (1995). Social identity, investment and language learning. *TESOL Quarterly, 29*(1), 9–31.

Perry, W. G. Jr. (1970). *Forms of intellectual and ethical development in the college years*. New York: Holt, Rinehart & Winston.

Piaget, J. (1952). *The origins of intelligence in children*. New York: International Universities Press.

Piaget, J. (1963). *The child's conception of the world*. Patterson, NJ: Littlefield, Adams.

Piaget, J. (1965). *The moral judgment of the child*. New York: Free Press.

Pollack, W. (1998). *Real boys: Rescuing our sons from the myths of boyhood*. New York: Random House.

Pollack, W. (2000). *Real boys' voices*. Melbourne: Scribe Publications.

Popp, N. (1993). The concept and phenomenon of psychological boundaries from a dialectical perspective: An empirical investigation. Unpublished doctoral dissertation. Harvard University Graduate School of Education, Cambridge, MA.

Popp, N. (2001, August). Appendix B: Developmental skills matrices. In R. Kegan, M. Broderick, E. Drago-Severson, D. Helsing, N. Popp, & K. Portnow, (Eds.), *Toward a "new pluralism" in the ABE/ESOL classroom: Teaching to multiple "cultures of mind"* (p. 727). NCSALL Research Monograph #19. Boston: World Education.

Popp, N., & Boes, L. (2001, August). Competence as a developmental process. In R. Kegan, M. Broderick, E. Drago-Severson, D. Helsing, N. Popp, K. Portnow, & Associates (Eds.), *Toward a "new pluralism" in the ABE/ESL classroom: Teaching to multiple "cultures of mind"* (pp. 615–662). NCSALL Research Monograph #19. Boston: World Education.

Popp, N., & Portnow, K. (2001, August). Our developmental perspective on adulthood. In R. Kegan, M. Broderick, E. Drago-Severson, D. Helsing, N. Popp, & K. Portnow (Eds.), *Toward a "new pluralism" in the ABE/ESOL classroom: Teaching to multiple "cultures of mind"* (pp. 43–76). NCSALL Research Monograph #19. Boston: World Education.

Portnow, K. (1996). *Dialogues of doubt: The psychology of self-doubt and emotional gaslighting in adult women and men.* Unpublished doctoral dissertation, Harvard University Graduate School of Education, Cambridge, MA.

Portnow, K., Diamond, A., & Rimer, K. P. (2001, August). "Becoming what I really am": Stories of personal creation, recreation, and "refreshment" in an Even Start ABE/ESL family literacy program: A developmental perspective. In R. Kegan, M. Broderick, E. Drago-Severson, D. Helsing, N. Popp, K. Portnow, & Associates (Eds.), *Toward a "new pluralism" in the ABE/ESL classroom: Teaching to multiple "cultures of mind"* (pp. 229–378). NCSALL Research Monograph #19. Boston: World Education.

Portnow, K., Popp, N., Broderick, M., Drago-Severson, E., & Kegan, R. (1998). Transformational learning in adulthood. *Focus on Basics, 2*(D), 22–27.

Purcell-Gates, V. (1995). *Other people's words: The cycle of low literacy.* Cambridge, MA: Harvard University Press.

Quigley, B. A. (1989). Literacy as social policy: Issues for America in the Twenty-first century. *Thresholds in Education, 15*(4), 11–15.

Quigley, B. A. (1993). To shape the future: Towards a framework for adult education, social policy research and action. *International Journal of Lifelong Education, 12*(2), 117–127.

Quigley, B. A. (1997). *Rethinking literacy education: The critical need for practice-based change.* San Francisco: Jossey-Bass.

Riggs, M. L., Warka, J., Babasa, B., Betancourt, R., & Hooker, S. (1994). Development and validation of self-efficacy and outcome expectations for job-related applications. *Educational and Psychological Measurement, 54*(3), 793–802.

Rockhill, K. (1982). *Language training by Latino immigrant workers: The sociocultural context.* Unpublished report to the National Institute of Education, Washington, DC.

Rogers, D. L., & Babinski, L. (1999). Breaking through isolation with new teacher groups. *Educational Leadership, 56*(8), 38–40.

Ross-Gordon, J. (1999). Gender development and gendered adult development. In M. C. Clark & R. S. Caffarella (Eds.), *An update of adult development theory: New ways of thinking about the life course* (pp. 29–38). San Francisco: Jossey-Bass.

Rossiter, M. (1999). A narrative approach to development: Implications for adult education. *Adult Education Quarterly, 50*(1), 56–71.

Scarf, M. (1980). *Unfinished business: Pressure points in the lives of women.* New York: Ballantine Books.

Schön, D. A. (1983). *The reflective practitioner: How professionals think in action.* New York: Basic Books.

Selman, R., & Schultz, L. H. (1990). *Making a friend in youth: Developmental theory and pair therapy.* Chicago: University of Chicago Press.

Skilton-Sylvester, E., & Carlo, M. S. (1998). *"I want to learn English": Examining the goals and motivations of adult ESL students in three Philadelphia learning sites.* National Center for the study of adult learning and literacy. Philadelphia: University of Pennsylvania. NCAL Technical Report TR98–08.

Smith, B., & MacGregor, J. (1992). What is collaborative learning? In A. Goodspell et al. (Eds.), *Collaborative learning: A sourcebook for higher education.* University Park, PA: National Center on Postsecondary Teaching and Learning Assessment.

Smith, M. C., & Pourchot, T. (1998). Toward adult educational psychology. In M. C. Smith & T. Pourchot (Eds.), *Adult learning and development: Perspectives from educational psychology* (pp. 259–266). Mahwah, NJ: Lawrence Erlbaum Associates.

Stein, S. (2000). *Equipped for the Future content standards: What adults need to know and be able to do in the twenty-first century.* Washington, DC: National Institute for Literacy.

Stein, S. (2002). *What family life demands: A purposeful view of competent performance.* Paper presented at the OECD Program DeSeCo Definition and Selection of Key Competencies Symposium, February 11–13, in Geneva, Switzerland. Swiss Federal Statistics Office.

Stites, R. (2002). *Assessing results that matter: Equipped for the future's approach to assessment for adult basic education accountability and improvement.* Working draft presented at the EFF Assessment Consortium.

Strauss, A., & Corbin, J. (1998). *Basics of qualitative research: Techniques and procedures for developing grounded theory.* Thousand Oaks, CA: Sage.

Taylor, F. W. (1911). *The principles of scientific management.* New York: Harper & Brothers.

Taylor, K. (1996). Why psychological models of adult development are important for the practice of adult education: A response to Courtenay. *Adult education quarterly, 46*(4), 54–62.

Taylor, K. (2000, June). *Relational aspects of adult development theory.* Paper presented at the Adult Education Research Conference, Vancouver, British Columbia.

Taylor, K., Marienau, C., & Fiddler, M. (2000). *Developing adult learners: Strategies for teachers and trainers.* San Francisco, CA: Jossey-Bass.

Teitel, L. (1997). Understanding and harnessing the power of the cohort model in preparing educational leaders. *Peabody Journal of Education, 72*(2), 66–85.

Tennant, M., & Pogson, P. (1995). *Learning and change in the adult years: A developmental perspective.* San Francisco: Jossey-Bass.

Tinberg, H., & Weisberger, R. (1997). In over our heads: Applying Kegan's theory of development to community college students. *Community College Review, 26*(2), 43–56.

Torff, B., & Sternberg, R. J. (1998). Changing mind, changing world: Practical intelligence and tacit knowledge in adult learning. In M. C. Smith & T. Pourchot (Eds.), *Adult learning and development: Perspectives from educational psychology* (pp. 109–126). Mahwah, NJ: Lawrence Erlbaum Associates.

Trimbur, J. (1993, March 5). Keynote address to the Indiana University Colloquium on Collaborative Learning, Indianapolis.

Vaillant, G. E. (1977). *Adaptation to Life.* Boston: Little, Brown.

Vaishnav, A., & Greenberger, S. (2001, January 7). Workers in state lack new job skills. *The Boston Globe,* pp. 1, 22.

Valentine, T. (1990). What motivates non-English-speaking adults to participate in the federal English-as-a-second-language program? *Research on adult basic education, 2.*

Weathersby, R. (1976). *A synthesis of research and theory on adult development: Its implications for adult learning and postsecondary education.* Unpublished qualifying paper. Harvard Graduate School of Education, Cambridge, MA.

Whitehurst, R. (2002). OERI chief lectures state officials on "evidence-based" curricula. *Report of Literacy Programs: The Biweekly Newsletter on Basic Skills and Workplace Literacy, 14*(20), 153–160.

Wigfield, A., Eccles, J. S., & Pintrich, P. R. (1996). Development between the ages of 11 and 25. In D. C. Berliner & R. C. Calfee (Eds.), *Handbook of educational psychology* (pp. 148–185). New York: Simon & Schuster Macmillan.

Wikelund, K., Reder, S., & Hart-Landsberg, S. (1992). *Expanding theories of adult literacy participation: A literature review.* (Technical Report TR92–1). Philadelphia: NCAL.

Wiley, T. G. (1993). Back from the past: Prospects and possibilities for multicultural education. *Journal of General Education, 42*(4), 280–300.

Winnicott, D. (1965). *The maturation processes and the facilitating environment.* New York: International Universities Press.

Wortley, D., & Amatea, E. (1982). Mapping adult life changes. *Personnel and Guidance Journal, 480.*

Wrigley, H. S., & Guth, G. J. A. (1992). *Bringing literacy to life: Issues and options in adult ESL literacy.* San Mateo, CA: Aguille International, U. S. Department of Education Office of Vocational and Adult Education. (ERIC Document Reproduction Service No. ED 348 896)

Index

ABE. *See* Adult Basic Education (ABE) programs/field
Abstract thinking, 25, 26, 27, 73, 115, 131–32, 133, 147, 161
Academic learning, 12, 65, 71, 72, 82, 89, 99, 156, 157
Acculturative change, 13, 129–30
Adult Basic Education (ABE) programs/field
  ancillary supports for, 160
  and constructive-developmental approach, 3
  contributions of research study to, 14–16
  expansion of, 5–8
  and implications of new pluralism, 154
  and influence of cohorts, 66
  need for research about, 5–6
  overview of, 3–8
  as principal support for helping adult literacy, 3
  purposes and outcomes of, 7–8, 103
  reconceptualization of, 15
  retention rates in, 103–4, 155–56, 157
Adult Diploma Program. *See* Continuing Education Institute (CEI) Adult Diploma Program
Adult Education and Family Literacy Act, 175
Amey, M., 162
Ancillary supports, 160
Angelina (Polaroid learner), 114, 115, 134–37
Applied Knowledge Program (Polaroid), 55, 141–42

Asghar, A., 158
Aslanian, C. B., 72
Atkinson, P., 48, 49
Atwell, N., 7

Babasa, B., 44
Babinski, L., 170
Barnett, B. G., 67
Barton, D., 175
Basom, M., 67
Basseches, M., 20
Baumgartner, L., 164
Baxter Magolda, M. B., 20
Beder, H., 3, 66, 103, 104, 155–56, 175
Belenky, M., 17, 20, 126
Beliefs, acting on, 122–23
Benchmarking, 59
Berdrow, I., 4, 8, 103
Berger, J. G., 9, 36, 65, 66, 129, 154, 157
Betancourt, R., 44
Bill (Polaroid learner)
  and change in learners' conceptions of self, skills, and relationship to work, 127, 131–32, 133
  and learners' expectations of teachers, 106–13, 116, 124
  and power of cohorts and collaborative learning, 73–76, 90, 91, 94–96, 98, 99
Bingman, B., 9, 66, 163, 173, 174
Bitterman, J., 162
Boes, L., 9, 44, 129, 154, 168, 172
Books and print materials, referencing, 166–67

Bosworth, K., 66, 68, 89, 90
Bransford, J. D., 164
Brickell, H. M., 72
Bridge to Learning and Literacy (Harvard University), 158–60, 174
Brod, S., 104
Broderick, M. A.
  and ABE/ESOL as expanding field, 5–8
  and change in learners' conceptions of self, skills, and relationship to work, 129, 130
  and cohorts and collaborative learning, 65, 66, 72
  and competencies, 167, 168
  and constructive-developmental approach, 7, 8, 9, 17, 18, 20, 21, 22, 23, 25, 33, 36, 172
  and contributions to ABE/ESOL field, 14, 15
  and curriculum, 160, 161, 163, 164, 168
  and holding environments, 11, 36
  and implications of new pluralism, 154, 155, 156, 157, 160, 161, 163, 164, 167, 168, 172, 174, 175, 176, 178
  and learners' expectations, 15
  as member of adult development study team, 8, 9, 10
  and pedagogy, 7
  and policymaking, 172, 174
  and program design, 156, 157
  and promising avenues for developmental research, 175, 176
  and research methods, 39, 40, 50
  and ways of knowing, 13, 14, 17, 18, 22, 23, 25, 33, 155, 172, 178
Brookfield, Stephen, 7, 19, 126, 170
Brooks, A., 161, 169–70
Brown, A. L., 164
Bunker Hill Community College (Chelsea, Massachusetts), 9, 38–39. See also Community college site

Calkins, L. M., 7
Carlo, M. S., 6
Cathedral High School (Boston, Massachusetts), 59, 181, 184
CEI. See Continuing Education Institute; Polaroid Learning Site
Center for Workforce Preparation, 129
Champy, J., 59
Change
  and core findings of research study, 11–12
  in learners' conceptions of self, skills, and relationship to work, 129–53
  motion of, 150
  and overview of book, 13
  See also type of change
Chappell, C., 8
Chevalier, M., 7
Christopher (Polaroid learner), 91–92, 94, 118, 119–20, 122, 127–28, 140, 142, 143–44
Ciulla, J. B., 4
Clark, C., 161, 169–70
Classrooms
  as communities, 7
  creating opportunities for development in, 168–71
  as holding environments, 11
  incorporating cohorts into, 157–58
  observations in, 46, 53
  See also Pedagogy
Clinchy, B., 17, 20, 126
Cochran-Smith, M., 6
Cocking, R. R., 164
Coffey, A., 48, 49
Cognitive development, 65, 71, 99, 143, 156, 157, 162–64
Cohorts
  benefits of, 66–67
  and change in learners' conceptions of self, skills, and relationship to work, 130, 151, 153
  characteristics of, 65, 71

as communities of connection, 7,
11–12, 155, 157, 159–60
and constructive-developmental approach, 66
and core findings of research study,
11–12
and curriculum, 162
definition of, 67–68
and developmental theory, 66
for emotional support, 90–94
as holding environments, 72, 73–99,
100
and implications of new pluralism,
13, 155–60, 162, 173, 175, 176
influence/power of, 12, 55, 65, 71,
72–102, 156, 158–59, 173
and learners' expectations of teachers, 103–28
for learning and teaching, 73–90
and overview of book, 12
and pedagogy, 13, 66, 71, 99, 100
for perspective broadening, 94–99
at Polaroid Learning Site, 57–58,
64–65
and policymaking, 173, 175
and program design, 13, 155–60
and research in ABE/ESOL field, 176
research about, 155–57
and site and participant selection,
38, 39
summary about, 99–102
Coleman, C., 160
Collaborative learning
and CEI Adult Diploma Program,
64, 70–71
and change in learners' conceptions
of self, skills, and relationship to
work, 151, 153
characteristics of, 69, 89
as component of basic skills, 5
and contextualizing the curriculum,
166
definition of, 67, 68–69
and implications of new pluralism,
155–60, 166, 173, 176

and overview of book, 12
and policymaking, 173
power of, 72–102, 173
and problem solving, 70
process of, 86–89, 92–94, 101
and program design, 155–60
and research, 176
and teachers, 69
and ways of knowing, 69
See also Cohorts; Popular democratic model; Postindustrial
model; Social constructionist
model
Collins, A. M., 164
Comings, J., 2, 3, 4–5, 66, 104, 151,
164, 167, 176, 177, 178
Communication
and CEI Adult Diploma Program, 64
and change in learners' conceptions
of self, skills, and relationship to
work, 131, 134–37, 140, 141,
144, 145–46, 147, 149, 150
as component of basic skills, 5
and implications of new pluralism,
178, 179
Communities, classrooms as, 7
Communities of connection, cohorts
as, 7, 11–12, 155, 157, 159–60
Community college site, 9, 13, 38–39,
41, 43, 53, 105, 130, 154, 168
Competency
and benefits of constructive-development approach, 11
and change in learners' conceptions
of self, skills, and relationship to
work, 129, 131, 140, 141, 145,
146, 149, 150, 151
and contributions of research study
to ABE/ESOL field, 16
definition of, 167, 168
as developmental continuum,
167–68
and implications of new pluralism,
167–68, 172, 173, 175, 177,
178–79

Competency (*continued*)
  and learners' expectations of teach-
    ers, 126
  and policymaking, 172, 173, 175
  and purposes and outcomes of ABE/
    ESOL programs, 8
  and research methods, 40, 44
  and ways of knowing, 167–68
Computer skills, 4, 5, 64, 148, 150,
    158, 160, 164–67, 178
Confidence
  and change in learners' conceptions
    of self, skills, and relationship to
    work, 139–42, 145, 146, 148–
    49, 151
  and graduation day, 182
  and implications of new pluralism,
    168, 178
  and overview of book, 13
Constructive-developmental approach
  benefits of, 11
  and change in learners' conceptions
    of self, skills, and relationship to
    work, 36, 150
  and contributions of research study
    to ABE/ESOL field, 14, 15–16
  and field of adult basic skills develop-
    ment, 3
  as focus of research study, 6
  and holding environment, 17, 35–36
  and implications of new pluralism,
    172, 173–74, 175
  and learners' expectations of teach-
    ers, 105
  and literacy, 9
  overview about, 17–18, 20–23
  and policymaking, 172, 173–74, 175
  premises of, 20–23
  and research about ABE/ESOL pro-
    grams, 7
  and research methods, 52, 54
  and self, 17, 18–20, 21, 22, 24, 25–
    26, 27, 28, 32–33, 36
  subphases in, 28, 31
  summary about, 36

theory of, 17–36
  and transformational learning, 18–
    20, 22, 35
  transitions in, 21–22, 23, 28, 31–33
  See also Kegan, Robert; Ways of
    knowing; *specific topic*
Context
  and cohorts and collaborative learn-
    ing, 101
  and learners' expectations of teach-
    ers, 122–23
Contextualizing the curriculum, 151,
    159, 160, 164–67
Continuing Education Institute (CEI)
    Adult Diploma Program
  assessment tests of, 57
  and cohorts and collaborative learn-
    ing, 99
  and collaborative learning, 64,
    70–71
  curriculum for, 64, 70, 150–51
  design of, 59, 70, 150–51
  founding and aims of, 183
  graduation day for, 181–85
  and implications of new pluralism,
    178, 179
  and overview of book, 12
  overview of program at, 58–59, 64,
    70
  at Polaroid Learning Site, 39, 58–64
  process for applying to, 57
  selection for study of, 70–71
  and site and participant selection, 40
  standards for, 64, 150
  structure of, 99
  teachers in, 59, 64
  and transformational learning, 59
  See also Polaroid Learning Site; *spe-
    cific person*
Continuous enrollment, 156, 157
Corbin, J., 48, 49, 50
Counseling, 160
Cranton, P., 19, 22, 126, 130, 170
Critical teaching, 170
Critical thinking skills, 2, 4, 64, 150

Cuban, S., 104, 151, 164, 176
Culture, 126–28. *See also* Accultura-
    tive change
Curriculum
    and applying skills to real life, 162
    for CEI Adult Diploma Program, 64,
        70, 150–51
    and change in learners' conceptions
        of self, skills, and relationship to
        work, 150–51, 153
    and cognition of different individu-
        als, 162–64
    contextualizing, 151, 159, 160,
        164–67
    and contributions of research study
        to ABE/ESOL field, 15
    creating a developmental, 160–64
    and goal setting, 164–67
    "hidden," 168
    implications of new pluralism for,
        159, 160–67, 169, 172, 173
    and making connections to learners'
        lives, 161–62
    and pedagogy, 163, 164, 169
    and policymaking, 172, 173
    and program design, 164
    and research methods, 38
    and teachers, 160–61, 164–67
    and ways of knowing, 160–61, 162–
        63, 164, 165–66

Daloz, L., 8, 10, 20, 168
D'Amico, D., 176
Daniel (Polaroid learner), 118, 120–22,
    125, 142, 143
Data
    analysis of, 48–51, 53–54
    collection of, 40–48, 51–53
David, Lloyd, 59, 64, 181, 183, 184
Decision making
    and change in learners' conceptions
        of self, skills, and relationship to
        work, 143, 146, 150
    and cohorts and collaborative learn-
        ing, 73, 80

and implications of new pluralism,
    178
and learners' expectations of teach-
    ers, 125
and research methods, 43, 44
and ways of knowing, 33, 35
"Developing learning" (Granott), 18
Development
    and appetite for learning, 177–79
    and assumptions in research study,
        11
    and cohorts, 66
    and constructive-developmental ap-
        proach, 21–23
    and contributions of research study
        to ABE/ESOL field, 15–16
    definition of, 21
    and developmental diversity, 154–79
    as gradual process, 28, 31
    and implications of new pluralism,
        154–79
    learning as, 18–20, 171–75
    as lifelong process, 21
    microdevelopment, 18
    and policymaking in support of de-
        velopmental learning, 171–75
    premises about nature of, 21–23
    and promising avenues for develop-
        mental research, 175–76
    See also Ways of knowing
Diamond, A., 9, 13, 39, 65, 129, 130,
    154
Diener, E., 44
Digby, J. E., 66, 68, 90
Dirkx, J. M., 162
Diversity
    in ABE/ESOL programs, 104
    and assumptions in research study,
        11
    and cohorts and collaborative learn-
        ing, 73–90, 94–99, 101
    and contributions of research study
        to ABE/ESOL field, 14, 15, 16
    cultural, 12–13
    developmental, 33, 73–90, 154–79

Diversity (*continued*)
  and implications of new pluralism,
    14, 154, 162–64, 172, 173, 178
  importance of, 5
  and learners' expectations of teach-
    ers, 105
  and overview of book, 12–13
  pedagogical, 13
  and policymaking, 172, 173
  race/ethnic, 33, 38, 57, 58, 70, 94–
    99, 104, 105
  and research about ABE/ESOL pro-
    grams, 5
  and research methods, 38, 41
  valuing of, 120–22
  See also Ways of knowing
Drago, Betty L. Brisgal, 1
Drago, Eleanora Locasia, 2
Drago, Rosario P., 1
Drago-Severson, E.
  and ABE/ESOL as expanding field,
    5–8
  and change in learners' conceptions
    of self, skills, and relationship to
    work, 129, 130
  and cohorts and collaborative learn-
    ing, 65, 66, 72
  and competencies, 167, 168
  and constructive-developmental ap-
    proach, 7, 8, 9, 17, 18, 20, 21,
    22, 23, 25, 33, 35, 36, 172
  and contributions to ABE/ESOL
    field, 14, 15
  and curriculum, 160, 161, 163, 164,
    165, 168
  and data collection and analysis, 42,
    49, 52, 53, 54
  and holding environments, 11, 36
  and implications of new pluralism,
    154, 155, 156, 157, 158, 160,
    161, 163, 164, 165, 167, 168,
    169, 170, 172, 174, 175, 176,
    178
  and learners' expectations, 15
  as member of adult development
    study tema, 8, 9, 10

  and pedagogy, 7, 169, 170
  personal background of, 1–2
  and policymaking, 172, 174
  and program design, 156, 157, 158
  and promising avenues for develop-
    mental research, 175, 176
  and research methods, 40, 42, 49,
    50, 52, 53, 54
  and ways of knowing, 13, 14, 17,
    18, 22, 23, 25, 33, 35, 155,
    172, 178
Drennon, C., 174

Eberly, M., 3, 104, 175
Eble, K. E., 7, 68–69
Ecclestone, K., 8
Education Department, U.S., 172
Educational leadership programs,
    67–68
EFF. *See* Equipped for the Future
Egan, K., 37
Ego Development Sentence Completion
    Test, 43, 50, 52
Emmons, R. A., 44
Emotional/psychological well-being
  and change in learners' conceptions
    of self, skills, and relationship to
    work, 132, 133, 139, 143, 145
  and cohorts and collaborative learn-
    ing, 72, 76, 77, 79, 82, 89, 90–
    94, 99, 100
  cohorts as holding environment for,
    90–94
  and implications of new pluralism,
    156, 157
  and influence of cohorts, 65–66, 71
  and overview of book, 12
English literacy, 4. *See also* Compe-
    tency; ESOL (English for Speakers
    of Other Languages) programs/
    learners; Skills
Equipped for the Future (EFF) (Na-
    tional Institute for Literacy), 9, 64,
    103, 156, 163, 165, 167, 168,
    173–75, 177, 178
Erdmann, D., 7

ESOL (English for Speakers of Other
    Languages) programs/learners, 3,
    5–8, 14–16, 57–58, 66, 88, 104,
    154, 158, 160
Even Start Family Literacy Site (Massa-
    chusetts), 9, 39. *See also* Family lit-
    eracy site
Evers, F. T., 4, 8, 103
Exemplary model, Equipped for the Fu-
    ture as, 174–75
Expectations
    and change in learners' conceptions
        of self, skills, and relationship to
        work, 147
    and cohorts and collaborative learn-
        ing, 73, 91
    and constructive-developmental ap-
        proach, 17, 26, 27, 28, 32–33
    and contributions of research study
        to ABE/ESOL field, 15
    and goals of research study, 10
    and implications of new pluralism,
        154, 172
    and learners' expectations of teach-
        ers, 103–28
    and policymaking, 172
    and research methods, 38
    of their teachers by learners, 103–28
    and ways of knowing, 26, 27, 28,
        32–33
Experiences of learning interviews, 42,
    45, 53

Family literacy site, 13, 14, 38, 41, 43,
    130, 154, 168
Felix, S., 14, 31, 32, 42, 49, 52
Fiddler, M., 124, 126, 165
Fingeret, H. A., 174
Fischer, K., 18
Flannery, J., 7, 69
Focus groups, 42, 45, 52–53
Fogg, W. N., 3, 4–5, 177, 178
Funding, 174, 175

Garner, B., 66
Geertz, C., 48

Gender issues, 4, 125–26, 176
General Educational Development
    (GED), 103–4, 158
Gerlach, J. M., 68–69
Gillespie, M. K., 9, 163, 164, 165,
    168, 173, 174
Gilligan, C., 20
Glaser, B. G., 51
Glaser, R., 164
Goals
    for ABE/ESOL programs, 7–8
    and change in learners' conceptions
        of self, skills, and relationship to
        work, 149, 150
    and constructive-developmental ap-
        proach, 17, 25
    and curriculum, 164–67
    and implications of new pluralism,
        161, 164–67, 169, 170, 172
    and overview of book, 12–13
    and pedagogy, 169, 170
    at Polaroid Learning Site, 12–13
    and policymaking, 172
    of research study, 10
    of teachers, 45
    and ways of knowing, 25
    writing about learning, 166
Goldberger, N., 17, 20, 126
Golden Rule, and ways of knowing,
    25, 26, 28
Goodman, R., 14, 31, 32, 42, 49, 52
Gore, Al, 58
Gowen, S. G., 4, 66, 104
Graduation, 181–85
Granott, N., 18
Graves, D. H., 7
Green, B., 8
Greenberger, S., 4
Greeno, J. G., 164
Griffen, S., 44
Grow, G., 7
Growth, personal
    and assumptions in research study, 11
    and change in learners' conceptions
        of self, skills, and relationship to
        work, 130, 133–34

Growth, personal (*continued*)
  and cohorts and collaborative learn-
    ing, 94–99, 101
  cohorts as holding environment for,
    94–99
  and constructive-developmental ap-
    proach, 21–23, 35–36
  and goals of research study, 10
  as gradual and progressive, 21
  and graduation, 184
  holding environment as dynamic con-
    text for, 35–36
  and implications of new pluralism,
    154
  and learners' expectations of teach-
    ers, 106–7, 110–13, 117, 119,
    120–22
  as lifelong process, 21
  premises about nature of, 21–23
  and ways of knowing, 106–7, 110–
    13, 117, 119, 120–22
Guth, G.J.A., 7

Hamilton, M., 175
Hamilton, S. J., 7, 66, 68, 69, 76, 79,
  89, 90, 99, 100, 101
Hammer, M., 59
Hammerman, J., 9, 13, 39, 65, 129,
  130, 154
Harbison, A., 37, 59
Harman, D., 6
Hart-Landsberg, S., 6
Harvard University
  Bridge to Learning and Literacy pro-
    gram at, 158–60, 174
  Extension School at, 158
  Graduate School of Education at, 3,
    8, 175
Hassey, Kathy, 183, 184
Haston, L., 162
Heard, G., 7
Helena (Polaroid learner), 90–91, 92,
  94, 114, 115–17, 133–34
Helsing, D.
  and ABE/ESOL as expanding field,
    5–8

and change in learners' conceptions
  of self, skills, and relationship to
  work, 129, 130
and cohorts and collaborative learning, 65, 66, 72
and competencies, 168
and constructive-developmental approach, 7, 8, 9, 17, 18, 20, 22,
  23, 25, 33, 36, 172
and contributions to ABE/ESOL
  field, 14, 15
and curriculum, 160, 161, 163, 164,
  168
and holding environments, 11, 36
and implications of new pluralism,
  155, 156, 157, 160, 161, 163,
  164, 168, 170, 172, 174, 175,
  176, 178
and learners' expectations, 15
as member of adult development
  study team, 8, 9, 10
and pedagogy, 7, 170
and policymaking, 172, 174
and program design, 156, 157
and promising avenues for developmental research, 175, 176
and research methods, 39, 40, 50
and ways of knowing, 13, 14, 17,
  18, 22, 23, 25, 33, 155, 172,
  178
Hill, Marie Somers, 67–68
Holding environment
  and assumptions in research study,
    11
  and change in learners' conceptions
    of self, skills, and relationship to
    work, 139, 152–53
  classrooms as, 11
  cohorts as, 72, 73–99, 100
  and cohorts and collaborative learn-
    ing, 72, 100, 101
  and constructive-developmental ap-
    proach, 17, 35–36
  definition/functions of, 35–36, 50,
    52, 72
  for emotional support, 90–94

and learners' expectations of teachers, 105
for learning and teaching, 73–90
for perspective broadening, 94–99
and research methods, 50, 52
summary about, 99–102
and ways of knowing, 36, 152–53
Hooker, S., 44
Hope (Polaroid learner)
  and change in learners' conceptions
    of self, skills, and relationship to
    work, 132, 137–39
  and cohorts and collaborative learn-
    ing, 72, 76–79, 80, 82, 90, 94,
    96–97, 99
  and graduation, 181, 183–84
  and learners' expectations of teach-
    ers, 114, 115, 128
Horsman, J., 5–6, 103
Huberman, A. M., 48
Hunter, C., 6
Hyland, T., 8

Imel, S., 162
Impulsive ways of knowing, 23
Informational learning, 19, 21, 162
Informative change, 13, 129–30
Instrumental way of knowing
  and change in learners' conceptions
    of self, skills, and relationship to
    work, 131–39, 149, 151–53
  and cohorts and collaborative learn-
    ing, 73–80, 81, 83–84, 89, 90,
    94–97, 100, 101–2
  and constructive-developmental ap-
    proach, 17, 22, 23–25, 31–32,
    33
  and continuum and progressive
    change in ways of knowing,
    151–53
  and curriculum, 161, 165–66
  and emotional support, 90–91
  and implications of new pluralism,
    155, 161, 165–66
  and importance of knowing about
    ways of learning, 33

and learners' expectations of teachers, 106–7, 110–17, 124, 127
and learning and teaching, 73–79
and motivation, 7
outcomes for, 134–39
overview/characteristics of, 23–25,
  33
and personal growth, 94–97, 106–7,
  110–13
transitioning from, 22, 31–32, 76–
  79, 90–91, 96–97
Interindividual ways of knowing, 23
Interviews
  experiences of learning, 42, 45, 46,
    53
  "non-completer," 38, 48
  of program directors, 41
  subject-object (SOI), 42, 46, 49–50,
    52, 53
  of teachers, 41, 45, 47

Jeff (Polaroid learner), 86–89, 92–94,
  97–98, 99, 119, 122–23, 127,
  129, 143, 149
John (CEI teacher), 64, 74, 83, 87, 88,
  98, 110–12, 115, 117, 119, 123
Josselson, R. E., 14
Journal writing, 169–70
Judith (CEI teacher), 64, 95, 112–13,
  116

Kegan, Robert
  and ABE/ESOL as expanding field,
    5–8
  and benchmarking, 59
  and change in learners' conceptions
    of self, skills, and relationship to
    work, 130, 150, 151
  and cohorts and collaborative learn-
    ing, 65, 66, 72, 80
  and competencies, 167, 168
  constructive-developmental approach
    of, 3, 7, 8, 9, 10, 12, 14, 17,
    18, 19–23, 36, 44, 46, 47, 172
  and contributions to ABE/ESOL
    field, 14, 15

Kegan, Robert (*continued*)
  and curriculum, 160, 161, 163, 168
  and "hidden curriculum," 168
  and holding environments, 11, 12,
    17, 35
  and implications of new pluralism,
    155, 156, 157, 160, 161, 163,
    164, 167, 168, 170, 172, 174,
    175, 176, 178
  on influences on person's life, 1
  and learners' expectations of teach-
    ers, 15, 119
  and nature of growth and develop-
    ment, 21
  and pedagogy, 7
  and policymaking, 172, 174
  as principal investigator of team, 8
  and program design, 156, 157
  and promising avenues for develop-
    mental research, 175, 176
  and reflective practice for teachers,
    170
  and research methods, 37, 40, 42,
    44, 46, 47, 49, 50, 52
  and skills and competencies, 9
  and transformational learning,
    19–20
  and ways of knowing, 5, 13, 14, 17,
    18, 22, 23–33, 84, 85, 119,
    151–53, 155, 164, 172, 178
Kerka, S., 8, 161, 169
Killion, J., 170
King, P., 20, 169, 170
Kirk (CEI teacher), 123
Kitchener, K. S., 20, 169, 170
Knowing. *See* Ways of knowing
Knowles, M. S., 7, 72, 167
Kohlberg, L., 20
Kolenik, Carol, 158, 159
Kottkamp, R. B., 170, 171

Lahey, L. L., 10, 14, 20, 21, 22, 25,
    31, 32, 42, 49, 52, 130, 170
Larsen, R. J., 44
Learner-centeredness, 169

Learning experience participant inter-
    views, 42, 45, 46, 53
Lentz, D., 176
Levy, F., 4–5, 177, 178
Life Skills Workshop, 160
Life stories/autobiographies, 94–99,
    161, 162
Literacy
  and constructive-development ap-
    proach, 9
  Harvard program Bridge to Learning
    and, 158–59
  importance of, 2–3
  meaning of, 2
  as a social practice, 175
Locus of Control Scale (LOC), 44,
    47
Loevinger, J., 43, 52
Luttrell, Wendy, 125–26, 175
Lytle, S. L., 6

McEwan, H., 37
Magda (Polaroid learner), 118, 142,
    143, 148–49
Malicky, G., 6
Maps, self as learner, parent, or
    worker, 44–46, 47–48, 50, 53
Margaret (CEI teacher), 64, 121
Marienau, C., 124, 126, 165
Marmor, T., 6
Marsick, V. J., 162
Massachusetts Institute for a New Com-
    monwealth, 4
Mathematics, 4, 5. *See also* Compe-
    tency; Skills
Maxwell, J. A., 48, 49, 51
Meaning-making system. *See* Ways of
    knowing
Medina, P., 3, 66, 104, 155–56, 175
Merriam, S. B., 51, 164
Meyers, C., 7
Mezirow, J., 7, 19, 20, 22, 130
Miles, M. B., 48
Miller, B., 49
Motion of change, 150

Motivation
    and cohorts and collaborative learn-
        ing, 74, 93
    and constructive-developmental ap-
        proach, 17
    and goals of research study, 10
    and implications of new pluralism,
        177
    and learners' expectations of teach-
        ers, 122, 125
    and overview of book, 12–13
    and research about ABE/ESOL pro-
        grams, 6–7
    and research methods, 40
    and ways of knowing, 122
Murnane, R., 4–5, 177, 178
Muse, I. D., 67

Nash, A., 9, 173, 174
National Adult Literacy Survey
    (NALS), 3
National Center for the Study of Adult
    Learning and Literacy (NCSALL),
    3, 5, 8–9, 12
National Evaluation of the Adult Edu-
    cation Program (NEAEP), 3
National Institute for Literacy Policy,
    103, 175
New pluralism, implications of, 13,
    154–79
No Child Left Behind Act, 172
"Non-completer" interviews, 38, 48
Noonan, J. F., 7, 68–69
Norman, C., 6
Norris, C., 67

Observations, classroom, 46, 53
Osterman, K. F., 170, 171

Palma, S., 3, 4–5, 177, 178
Parenting, 44–46, 47–48, 50, 53, 136–
    37, 147, 150. See also Family liter-
    acy site
Parrella, A., 104, 151, 176
Participant selection, 37–40

Patrice, Sister, 184
Paulo (Polaroid learner), 83–85, 118,
    142, 144–47
Pearlin, L., 44
PEBS (Perceived Self-Efficacy Scale),
    44, 53
Pedagogy
    and change in learners' conceptions
        of self, skills, and relationship to
        work, 143, 151, 153
    and cohorts and collaborative learn-
        ing, 13, 66, 71, 99, 100
    and contributions of research study
        to ABE/ESOL field, 15, 16
    and curriculum, 163, 164, 169
    and development in classroom,
        168–71
    and goals, 169, 170
    implications of new pluralism for, 13,
        158, 163, 164, 168–71, 172, 173
    and learners' expectations of teach-
        ers, 126–28
    need for diversity in, 13
    and overview of book, 13
    and policymaking, 172, 173
    and research about ABE/ESOL pro-
        grams, 7
    and research methods, 38, 40, 45
    and ways of knowing, 169
Pedersen, J. E., 66, 68, 90
Peirce, B. N., 6–7
Penner, F., 6
Perceived Self-Efficacy Scale (PEBS),
    44, 53
Perry, W. G. Jr., 20
Personality, 17, 120–22, 123
Perspective broadening. See Growth,
    personal
Piaget, Jean, 20
Pierre (Polaroid learner), 79–82, 89,
    117–18, 124–25, 127–28, 139–41
Pogson, P., 154
Polaroid Corporation, 3, 9–10, 55–58,
    70, 184–85. See also Polaroid
    Learning Site

Polaroid Learning Site
  and change in learners' conceptions
    of self, skills, and relationship to
    work, 129, 130, 150–51
  and cohorts, 64–65
  Continuing Education Institute
    (CEI), and Polaroid Learning
    Site, 55, 57
  and contributions of research study
    to ABE/ESOL field, 16
  data analysis and collection at, 41,
    43–44, 45, 48
  as focus of research study, 17
  goals at, 12–13, 38
  graduation for learners at, 181–85
  and implications of new pluralism,
    168
  learners in cohort at, 57–58
  overview about, 3, 12–13
  and research methods, 38, 39–40,
    41, 43–44, 45, 48, 53
  and site and participant selection,
    38, 39–40
  summary about, 70–71
  See also Continuing Education Insti-
    tute (CEI) Adult Diploma Pro-
    gram; specific person or topic
Policymaking, 14, 15, 171–75, 176
Popp, N.
  and ABE/ESOL as expanding field,
    5–8
  and change in learners' conceptions
    of self, skills, and relationship to
    work, 129, 130
  and cohorts and collaborative learn-
    ing, 65, 66, 72
  and competencies, 167, 168
  and constructive-developmental ap-
    proach, 7, 8, 9, 17, 18, 20, 21,
    22, 23, 24–25, 26, 28, 31, 32,
    33, 36
  and contributions to ABE/ESOL
    field, 14, 15
  and curriculum, 160, 161, 163, 164,
    168

  and holding environments, 11, 36
  and implications of new pluralism,
    154, 155, 156, 157, 160, 161,
    163, 164, 167, 168, 172, 174,
    175, 176, 178
  and learners' expectations, 15
  as member of adult development
    study team, 8, 9, 10
  and pedagogy, 7
  and policymaking, 172, 174
  and program design, 156, 157
  and promising avenues for develop-
    mental research, 175, 176
  and research methods, 40, 44, 50
  and ways of knowing, 17, 18, 22,
    23, 24–25, 26, 28, 31, 32, 33,
    155, 172, 178
Popular democratic model (Trimbur),
  69, 89, 99, 101–2
Portnow, K.
  and ABE/ESOL as expanding field,
    5–8
  and change in learners' conceptions
    of self, skills, and relationship to
    work, 129, 130
  and cohorts and collaborative learn-
    ing, 65, 66, 72
  and competencies, 167, 168
  and constructive-developmental ap-
    proach, 7, 8, 9, 17, 18, 20, 21,
    22, 23, 24–25, 26, 28, 31, 32,
    33, 36
  and contributions to ABE/ESOL
    field, 14, 15
  and curriculum, 160, 161, 163, 164,
    168
  and holding environments, 11, 36
  and implications of new pluralism,
    154, 155, 156, 157, 160, 161,
    163, 164, 167, 168, 172, 174,
    175, 176, 178
  and learners' expectations, 15
  as member of adult development
    study team, 8, 9, 10
  and pedagogy, 7

and policymaking, 172, 174
and program design, 156, 157
and promising avenues for develop-
    mental research, 175, 176
and research methodology, 39, 40,
    50
and ways of knowing, 13, 14, 17,
    18, 22, 24–25, 26, 28, 31, 32,
    33, 155, 172, 178
Postindustrial model (Trimbur), 69, 76,
    79, 89, 99, 100, 101–2
Power relations, 175
Problem solving
    and CEI Adult Diploma Program,
        64, 70
    and change in learners' conceptions
        of self, skills, and relationship to
        work, 150, 151
    and cohorts and collaborative learn-
        ing, 69, 70, 87
    as component of basic skills, 4, 5
    and curriculum, 162
    and implications of new pluralism,
        162, 169, 170, 178
    and learners' expectations of teach-
        ers, 107
    and pedagogy, 169, 170
    and research methods, 43, 44
Program design
    and change in learners' conceptions
        of self, skills, and relationship to
        work, 150–51, 153
    and cohorts and collaborative learn-
        ing, 13, 66, 71, 100, 155–60
    and curriculum, 164
    implications of new pluralism for,
        13, 14, 155–60, 164, 174
    and policy making, 174
    and research methods, 38
Program directors, interviews of, 41
Program, exemplary, Bridge to Learn-
    ing and Literacy as, 158–59
Psychological well-being. See Emo-
    tional/psychological well-being
Purcell-Gates, V., 178

Quantitative survey measures, 44, 47,
    49, 51, 53
Questions, research, 40
Quigley, R., 66, 103–4, 105, 173

Race/ethnicity, 4, 33, 38, 57, 58, 70,
    94–99, 104, 105
Ramirez-Soto, Ismael, 182, 184
Reder, S., 2, 3, 4, 6, 151, 176
Referencing books and print materials,
    166–67
Reflective practices, 169–71
Renada (Polaroid learner), 90, 91, 101,
    106–13, 124, 131–32, 133
Report on Literacy Programs, 171–
    72
Research
    developmental, 175–76
    implications of new pluralism for,
        175–76
    importance of, 5
    and policymaking, 176
    promising avenues for develop-
        mental, 175–76
    and teachers, 176
    See also Research methods; Research
        study
Research methods
    and challenges to administration of
        measures, 52–53
    and constructive-development the-
        ory, 54
    and data analysis, 48–51, 53–54
    and data collection, 40–48, 51–53
    implications of, 54
    and research questions, 40
    and site and participant selection,
        37–40
    summary about, 51–54
Research study
    adult development team for, 8–10
    aims/goals of, 10, 16, 37
    assumptions in, 11
    core findings of, 11–12
    measures used in, 42–48

Research study (*continued*)
  See also Research methods; *specific
    site or topic*
Resnick, L. B., 164
Retention rates, 103–4, 155–56, 157,
    173
Riggs, M. L., 44
Rimer, K. P., 9, 13, 39, 65, 129, 130,
    154
Rita (Polaroid learner), 57, 118, 132,
    139, 140, 141–42
Rockhill, K., 6
Rogers, D. L., 170
Role models, teachers as, 114, 124
Roles
  and assumptions in research study,
    11
  and curriculum, 165
  and goals of research study, 10
  and implications of new pluralism,
    165, 168, 170, 172, 173, 178
  and pedagogy, 170
  and policymaking, 172, 173
  and research questions, 40
  of teachers, 170
  See also Research methods
Ross-Gordon, J., 72
Rossiter, M., 161, 163
Rush, J. C., 4, 8, 103

Sal (Polaroid learner), 132
Santos, Maricel, 3, 4–5, 159, 177, 178
Satisfaction with Life Scale (SWLS), 44,
    47, 50
Scaffolding, 153, 161, 162, 163, 169,
    173
Schön, D. A., 170
Schooler, C., 44
Schultz, K., 6
Schultz, L. H., 37
Self
  changes in learners' conceptions of,
    129–53
  and constructive-developmental ap-
    proach, 17, 18–20, 21, 22, 24,
    25–26, 27, 28, 32–33, 36
  definition of, 21
  development of, 18–20
  and goals of research study, 10
  and implications of new pluralism,
    154
  and influence/power of cohorts and
    collaborative learning, 65–66,
    73, 80
  and learners' expectations of teach-
    ers, 118
  and transformational learning,
    18–20
  and ways of knowing, 24, 25–26,
    27, 28, 32–33, 36
Self as learner, parent, or worker maps,
    44–46, 47–48, 50, 53
Self-authoring way of knowing
  and change in learners' conceptions
    of self, skills, and relationship to
    work, 142–47, 148–49, 150
  and cohorts and collaborative learn-
    ing, 73, 80, 83–85, 86–89, 92–
    94, 97–98, 100–102
  and constructive-developmental ap-
    proach, 17, 23, 27–28, 32–33,
    35
  and context, 122–23
  and curriculum, 161, 166
  and emotional support, 92–94
  and implications of new pluralism,
    155, 161, 166
  and importance of knowing about
    ways of learning, 33
  and learners' expectations of teach-
    ers, 118–23, 125, 127
  and learning and teaching, 83–85,
    86–89
  outcomes of learning from, 148–49
  overview/characteristics of, 27–28,
    35
  and personal growth, 97–98, 119,
    120–22
  transitioning to, 32–33, 83–85
Self-Directed Learning Center (Bunker
    Hill Community College), 38
Selman, R., 37

Site selection, 37–40
Skills
    applying, 162
    basic/core, 3–8, 9, 55, 57, 70, 151
    and benefits of constructive-development approach, 11
    building confidence from new, 141–42
    changes in learners' conceptions of, 129–53
    developing new, 137–39
    and field of adult basic skills development, 3–8
    and implications of new pluralism, 160, 167, 172, 173, 177, 178–79
    and overview of book, 13
    and Polaroid Learning Site, 55, 57, 70
    and policymaking, 172, 173
Skilton-Sylvester, E., 6
Smith, R. L., 176
Social constructionist model (Trimbur), 69, 79, 89, 99, 100, 101–2
Socializing way of knowing
    and change in learners' conceptions of self, skills, and relationship to work, 131, 132–47, 148–50, 151–53
    and cohorts and collaborative learning, 73, 76–82, 83–85, 86, 87, 89, 90–92, 93, 96–97, 100, 101–2
    and constructive-developmental approach, 17, 22, 23, 25–27, 28, 31–33, 35
    and continuum and progressive change in ways of knowing, 151–53
    and curriculum, 161, 166
    and emotional support, 90–92
    and implications of new pluralism, 155, 161, 166
    and importance of knowing about ways of learning, 33
    and learners' expectations of teach-
ers, 28, 106–7, 110–23, 124–25, 127
    and learning and teaching, 76–82, 83–85
    outcomes of learning from, 134–39, 148–49
    overview/characteristics of, 25–27, 33, 35
    and personal growth, 96–97, 106–7, 110–13, 117, 119, 120–22
    transitioning from, 32–33, 83–85
    transitioning to, 22, 31–32, 76–79, 90–91, 96–97
SOI (Subject-object interviews), 42, 46, 49–50, 52, 53
Soricone, L., 3, 4–5, 177, 178
Souvaine, E., 14, 31, 32, 42, 49, 52
Standards, 64, 66, 119, 125, 150
Star Model (Polaroid), 55, 70, 151
Stein, Sondra, 9, 21, 64, 103, 156, 160, 163, 168, 173, 174, 177–79
Stites, R., 173, 174
Strauss, A. L., 48, 49, 50, 51
Strength, learning for, 143–47
Stuebner Gaylor, S., 158
Subject-object interviews (SOI), 42, 46, 49–50, 52, 53
Sum, A., 2, 3, 4–5, 66, 104, 151, 176, 177, 178
Summers, Lawrence, 158
SWLS. See Satisfaction with Life Scale

Tarule, J., 17, 20, 126
Task Force on Adult Education, 66
Taylor, Frederick Winslow, 4
Taylor, K., 66, 105, 124, 126, 165
Taylor, M. L., 176
Teachers
    appreciation of techniques of, 119–20
    as caring, 114–17, 127
    in CEI Adult Diploma Program, 59, 64
    and change in learners' conceptions of self, skills, and relationship to work, 130, 137, 138, 143, 153

Teachers (*continued*)
   and cohorts and collaborative learn-
     ing, 69, 77, 78, 80, 81, 82, 83–
     84, 89–90, 101
   and contributions of research study
     to ABE/ESOL field, 15
   criticisms of, 118, 123, 125
   and curriculum, 160–61, 164–67
   and data collection, 41
   as experts, 117–18
   goals of, 45
   and implications of new pluralism,
     14, 154, 158, 160–61, 164–67,
     170–71, 172, 173–74, 176
   interviews of, 41, 45, 47
   and learners conceptualization of
     teacher-learner relationships,
     12–13, 105–23
   learners' expectations of, 103–28
   learners' trust of, 78
   as mentors, 126
   personality of, 120–22, 123
   philosophy of teaching, 45, 69, 101
   and policymaking, 172, 173–74
   professional development of, 173–74
   and program design, 158
   reflective practice groups for,
     170–71
   and research, 176
   and research study questions, 40, 41,
     45, 47
   as role models, 114, 124
   roles of, 170
   and ways of knowing, 33
   See also Pedagogy; *specific teacher*
Teaching
   cohort as holding environment for
     learning and, 73–90
   "critical," 170
   See also Pedagogy
Teaching and Learning Toolkit (EFF),
   163, 173–74
Technology, 2, 4. See also Computer
   skills
Teitel, L., 67

Tennant, M., 154
Teresina (Polaroid learner), 101, 114–
   15, 124, 134–37
Tinberg, H., 105, 163
Tough (Polaroid learner), 58, 128,
   139
Training, 19
Transformational learning
   and aims/goals of research study, 16
   and CEI Adult Diploma Program, 59
   and change in learners' conceptions
     of self, skills, and relationship to
     work, 150
   and constructive-developmental ap-
     proach, 18–20, 22, 35
   definition of, 19, 50, 52
   and implications of new pluralism,
     162, 171
   nature of, 18–20
   and pedagogy, 171
   and research methods, 40, 50, 51, 52
   and self, 18–20
   and ways of knowing, 35
Transformative change, 13, 129–30
Transitions, in ways of knowing, 21–
   22, 23, 28, 31–33, 76–79, 83–85,
   90–91, 96–97
Trimbur, John, 69, 76, 79, 89, 99,
   100, 101
Trub'skyy, M., 3, 4–5, 177, 178
"21st Century Skills for 21st Century
   Jobs" (Gore summit), 58–59

University of Massachusetts/Boston,
   181, 184
Uvin, J., 2, 3, 4–5, 66, 104, 176, 177,
   178

Vaishnav, A., 4
Valentine, T., 6, 104
Values, 96
Van der Veen, R., 162
Veronica (Polaroid learner), 57, 114,
   115, 133
Vignettes, 43–44, 47, 49, 53

Warka, J., 44
Ways of knowing
  and change in learners' conceptions
    of self, skills, and relationship to
    work, 13, 130, 149, 150, 151
  and cohorts and collaborative learn-
    ing, 69, 73, 90, 99, 101–2
  and constructive-developmental ap-
    proach, 11, 17, 18, 20, 21, 22–
    35, 36
  and contextualizing the curriculum,
    165–66
  continuum and progressive change
    in, 151–53
  and contributions of research study
    to ABE/ESOL field, 14, 15, 16
  and core findings of research study,
    11
  and curriculum, 160–61, 162–63,
    164, 165–66
  definition of, 5, 17, 20
  and holding environment, 36,
    152–53
  and implications of new pluralism,
    14, 154, 155, 156, 160–61,
    162–63, 164, 165–66, 167–68,
    169, 172, 176, 178
  importance of, 33–35, 36
  Kegan's perspective on, 5, 13, 14,
    17, 18, 22, 23–33, 84, 85, 119,
    151–53, 164
  and learners' expectations of teach-
    ers, 105, 106, 126, 127–28
  and methods of research study, 40,
    42, 46, 49–50
  and overview of book, 12–13
  and personal growth, 106–7,
    110–13
  and policymaking, 172
  and research in ABE/ESOL field,
    176
  and transformational learning, 35
  transitions in, 21–22, 23, 28, 31–
    33, 76–79, 83–85, 90–91, 96–
    97
  See also Instrumental way of know-
    ing; Self-authoring way of know-
    ing; Socializing way of knowing;
    specific topic
Weathersby, R., 20
Weisberger, R., 105, 163
Wessler, R., 43, 52
Whitehurst, R., 171–72
Wikelund, K., 6
Williams, Steve, 55, 57
Winnicott, D. W., 35
Work, relationship to, change in learn-
  ers' conceptions of, 131–42
Workforce Investment Act (WIA)
  (1988), 175
Workplace site. See Polaroid Learning
  Site
Wrigley, H. S., 7
Writing, about learning goals, 166

Yerkes, D., 67

About the Author

ELEANOR DRAGO-SEVERSON is a lecturer on education at Harvard University's Graduate School of Education, where she conducts research into and teaches courses on leadership for adult development and qualitative research methods. A developmental psychologist, Dr. Drago-Severson offers her readers the added experiences as both a teacher and program director in middle and upper schools. Her research and published writings focus on support for adult learning in K–12 schools, higher education, and ABE/ESOL programs. She is also known for her research, publications, and teaching in qualitative research methods and leadership for adult development.

Eleanor Drago-Severson's awards include recognition and support from: the Spencer Foundation (Spencer Grant); the Klingenstein Foundation (Klingenstein Summer Fellow); Harvard Graduate School of Education (Postdoctoral Fellow); and Harvard University's Extension School (Distinguished Teaching). She served as lead researcher on the Adult Development Team of the National Center for the Study of Adult Learning and Literacy (NCSALL), and is a consultant to schools and educational leaders on matters of adult learning, professional development, and leadership that support adult development. Author of *Helping Teachers Learn: Leadership for Adult Growth and Development* (2004, Corwin Press), Ellie lives in Cambridge, Massachusetts, with her husband, David.